The Development of Iran's Upstream Oil and Gas Industry

This book critically examines different forms of petroleum contracts, the historical perspective of the oil and gas industry and the political economy of the petroleum development in Iran.

In doing this, the author provides analysis of the concept of concession in oil and gas development. This is discussed through the main forms of concession contracts; namely, the classic concession contract (CCC) and the new concession contract (NCC). The book ties together much of the existing work on the history of oil and gas regulation in Iran and builds on that foundation to propose a coherent and balanced approach within the framework of the NCC. To consider the role of the NCC in developing national upstream oil and gas industry, comparative examples are drawn from countries currently using, or having previously used, NCC oil and gas contracts. The selected developed and developing countries are Brazil, Thailand, the United Kingdom, Australia and Norway. The analysis considers the extent to which the NCC has served to advance the objectives and national interests of the national governments in this industry. The book involves a comparative exploration of the utilisation of NCCs in other jurisdictions and synthesises a framework through which Iran may develop its underutilised oil and gas resources.

Of interest to academics, students and practitioners throughout the world, this book focuses on the relevant aspects of Iran's Constitution and natural resource laws and makes recommendations for law reform to Iran's legal frameworks.

Dr Mahmoud Fard Kardel has a PhD in law from Western Sydney University in Australia (2018). Kardel has published law articles in international journals in Europe, Australia, Asia and Iran. Dr Kardel has practiced law in Tehran (2007) and is due to take on an academic position as an Assistant Professor of Law at Shahid Beheshti University (National University of Iran) in 2020.

Routledge Research in Energy Law and Regulation

Regulation in the European Electricity Sector
Maciej M. Sokolowski

Law and Green Energy Policies
Roy Partain

Nuclear Energy Regulation, Risk and The Environment
Abdullah Al Faruque

Local Content Oil and Gas Law in Africa
Lessons from Nigeria and Beyond
Pereowei Subai

Host Government Agreements and the Law in the Energy Sector
The case of Azerbaijan and Turkey
Hakan Sahin

Iraq's Oil and Gas Industry
The Legal and Contractual Framework
Janan Al-Asady

The Development of Iran's Upstream Oil and Gas Industry
The Potential Role of New Concession Contracts
Mahmoud Fard Kardel

The Development of Iran's Upstream Oil and Gas Industry

The Potential Role of New Concession Contracts

Mahmoud Fard Kardel

Routledge
Taylor & Francis Group
LONDON AND NEW YORK

First published 2020
by Routledge
2 Park Square, Milton Park, Abingdon, Oxon OX14 4RN

and by Routledge
605 Third Avenue, New York, NY 10017

First issued in paperback 2021

Routledge is an imprint of the Taylor & Francis Group, an informa business

Publisher's Note
The publisher has gone to great lengths to ensure the quality of this reprint but points out that some imperfections in the original copies may be apparent.

British Library Cataloguing-in-Publication Data
A catalogue record for this book is available from the British Library

Library of Congress Cataloging-in-Publication Data
A catalog record has been requested for this book

ISBN 13: 978-1-03-224039-8 (pbk)
ISBN 13: 978-0-367-35087-1 (hbk)

Typeset in Galliard
by codeMantra

This book is dedicated to:

God Almighty, my creator, my source of inspiration, wisdom, knowledge and understanding;

My honourable father and all great martyrs who are eternal teachers;

My admirable mother, the symbol of sacrifice and a person who taught me that even the largest task can be accomplished if it is accomplished one step at a time; and

My beloved brother, who stood by me in difficult times and is always a symbol of loyalty.

Contents

Abstract

The types and forms of oil and gas contracts play an important role in the negotiation of financing, operations and risk and profit sharing in the development of the upstream oil and gas industry in Iran. Different forms of contracts co-exist in this globalised industry dominated by multinational oil and gas corporations. Increasingly, developed and developing countries have found it necessary to reconsider the forms of contract they enter into in consideration of whether they have served the nation's interests in oil and gas development in the past or are likely to in the future.

Iran has a unique historical context and legal system in relation to oil and gas exploration and exploitation. This book focuses on the legal and contractual framework of the Iranian oil and gas industry from discovery to present day. This has been classified into three periods: from exploration of oil in Iran to nationalisation (1901–1951), from nationalisation to the Islamic revolution (1951–1979) and from revolution to the present day (1979–2018). It considers the strengths and weaknesses of past and present contractual forms having regard to the national interests of the Iranian government.

Exerting State control over all oil and gas production stages, especially upstream stages, has been popular from a historical perspective. However, regard should be given to the high costs of investment in oil projects and the risks where profitability and return of the capital is doubtful. In addition, oil-rich countries like Iran generally lack the required technology to efficiently exploit its resource fields as well as the financial resources for infrastructure development. The result has been a distortion of negotiations, particularly over all aspects of financing, infrastructure and the allocation of project risks.

The central theme of this book is the analysis of the concept of concession in oil and gas development. This is discussed through the main forms of concession contract; namely, the classic concession contract (hereafter referred to as CCC) and the new concession contract (hereafter referred to as NCC). The present study examines the nature and features of the NCC as both a unique type of oil and gas contract and as a modified version of a concession contract. The research reviews other forms of contracts to have been adopted in Iran and compares them with other arrangement such as joint venture contracts, production sharing agreements, service contracts and buy-backs used internationally by sectors of the oil and gas industry.

To consider the role of the NCC in developing national upstream oil and gas industry, comparative examples are drawn from countries currently using, or having previously used, NCC oil and gas contracts. The selected developed and developing countries are Brazil, Thailand, the United Kingdom, Australia and Norway. The analysis considers the extent to which the NCC has served to advance the objectives and national interests of the national governments in this industry. The implications for future contractual arrangements for this sector in Iran are considered, having regard to the experiences of the NCC discussed.

The final chapters of the book focus on the relevant aspects of Iran's Constitution and natural resource laws and make recommendations for law reform to Iran's legal frameworks. It argues such reforms are required to implement the NCC as a contractual form for future upstream oil and gas development in Iran.

Selected acronyms

AGIP	Azienda Generale Italiana Petroli
AIOC	Anglo-Iranian Oil Company
APOC	Anglo-Persian Oil Company
BBL	unit of volume for crude oil and petroleum products
BOT	Build, Operate and Transfer
BP	British Petroleum
BPD	Barrels Per Day
BBC	Buy-Back Contract
CCC	Classic Concession Contract
CFP	Company France petroleum
DCF	Discounted Cash Flow
DA	Designated Authority
DMR	Department of Mineral Resources
ERAP	Entreprise de Rechereche et d'Activités Pétrolières
EBG	Exclusive Benefit to Government
EEA	European Economic Area
FIPPA	Foreign Investment Promotion and Protection Act
FDI	Foreign Direct Investment
GSF	Geological Stability Factor
ICJ	International Court of Justice
ICL	International Constitution Law
IEA	International Energy Agency
ILUA	Indigenous Land Use Agreements
IOC	International Oil Company
IPAC	Iran Pan American Corporation
IPC	Iran Petroleum Contract
JA	Joint Authority
JOA	Joint Operation Agreement
JVA	Joint Venture Agreement
LPG	Liquefied Petroleum Gas
LIBOR	London Interbank Offered Rate
LTEOSA	Long-Term Export Oil Sale Agreement
MEP	Minimum Exploration Plan

MCC	Modern Concession Contract
MLR	Modern licensing Regime
NCC	New Concession Contract
NCS	Norwegian Continental Shelf
NEPC	National Energy Policy Council
NIOC	National Iran Oil Company
NPA	National Petroleum Agency
NSW	New South Wales
OPGGSA	Offshore Petroleum and Greenhouse Gases Storage Act
OC	Oil Company
OPEC	Organization of Petroleum Exporting Countries
PEM	Plano Exploratorio Minimo
PEPR	Program for Environment Protection and Rehabitation
PRT	Petroleum Revenue Tax
PSA	Production Sharing Agreement
PSC	Production Sharing Contract
ROR	Rate Of Return
RSA	Risk Sharing Agreement
SA	Southern Australia
SIRIP	Societe Irano-Italienne des Petroles
SRB	Special Remunerator Benefit
SDFI	State Direct Financial Interest
TCF	Trillion Cubic Feet
UK	United Kingdom
US	United States
UGPC	Upstream Government Petroleum Contract
WA	Western Australia

Key definitions

Agreement: A mutual understanding between two or more persons about their relative rights and duties regarding past or future performances; a manifestation of mutual assent by two or more persons.[1]

Contract: An agreement between two or more parties creating obligations that is enforceable or otherwise recognisable at law.[2]
Upstream oil and gas industry: Exploration, extraction, exploitation and production of crude oil and natural gas.[3]

Downstream oil and gas industry: Transportation, refining and marketing of crude oil and natural gas.[4]

Classic Concession Contract: Specific privileges[5] to natural or juridical persons. The Concession is an arrangement whereby the International Oil Company (IOC) is granted the right to explore and exploit oil and gas in exchange for the payment of all costs and also specific taxes related to the operation.[6]

New Concession Contract: An agreement which retains the basic legal format of the classic concession, but which has significant modification to the financial terms and features of its prototype.[7]

Production Sharing Agreement: An oil and gas contract between a multinational oil and gas company and a host government, in which the corporation provides capital investment in exchange for control over an oil and gas field and access to a large share of the revenues from it.[8]

1 Henry Campbell, *Black's Law Dictionary* (MINN West, 4th ed, 1951) 89.
2 *Henry Campbell, Black's Law Dictionary* (MINN West, 4th ed, 1951) 89.
3 Paolo Macini and Ezio Mesini, *The Petroleum Upstream Industry: Hydrocarbons Exploration and Production* (Encyclopedia of Life Support System (EOLSS), 2011) 2.
4 Ibid.
5 Campbell, above n 1 361.
6 Keith W Blinn et al (eds), *International Petroleum Exploration & Exploitation Agreements: Legal, Economic, and Policy Aspects* (Barrows Company Inc, 2nd ed, 2009) 47.
7 Albert T Chandler, *Thailand Petroleum Concessions* (Research Discussion Paper, Chandler & Thong-ek Law Offices Ltd, 14 December 2015) 2–4.
8 Unravelling the Carbon Web, *About Production Sharing Agreement* <http://www.carbonweb.org/showitem.asp?article=58&parent=4&link=Y&gp=3>.

Joint Venture: One form of current oil and gas contract involving a business undertaking by two or more persons engaged in a single defined project.[9]

Buy-back Contract: A financing arrangement in which the developer sells a property to an investor and then buys it back under a long-term sales contract.[10]

License: Grants the investor the right to exploit a defined area in consideration of a fee and/or royalty payment.[11]

Exploration license: A permit to only geological and geophysical surveying and the drilling of shallow wells to get petroleum.

Production License: An exclusive right on the licensee to search and bore for petroleum.

Reservoir: A subsurface, porous, permeable rock formation in which oil and gas are found.[12]

Service Contract: An agreement whereby the government (state) would grant contractual (but not proprietary) right to an oil company, however retains majority control over the operations and the contractor provides the necessary services required to carry out the project.[13]

Oil and Gas Royalty: Payment expressed as a percentage of the oil and/or natural gas volumes produced by the licensee in a concession contract which is payable in cash or kind (as government prefers) to the owner of the petroleum in situ, to both onshore and offshore production.[14]

Oil and Gas Income Tax: is included in the profit oil and gas (that is calculated by subtracting the royalties paid, transportation cost, amortisation cost and exploitation costs from the gross income) received by the government.[15]

9 Campbell, above n 1, 973.

10 Willem J H van Groenendaal and Mohammad Mazraati, 'A Critical Review of Iran's Buyback Contracts' (2006) 34 *Energy Policy Journal* 1.

11 Mohammad Alramahi, *Oil and Gas Law in the UK* (Bloomsbury, 2012) 5.

12 Anthony Jennings, *Oil and Gas Exploration Contracts* (Sweet & Maxwell Publish, 2002) 56.

13 Alramahi, above n 11, 6.

14 Daniel Johnston, *International Petroleum Fiscal Systems and Production Sharing Contracts* (Pennwell, 1994) 3.

15 Alexander G Kemp, 'An Assessment of UK North Sea Oil and Gas Policies' (1990) 18(7) *Energy Policy Journal* 2.

Acknowledgements

I would like to express my deep thanks and appreciation to Professor Donna Craig and Professor Michael Adams for their great teaching, encouragement and invaluable ideas.

I would also like to acknowledge the wonderful support and assistance of Associate Professor Hossein Esmaeili for his constructive criticism and invaluable comments.

My sincere thanks go to the Western Sydney Law Librarians. They were significantly helpful with mastery of the databases and international library loan facilities.

The publisher and I would like to thank the copyright holders for their permission to reproduce the following materials:

Extract from Mahmoud Fard Kardel, 'Comparative Concession Contracts in the Gas and Oil Industries Globally' (2019) 14(1) *The Journal of Comparative Law* 244–274.

Extract from Mahmoud Fard Kardel, 'Evolution of the National Oil and Gas Legal Framework' (2018) 48(3–4) *Environmental Policy and Law* 233–249.

I am profoundly grateful to all legal advisors for their great advice and to those people who assisted me with valued and insightful comments. It is not possible to list all their names, but their cooperation and support are sincerely acknowledged.

1 Introduction

1.1 Classic concession contract

A CCC is a contract by which a government, or a governmental organ, hands over the administration of an organisation or a public service such as mines to natural or juridical persons. These persons put in their own capital to cover costs within a specified and limited time against which sums are collected from the users of the public services.[1] Payments are made to the government in consideration of the benefits gained from the use of public resources for a lengthy, but also fixed, period of time through mechanisms such as royalty payments.[2] The features of a CCC include a long time period public service lease (usually 75 years or more) and territorial coverage that in some cases includes the whole or large part of countries such as Iraq, Libya, Oman and Iran.[3] In these contracts, arbitration is used to resolve disputes between the parties, and the formula for calculating taxation is simple, or there is no provision for taxation.[4] This older form of concession contract is sometimes referred to as the CCC.

1.2 New concession contract

The NCC is an agreement between a government and an international oil company (IOC). The government authority grants rights and agrees to the obligations to be undertaken by the IOCs in relation to the construction, refurbishment or provision of infrastructure, or to explore for and exploit the country's petroleum. It also reserves and transfers considerable discretion over most aspects of development to the country.[5] The term 'new' not only suggests

1 Ezzatollah Taher Estakhti, *Concession on Tract and Its Legal Evolution* (Dissertation for LLM of Public Law, Shahid Beheshti Law Faculty, 1999) 22.
2 Sinturug Savana, *World Petroleum Arrangement and the Role of the State* (Dissertation submitted to the CEPMLP, University of Dundee, 1986) 117.
3 Keith W Blinn et al (eds), *International Petroleum Exploration and Exploitation Agreement* (Barrows Company Inc, 2nd ed, 2009) 60.
4 Taher Estakhti, above n 1, 32.
5 Rainer Geiger and Aril Seren, *Basic Elements of a Law on Concession Agreements*' (Organization for Economic Co-Operation and Development (OECD), Multilateral Centre for Private Sector Development Istanbul, 2001) 8.

a new area in which the contracts are concluded but also refers to the incorporation of new trends into the contract and an attempt at a rational development of the country's natural resources. To take control over resources, the relationship between developing countries and IOCs evolved from collector of royalty payments to equal profit sharing. In addition, the role of the host country had essentially changed from a passive rent collector to an active partner. An example of an NCC is provided by Thailand. The Thailand concession system, patterned on the traditional concession agreement which is a model contract of standard terms and conditions, clearly represents an example of NCC, and this is discussed in Chapter 4 of this book.

The NCC has several distinguishing features from the CCC such as shorter contract periods, a work obligation, relinquishment clause, bonus payment and higher royalty.[6] In fact, the NCC provides for the host country to have a more active role and a corresponding decrease in the responsibilities and rights of the IOC. Such modifications, however, did not alter the legal nature of the concession agreement. Only the terms were different under the early concession systems with the result that the features most disadvantageous for the host country were progressively eliminated.

It should be noted that the NCC has advantages and satisfies most of the major demands of the host countries including its authority to exercise some review of, and control over, the concessionaire's decision. However, it is extremely persuasive IOCs to expand their investments in new oil and gas fields and its high revenues.

1.3 Need for Iran to transition to NCC

Governments can select different kinds of contracts depending on their circumstances; resource geology and economic, social and political conditions. A state can negotiate many types of contractual frameworks, taking into consideration different conditions in matters such as global markets, geographical situation, production costs and field-related risk factors. Iran requires hundreds of billions of dollars in investments to explore and exploit its oil and gas fields over the next two decades. For this to occur, Iran needs to address the desirability and interests of international investing companies in the types of concession contracts it offers.[7]

The NCC and associated legal regime for Iranian oil and gas fields may help to attract overseas investors with the appropriate technical expertise. The costs and risks are high in some Iranian oil and gas fields such as those which have no exploitation record, no extraction infrastructure installations, the possibility of

6 Blinn et al, above n 3, 276.

7 F. Ameri and M. Shirmardi, 'The New Concession Agreements and the Interests of Oil Producer Countries: With Specific Reference to Ownership of the Oil, Host State's Control and Management and the Fiscal Regime of the Agreements' (2016) 4(15) *Journal of Private Law Research*.

yielding no product and located in difficult and mountainous regions.[8] While an NCC often grants an oil company exclusive rights to explore, extract, develop, sell and export oil or minerals extracted from a specified area for a fixed period of time, the biggest advantage of NCC for a country like Iran is that the state bears no liability as to the different risks inherent to every oil and gas project.[9]

This research study examines the legal framework of Iran's oil and gas contracts with legal and comparative analysis between them (Chapter 2). The analysis involves identifying the distinguishing characteristics of NCC and CCC (Chapter 3), discussing comparative contractual approaches in selected countries (Brazil, Thailand, Australia, the UK and Norway) that used, or are still using, the NCC in their oil and gas fields (Chapter 4). The purpose of the comparative examples is to consider the appropriateness of NCCs for the future development of Iran's upstream oil and gas industry. This book considers other current oil and gas contract frameworks (e.g., production sharing agreement, participation agreement, joint venture, service contract), and the book also considers the positive and negative aspects of the CCC and NCC compared to these other contracts (Chapter 5). Finally, the book reviews the existing legal framework in Iran and the opportunities and barriers to adopting the most appropriate form of contract (Chapter 6).

1.4 Main question

The main question addressed is:

How desirable is the NCC for the future development of Iran's oil and gas fields?

This is the major focus of the related main questions detailed below:

1. What are the legal frameworks and key characteristics of past and present oil and gas contracts in Iran?
2. What are the strengths and weaknesses of these past and present contractual forms (considered through comparative legal analysis) having regard to Iran's national interest in the development of the upstream oil and gas industry and in the context of Iran's legal system?
3. What contractual form is most appropriate to develop the future upstream oil and gas industry in Iran having regard to the interest of the government of Iran?
4. To what extent would the chosen contractual form need to be modified to overcome weaknesses in prior practices and to meet the future needs of developing Iran's upstream oil and gas industry?
5. What reform is necessary to Iran's legal frameworks that would be required to implement this recommendation?

8 Abbas Ansari, *The Nature and Efficiency of Buy-Back Contracts* (Dissertation for LLM of International Trade Law, Shahid Beheshti University, Persian Abstract, 1387).

9 Ameri and Shirmardi, above n 7, 89.

1.5 Background of Iran's oil and gas contracts

Iran, as one of the Organisation of Petroleum Exporting Countries' (OPEC)[10] founding members, is the OPEC's second largest oil producer and the fourth-largest crude oil exporter in the world. Iran holds around 158 billion barrels of proven oil reserves,[11] which is approximately 10 percent of the world's total proven petroleum reserves. Iran also holds the world's second-largest natural gas reserves.[12] The legal frameworks of the Iranian oil industry have generally been classified into three distinct time periods.[13]

1.5.1 Pre-nationalisation period (1901–1951)

There was never an oil law before the oil Nationalisation Law of 1951.

Generally, in that time, agreements were through bilateral negotiations for producing oil. In other words, there were no existing legal frameworks in place to inform the negotiation process between the two parties.[14]

Basically, concessions were typically signed between Iranian rulers and foreign individuals or companies like other oil-rich countries at the time. Regarding the absence of oil legislation, the rulers were not subjected to legal restrictions on the type of contracts, terms and conditions that they could agree upon. The two main agreements entered into, before the nationalisation of Iran's oil industry in 1951, were the D'Arcy Concession (1901) and the 1933 Concession Agreement.[15] Regarding the D'Arcy Concession (1901), D'Arcy was given exclusive privilege to Iran's oil exploration throughout all of Iran (except five provinces) for a period of 60 years. In exchange, D'Arcy agreed to pay to the government a few bonuses and 16 percent of the company's annual profit.[16] Regarding the 1933 Concession Agreement, the Anglo-Iranian Oil Company (AIOC) sought to extend the D'Arcy Concession by 20 years. After long negotiation, though the AIOC and the government agreed to a payment of 750,000 pounds annually plus a royalty to the government however, the concession structure remained in place. These concessions will be described in greater detail in Chapter 2.

10 OPEC was formed in 1960 when five oil-producing nations: Iran, Iraq, Kuwait, Saudi Arabia and Venezuela met to address the question of falling oil prices.

11 OPEC ASB, *OPEC Annual Statistical Bulletin* (2016) 8 <http://www.opec.org/opec_web/static_files_project/media/downloads/publications/ASB2016.pdf>.

12 Energy Information Administration (EIA), Official Energy Statistics from the U.S. Government, Country Analysis Brief, Iran <https://www.eia.gov/beta/international/analysis.cfm?iso=IRN> (accessed 28/03/2013).

13 Nima Nasrollahi Shahri, 'The Petroleum Legal Framework of Iran: History, Trends and the Way Forward' (2010) 8(12) *China and Eurasia Forum Quarterly Journal* 112.

14 Ibid. 113.

15 Ibid. 113.

16 Anglo-Persian Oil Company, *Agreement of 28th May, 1901 (the D'Arcy Concession) between, the Governments of His Imperial Majesty the Shah of Persia Ad William Knox D'Arcy* (London) appendix to annex 1419.

1.5.2 Hybrid period (1951–1979)

Nationalisation in Iran, like every country with nationalisation experience, was impacted by several factors such as financial inequalities, rampant poverty, revival of lost dignity and the non-acceptance of foreign interference. These factors gave rise to a nationalistic movement in Iran pioneered by Prime Minister Mosaddegh, which culminated in the nationalisation of the Iranian oil and gas industry in 1951. The Nationalisation Law was validated by the Iranian parliaments in 1951.[17] Before the 1979 revolution, two parliaments (the National Parliament and the Senate) were both required to validate concessions before they could come into force. The entire oil and gas industry was nationalised and all relevant stages "including exploration, development and exploitation were to be carried out and controlled solely by the Iranian government".[18] For the first time in the history of Iran, the country was legally considered the owner of its petroleum wealth.

At the time of the nationalisation of Iran's oil and gas industry, Britain and America felt that their economic interests were being threatened and orchestrated a political coup in Iran in 1953.[19] In the summer of 1953, the Iranian coup d'état, known in Iran as the 28 Mordad coup, ended in the downfall of Mosaddegh and his cabinet. The coup was orchestrated by the United Kingdom (UK) under the name, 'Operation Boot' and the United States (US) under the name, *TPAJAX* Project.[20] As *Palash Ghush* mentioned: "Mosaddegh's 'crime' had been to support the nationalization of Iran's key oil industry – a grave affront to British oil companies. The 1953 coup ended Iran's attempt to control its own hugely lucrative petroleum sector".[21]

Following the political coup, the 1954 Consortium Contract was signed with IOC. The consortium consisted of the AIOC (which later changed to British Petroleum Company), Royal Dutch-Shell, the five US companies (Standard Oil (NJ), Socony, Socal, Texas and Gulf) and Compagnie Française des Pétroles. The Consortium Contract 1954 was thus a contract between Iran and a consortium of IOCs for the exploration of Iran's resources which substantially revised to provide more benefits to the IOCs.

This contract, called an 'Amini-Page Contract', involved the Iranian government granting rights to oil and gas exploration, extraction and selling phases to IOCs, despite the 1951 Nationalisation Oil Act.[22] Also, Iran agreed to royalty

17 Nasrollahi Shahri, above n 13, 4.

18 *Nationalization Act 1951* (Iran) National Parliament.

19 Mark Gasiorowski, *Mohammad Mosaddeq and the 1953 Coup in Iran* (Syracuse University Press, 2004) 130.

20 Ibid. 137.

21 Palash Ghush, 'Iran: The Long Lasting Legacy of the 1953 U.S./CIA Coup' (20 March 2012) International Business Times <http://www.ibtimes.com/iran-long-lasting-legacy-1953-uscia-coup-214329>.

22 The major objectives of Iran's nationalisation consisted of: the establishment of Iran's sovereignty, ownership and control of the country's oil industry and resources, and to control all operations of exploration, extraction, and exploitation.

payments (under the somewhat vague name of 'declared payment'). The consortium agreed to share profits on a 50-50 basis with Iran, "but not to open its books to Iranian auditors or to allow Iranians onto its board of directors".[23]

During this period, both the Petroleum Act 1957 (as Iran's first Petroleum Act)[24] and the Petroleum Act 1974 were approved. The Petroleum Act 1957 permitted production sharing agreements and the Petroleum Act 1974 permitted service contracts[25] (the concept of "Risk Service Contract" (RSC) was introduced for the first time in Article No. 3)[26] for Iran's oil and gas sectors.

1.5.3 Contemporary period (1979–2018)

The 1954 Consortium agreements, as well as all other contracts thought of as contrary to Iranian law, were unilaterally ended after the 1979 Islamic Revolution. All petroleum contracts now had to accord with Iran's new Constitution (Islamic Republic of Iran Constitution),[27] the 1987 Petroleum Act and other petroleum Acts and legislations.[28] The significance of this Act was that it outlawed foreign investment completely, rendering Iran's petroleum industry independent from any foreign assistance or participation. For this reason, the Petroleum Act of 1987 ratified on 1st October of that year cancelled all foreign investments in Iran's petroleum industry.[29]

1.6 Overview of Iran's oil and gas legal development

The beginning of the oil and gas industry in Iran was marked by the exploration of the nation's sedimentary basins. Officially, it commenced with the concession granted to W.K. D'Arcy by the Iranian government (Persia) in 1901 for the extraction and production of oil. Therefore, the early concessions go back more than 100 years.[30] The first significant point regarding the early concessions was that the geographic area of operation was very wide. The next distinguishing

23 Stephen Kinzer, *All the Shah's Men: An American Coup and the Roots of Middle East Terror* (John Wiley & Sons, 2008) 195.

24 E H Wall, 'The Iranian-Italian Oil Agreement of 1957' (1958) 7(4) *The International and Comparative Law Quarterly* 786.

25 In this contract, the contractor (IOC) had to conduct upstream exploration entirely at its own risk, and had no right to the reserves discovered or to the production from any field developed. If exploration led to a commercial discovery, the IOC had to develop the oil field under the supervision of the NIOC.

26 The text of the *Act* was published by Public Relations Affairs, Iranian Oil Industry in 1974.

27 *Iranian Constitution 1979* (Iran) (to view the Constitution in English, go to: <http://www.iranonline.com/iran/iran-info/government/constitution.html> (accessed 18/02/2017).

28 *The Petroleum Act of 1987* (Iran) (to view *The Petroleum Act of 1987* in English, go to: <http://www.alaviandassociates.com/documents/petroleum.pdf> (accessed 18/02/2017).

29 Leila Zabbah, 'Investment Challenges in Iranian Oil & Gas Sectors – A Legal Approach' (2011) *Institute for International Energy Studies* 10.

30 Earnest Smith and John Dzienkowski, 'A Fifty-Year Prospective on World Petroleum Arrangements (2005) 3(1) *Oil, Gas & Energy Law Intelligence OGEL* 17.

feature of early concessions is related to the duration of the agreement. Sometimes, this sort of agreement was binding for more than 60 years – a very long time. The remarkable point in respect to these kinds of agreements is that the foreign companies were regarded as the exclusive owner of the petroleum reserves in the area covered by the agreement. The ownership and control over equipment and installations used for the purpose of the contract remained with the concessioner.[31]

For this reason, from 1954 the concession regimes and associated Consortium Contracts in Iran's oil and gas sector were amended and revised. In order to encourage private investment in oil and gas, the Iranian Parliament passed a new Petroleum Law in July, 1957.[32] It aimed at providing a different basis for Iranian oil and gas operations that provided a middle way between the concession system (where the Iranian Government had to assume the role of bystander and rent collector with no control over the management or direction of this most strategic industry) and the opposite extreme epitomised by the Nationalisation Law of 1951.[33] The Iranian parliament decided to revise the structure of the oil and gas concession framework soon after Iran's independence as it desired to earn higher oil and gas revenues with more direct participation by the national government.[34] This placed heavier financial burdens and greater risks on the international companies.[35] The government sought to control all operations of exploration, extraction and exploitation.[36]

The severe economic consequences following the ratification of the 1951 Oil Nationalisation Act demonstrated that a more pragmatic approach was required to attract and retain investment in Iran's crucial oil and gas sector. In July 1957, the parliament passed the Petroleum Act 1957. Based on this law, the government wanted active involvement in this key industry through partnerships with foreign corporations holding the expertise and capital to undertake the risky and invariably long-term investments that characterised it. The Petroleum Act 1957 was an enabling statute authorising the National Iran Oil Company (NIOC) to enter into agreements with Iranian or foreign companies with a view to extending as rapidly as possible the research, exploration and petroleum extraction operations throughout the country and the continental shelf.[37]

31 Blinn et al, above n 3, 54.
32 Wall, above n 24, 8.
33 Mostafa Elm, *Oil, Power, and Principle: Iran's Oil Nationalization and Its Aftermath* (Syracuse, 1992) 91–93.
34 Edward Henniker, 'Nationalisation: The Anglo-Iranian Oil Company, 1951 Britain vs. Iran' (2013) 2(2) *Moral Cents: The Journal of Ethics in Finance* 19.
35 Homayoun Mafi, 'Iran's Concession Agreements and the Role of the National Iranian Oil Company: Economic Development and Sovereign Immunity' (2008) 48 *Natural Resources Journal* 410.
36 Rouhollah K Ramazani, 'Choice-of-Law Problems and International Oil Contracts: A Case Study' (1962) 11(2) *The International and Comparative Law Quarterly* 56.
37 Wall, above n 24, 8.

Immediately after the passing of the Petroleum Act 1957, several oil and gas contracts were concluded between the NIOC and foreign companies. The first, in 1957, was with the Italian government-owned AGIP Mineral, which provided for the formation of an Iranian company, SIRIP. A second oil and gas contract was signed with Pan American Petroleum Corporation and led to the formation of the Iran Pan American Corporation (IPAC) in 1958. At the time, there was considerable media speculation about the fiscal terms of these contracts, which appeared to give the NIOC 75 percent of net profits realised from the investment. Such fiscal terms were unheard-of in petroleum investments at this time.[38] In fact, the new contracts were participation agreements with IOCs in which risks and rewards were shared equally with the NIOC. However, because the IOC had to pay 50 percent of its share of profits as tax to the government of Iran, it effectively meant that 75 percent of the profit share went to Iran (i.e., the NIOC's 50 percent share plus 50 percent of the second party's profit of 50 percent). However, the IOC still received 50 percent of profits realised from its actual investment.[39]

This type of contractual arrangement continued to operate in Iran as the basis of upstream contracts with the IOCs until 1974, when the worldwide petroleum industry's fiscal system took on another dimension because of the first oil price shock, driving changes in Iran's regime. Until the late 1960s, the global oil price had remained relatively low. However, there was an almost three-fold increase in crude oil prices from US$3.39 to US$9.35/Per Oil Barrel (BBL) during the five-year period from 1970 to 1974.[40] This led to excessive profits for oil companies and drove home the disadvantages of the concession system to the host countries. This situation was one of the major factors that gave birth to new types of petroleum agreements. Indeed, many host countries introduced RSCs – whereby the contractor bears the entire financial risk and has no ownership rights either to the reserves discovered or to the production from the agreed area – and other service contracts. Alternatively, some host countries amended existing participation agreements.[41]

After the Iranian Islamic Republic revolution of 1979, Iran implemented new Petroleum Law as part of the Petroleum Act 1987.[42] This permitted buy-back contracts between the Ministry of Petroleum, state companies and local and foreign nationals. Buy-back contracts have similar features to RSCs. The contracts were originally designed in 1995 to develop existing oil and gas fields, but by

38 Golam-Reza Afkhami, *Evolution of Iran's Oil Industry: An Industry's* View (translated by author, Iran's Study Institute, 1978) 84 [trans of: *Tahawwole-e- San'te-e Naft: Negahi az Darun* (1357)].

39 W A Otman, 'The Iranian Petroleum Contract: Past, Present and Future Perspectives' (2007) 44(5) *Oil, Gas & Energy Law Intelligence* 7.

40 Michael Corbett, 'Oil Shock of 1973–74' (22 November 2013) Federal Reserve History <http://www.federalreservehistory.org/Events/DetailView/36>. Also, See 'The Price of Oil-In Context' (Media Released, 18 April 2006) 1 <https://web.archive.org/web/20070609145246/http://www.cbc.ca/news/background/oil/>.

41 Otman, above n 39, 8.

42 Nasrollahi Shahri, above n 13, 9.

2003 they had been extended to include the exploration and development phases for onshore and offshore oil and gas fields.[43] The main features of a buy-back contract include contract duration of between five and seven years, and a fixed rate of return of 15 percent to 20 percent.[44] The IOC is also required to transfer capital, technology and management skills.[45] The project's executive management is formed under the supervision of a six-member committee, comprising three representatives from each side.[46] In the first year, the chairman of the committee is Iranian, with the nationality of the chair rotating thereafter on an annual basis.[47] In addition:

- 'the contractor has no further interest in the field after all costs have been recovered at the end of the amortisation period;
- the NIOC takes over the operation of the field upon the commencement of production and is responsible for the operating costs; and
- the contractor holds no equity in the field'.[48]

Exerting government control over all oil and gas production stages, especially upstream stages, has been popular from an historical point of view as well as politically popular. However, due to problems such as the high costs of investment in oil and gas projects, the high level of risk, the costs the government is bound to pay in these agreements and the Iranian government's reluctance to invest public funds in fields where the profitability and return of the capital is doubtful, the realisation of these policies was improbable. This gap requires a better understanding of the reality that oil rich countries, like Iran, often face the problem of a lack of adequate financial resources for infrastructure investments. This led to a practice in the various contracts concluded by Iran whereby, irrespective of which contractual framework was utilised, a clause was incorporated stating that if the operating company incurs costs from the exploration phase up to the time the production becomes commercial, the government is bound to pay the investment costs only if the operation leads to the commercial outcome.[49] Therefore, the oil- and gas-producing states could devise a formula which exempts them from the heavy costs of investment and at the same time recognise the share of the state in the revenues of the project.[50] Different projects required different

43 Abdolhossein Shiravi and Seyed Nasrollah Ebrahimi, 'Exploration and Development of Iran's Oilfields through Buyback' (2006) 30(3) *Natural Sources Forum* 203–204.

44 Ibid. 205.

45 Ibid. 206.

46 Ibid. 201.

47 Abdulaziz Al-Attar and Osamah Alomair, 'Evaluation of Upstream Petroleum Agreements and Exploration and Production Costs' (2005) 29(4) *OPEC Review: Energy Economics & Related Issues* 254.

48 Otman, above n 39, 10.

49 Shiravi and Ebrahimi, above n 43, 202–205.

50 Sakhaei Ehsan, *Oil Contracts of Production Sharing and their Applicability in the Oil Industry of Iran* (Dissertation for LLM of International Trade Law, Shahid Beheshti University, 2009) 83.

frameworks and, in this sense, using a single type of contractual form for all projects was not justifiable.[51]

History has shown that the government may be forced to resort to complicated or indirect mechanisms such as buy-back contracts, with ambiguous rights and duties of parties that are subject to misinterpretation because of the complex structure of such mechanisms. Because of its long history, the concession system has a track record of making the rights of the parties more transparent in a dispute about the interpretation of contract provisions where a wide range of legal and judicial precedents and customs exist.[52]

The literature also suggests that the advantage of the concession system for a country like Iran is that the state bears no liability as to different risks inherent to every oil and gas project.[53] Costs may put added pressure upon the public budget, and considering the economic problems the Iranian government must deal with to regulate its public finance, it is a matter which is undoubtedly unpleasant to the Iranian government. In buy-back systems, the government tried to discharge its financial obligations by incorporating clauses into the contracts, but in the concession system the discharge of the state's financial liabilities is the essence of the contract.[54]

Finally, there is evidence that the concession contractual framework may more efficiently deal with the lack of adequate financial resources for investment for the discovery and exploitation of oil and gas in many of the regions of the Iran Plateau.[55] It is important to consider the viability of the NCC, and its transformation to one of the recognised and accepted types in the Iranian legal system, as a way to provide an improved contractual framework for attracting investment in new fields and improved trade competitiveness (particularly with Saudi Arabia).[56]

1.7 Methodology

This book follows a qualitative research method. Qualitative research methods attempt to glean the insider's view of the topic, not necessarily the objective truth, but the truth as the information perceives it.[57] Qualitative methods have links with postmodernism, whereby the multifaceted aspects of experience are duly recognised. Qualitative research methodologies acknowledge that there is

51 Ansari, above n 8, 98.

52 Jenik Radon, 'The ABCs of Petroleum Contracts: License-Concession Agreement, Joint Ventures, and Production Sharing Agreements' 63–64.

53 Faranak Rabiei, *Contracts Law* (translated by author, Behnami, 2002) 71 [trans of: *Hoghoogh-e-Gharardadha* (1381)].

54 Shiravi and Ebrahimi, above n 43, 201.

55 David N Smith and Louis T Wells, 'Mineral Agreement in Developing Countries, Structures and Substance' (1975) 69(3) *The American Journal of International Law* 591.

56 Iran and Saudi Arabia are traditional rival in OPEC and they have continuous competitive in terms of oil production amount.

57 Robert E Burns, *Introduction to Research Methods* (Longman, Cheshire, 4th ed, 2000) 11.

not one overriding reality, but that reality is situational, personal and between context and individuals. In other words, qualitative research methods are particularly suitable for gaining an in-depth understanding of underlying reasons and motivations. It provides insights into the setting of a problem. At the same time, it frequently generates ideas.[58] It also uses theoretical, analytical, historical and comparative approaches to oil and gas contractual forms and evolution in selected comparable countries. This book, like most legal books and researches, applies the two-part doctrinal method: locating the sources of the law in legal system in Iran, and then interpreting and analysing the text of these laws. It also uses form-oriented approaches that have regard to the national interests of the government of Iran in the future development of upstream oil and gas fields.

This book reviews current Iranian legal regimes governing oil and gas contracts for the development of the upstream oil and gas industry. This review, as well as the comparative theoretical analysis of contractual forms, provides the basis for recommendations on the future development of oil and gas contracts in Iran.

This research includes secondary resources such as articles, books, Iran's Foreign Ministry and oil and gas documents, magazines, theses and dissertations undertaken at domestic and foreign universities, expert bulletins of multinational oil and gas companies, international investment recommendations of United Nations (UN) Economic and Social Council and the publicly available texts of concluded contracts in the field of oil and gas in Iran and other countries relying on the upstream oil and gas industry. The focus is on the CCC and NCC.

Issues of confidentiality and access to commercial negotiations mean that it was necessary to heavily rely on secondary resources such as those described above. The important research dimension is the application of research to the relevant aspects of the Iranian legal system for the future development of Iranian oil and gas contractual frameworks.

1.8 Book structure

To achieve the above goals, this book has been divided into six separate chapters, each divided into several parts.

Chapter 2 outlines the history and legal framework of Iran's oil and gas contracts such as concession contracts, production sharing agreements, service contracts and buy-back contracts with legal and comparative analysis between them. In addition, the characteristics of the upstream oil and gas industry in Iran and related exploration issues are discussed.

Chapter 3 explains the nature and features of the CCC and the characteristics that distinguish it from the NCC. Part one considers the nature and features of CCC, part two explains the nature and features of NCC and part three distinguishes the difference between them.

58 Terry Hutchinson, *Researching and Writing in Law* (Thomson Reuters, 3rd ed, 2010) 106.

Chapter 4 examines the NCC in upstream oil and gas industries including Brazil, Thailand, Australia, the UK and Norway, with a critique of the special features of NCC having regard to the circumstances of Iran.

Chapter 5 considers the regimes competing with the NCC such as production sharing agreement, joint ventures, service contract and buy-back contracts as current oil and gas contractual agreements in Iran. The new Iranian Petroleum Contract is examined. Attention is also given to the positive and negative points of the NCC having regard to these other contract forms.

Chapter 6 critiques the NCC under the Iranian legal system and the viability of these contract types to support Iran's oil-based economy to attract more foreign investment. This chapter also considers what reforms to Iran's legal frameworks are necessary and what reforms to the NCC framework are necessary to better comply with Iran's statutes. This requires the context of Islamic law in Iran, an overview of existing oil and gas legal framework in Iran and consideration of the opportunities and barriers to adopting the NCC for upstream oil and gas development. Regard is given to the Iranian legal system and to proposing the NCC framework for Iran's upstream oil and gas industry.

1.9 Conclusion

This chapter defines the key terms and concepts used throughout this book. The central questions for this book are identified and the associated methodology and book structure are outlined. Further, a brief review of Iran's oil and gas legal history and framework since the discovery and extraction of Iran's oil is provided, along with details of the development of the original CCC in Iran. The potential NCC is also discussed.

2 History and legal framework of Iran's oil and gas contracts and sectors of oil and gas industry

2.1 Oil and gas industry of Iran

The oil and gas industry has a lot of influence in the world today. To really understand the processes involved in the oil and gas industry, it makes sense to consider its subdivision. The oil and gas industry is essentially subdivided into three phases: the upstream sector, the midstream sector and the downstream sector. Before examining these phases, it is important to note that the midstream sector is also included in the downstream sector.[1]

2.1.1 The upstream sector

The upstream oil and gas industry involves processes including the searching for and recovery of crude oil[2] as well as its production.[3] In the upstream sector, discovery or exploration of crude oil involves intensive and extensive efforts towards

1 Professors Macini and Mesini, and other oil experts believe the midstream sector is included in the upstream sector. The oil and gas industry is usually divided into three main areas: the upstream sector (exploration and production), midstream sector (transport) and the downstream sector (refining and marketing). The midstream sector is often included in the upstream. Paolo Macini and Ezio Mesini, *The Petroleum Upstream Industry: Hydrocarbons Exploration and Production* (Encyclopedia of Life Support Systems (EOLSS), 2008) 2.

2 Macini and Mesini define crude oil as fossil fuels such as coal and natural gas that has originated from the remains of plants and animals that died hundreds of millions of years ago. The plants and animals, just like today, have accumulated energy from the sun and, after being buried for millions of years, the energy turns into oil, gas and coal. Prehistoric plants and animals give back the solar energy accumulated in the past. Ibid. 2–5.

3 The types of oil and gas products depend partly on the natural structure of the hydrocarbons and partly on the post-extraction production processes.

- *Crude oil* – It comes in three types depending on its chemical structure, which also determines its density:
- *Paraffin-based crudes* – These are mostly composed of paraffin molecules. These tend to have a low density and are generally referred to as *light crudes.*
- *Asphalt-based crudes* – These are mostly composed of naphthenic molecules. These tend to have a high density and are generally referred to as heavy crudes.
- *Mixed-base crudes* – These contain paraffin, naphthenic and aromatic hydrocarbons. These are heavier than paraffin-based crudes, but lighter than asphalt-based crudes.

ascertaining the actual places where crude oil is located. Exploration is a very difficult process and therefore requires the services of experts in the field. Moreover, information technology plays an active role in the exploration or searching of crude oil to easily discover new grounds where oil is located.

The upstream sector includes different operations such as the searching for prospective underwater oil and gas fields, drilling of exploratory wells and making requisite operations on the wells to bring the crude oil or natural gas[4] to the ground surface.

The definition of the upstream sector is specific to Iran. This is because every country has a different definition for their upstream sector based on special geology, geophysics and geochemistry circumstances.[5] However, the upstream sector compromises four distinct phases of activities.

2.1.1.1 Exploration

The exploration phase focuses on the exploration of the geology of the region and involves aerial tracking, seismic surveying and the drilling of exploratory wells, in search for commercially viable hydrocarbon reservoirs. Governments develop and maintain publicly available databases which include petroleum occurrences, data concerning other minerals and natural resources and geological data.

This phase is heavily reliant on expensive specialist drilling rigs. In offshore marine exploration, these rigs can include floating platforms, jack-up rigs, drilling ships and semi-submersible vessels. They are all very expensive to hire, build or operate. In onshore exploration, there needs to be sufficient drilling rig capacity to undertake new phases of petroleum exploration and production. Exploration is currently taking place in Iran, particularly in the Persian Gulf.

2.1.1.2 Appraisal

The appraisal phase assesses the size and quality of the reservoirs and therefore the commercial potential of a discovery. This is usually done by drilling more appraisal wells near exploration wells. Production tests reservoir pressures and

4 *Natural gas* is mainly methane. It is treated before sale to remove the propane, butane, other liquid hydrocarbons and impurities that it often contains in its crude form.

- *Liquefied natural gas (LNG)* – It is a natural gas cooled to below -160 degrees Celsius, thereby rendering it a liquid. This reduces its volume by over 600 times, making storage and transportation viable.
- *Liquefied petroleum gas (LPG)* – It consists of propane and butane. It is found in gas and oil reservoirs and is also a refinery by-product. LPG liquefies under slight cooling and compression and is used as motor, domestic and industrial fuel. James H Gary et al, *Petroleum Refining Technology and Economics* (Taylor and Francis, 2007).

5 For instance, definition of upstream sector from the perspective of Australia government productive commission that published in *Review of regulatory burden on the upstream petroleum (oil and gas) sector* is "The upstream petroleum (oil and gas) sector encompasses exploration and appraisal, development and construction, and production. For oil, natural gas and liquefied natural gas (LNG), the definition of upstream includes processing and delivery to export terminals or to the intakes of domestic gas transmission pipelines."

flow rates. Geochemical and petrophysical analyses give information about the hydrocarbons (e.g., viscosity and chemistry) and the porosity of the reservoir. Some countries require the certification of reserves by a government body as a precondition of the development phase.

2.1.1.3 Development

The development phase involves establishing the commercial viability of the field, as well as the subsequent planning process to commercially exploit the underlying petroleum resources. Planning includes the engineering and construction of production facilities. Planning also includes the depletion of the reservoir and rates of production, as well as the design and engineering of production facilities and pipelines, environmental concerns, safety and community and work force issues.

The development stage also includes economic considerations such as capital and production costs, taxation and royalties. In Iran, as in many countries, before production can commence, the government will have to approve the developer's detailed field development plan for the proposed development.

The final step prior to commencing construction, usually called the final investment decision, is the formal commitment to allocate funds to develop the project and commence engineering, procurement and construction. This phase can take from one to 10 years or more, depending on the size of the field and complexity of the technical, economic, commercial and regulatory hurdles.

2.1.1.4 Production

During the production phase, petroleum commences flowing, the rate of flow depending on the geology of the field and the requirement of the field development plan. The production capacity of a well is normally reached gradually as new production wells are slowly brought on-stream. Initially wells will often flow under their own pressure. However, as the field loses pressure, enhanced oil recovery techniques, often involving gas or water injection, are usually required. This phase can last many years, often up to 40 years or more for large fields in Iran. Major costs during this phase are associated with the development of techniques to improve recovery from a well and the drilling of further wells to enhance production.

2.1.2 The downstream sector

The downstream sector of the oil and gas industry involves the refining of the crude oil and/or raw natural gases obtained in the upstream sector, as well as selling or distributing the products obtained. Many products are derived from the refining of crude oil including diesel oil, liquefied petroleum gas (LPG), asphalt, petroleum coke, gasoline, fertilisers, antifreeze, plastic, rubbers, pesticides, synthetic rubber, jet fuel and many more.

The downstream sector of the industry is the sector that relates to the consumers. Facilities involved in this sector include petrochemical plants, oil refineries, natural gas distribution companies, retail outlets and so forth. Indeed, the downstream sector is an industry which is beyond the initial extraction and processing stages and it includes refining and marketing. The main processes involved in the upstream and downstream oil and gas operations include exploration, extraction, development, exploitation, production, refining, transporting and marketing.

2.2 History and legal frameworks of Iran's oil and gas

The history and legal frameworks of the Iranian oil industry have generally been classified into three periods. The first period consists of the individually negotiated agreements that instigated the discovery and exploration of oil in Iran (1901). The most important feature of this period was a lack of legal grounds and the prevalence of concessions. The second period was from the nationalisation of the oil and gas industry in 1951 until the Islamic revolution in 1979. The final period is the General Legislative Period that started from the Islamic revolution and which is in place to present day, whereby all petroleum contracts have to accord with Iran's Constitution, laws and petroleum acts.

2.2.1 From exploration to nationalisation (1901–1951)

The period from the first exploration of oil in Iran until the nationalisation of Iran's oil industry by parliament in 1951 was characterised by a lack of legislative framework, contractual form and agreements; except individually negotiated with no pre-conditions. The first governance system in Iran followed the pattern of concession, taking into consideration the current structure of oil contracts at that time. Similar to other countries which have resources in oil in the region, the ruler of Iran (Shah) used to sign off all the concessions with other foreign companies. Since, there was no rule about this concession; the rulers had not legal restrictions about the type of contracts and conditions applying to them. The D'Arcy Concession and the 1933 Concession Agreement are considered two of the main agreements entered before the nationalisation of the oil industry in 1951.[6]

2.2.1.1 D'Arcy Concession

More than a century has elapsed since the beginning of the oil industry in Iran's sedimentary basins. Officially, it commenced with the concession granted to William Knox D'Arcy (a British citizen, and an entrepreneur and financer who had made a fortune in gold mining in Australia) by Shah of Iran in 1901.[7]

The first concession ever granted in the entire Middle East was the exclusive rights to oil exploration of the entire country, excepting the five provinces. The

6 Nima Nasrollahi Shahri, 'The Petroleum Legal Framework of Iran: History, Trends and the Way Forward' (2010) 8(12) *China and Eurasia Forum Quarterly Journal* 113.

7 Simon Chapman, 'Oil in Middle East and North Africa' in Lucy Dean (eds), *The Middle East and North Africa 2004* (Europa Publication, 50th ed, 2004) 116.

first site chosen for exploration was in southern region, an almost inaccessible plateau in the mountains of western of Iran. Meanwhile, D'Arcy was looking for financial support to cover mounting exploration costs to keep the concession.[8] However, D'Arcy resolved his financial difficulties by involving Glasgow-based British company and Burma Oil (named after its concession operations in Burma) in the exploration.[9] D'Arcy's protracted negotiation with Burma Oil resulted in the formation of a new company, Concession Syndicates Ltd, in mid-1905, with financial and technical support provided by Burma Oil. D'Arcy's operation thus became a subsidiary, and he was a director of the new enterprise.[10]

The first commercial oil discovery was recorded in the Masjid Solaiman concession area on 26 May 1908.[11] Shortly after the discovery of this huge oil field, the Anglo-Persian Oil Company (APOC) was established, which later became the AIOC in 1935. It is now better known today as British Petroleum (BP).[12] Regarding to the concession, the exclusive right to explore, develop, exploit and transport petroleum was granted to the concessionaire. The Iranian government received up to 16 percent of the net profit on all operations, in return. However, the concession was protested through Shah of Iran because of its less share in oil revenue.[13]

2.2.1.2 The 1933 Concession Agreement

By the late 1920s, the APOC was seeking a 20-year extension on the original 1901 concession. Consequently, a special commission was established for the purposes of negotiation. Negotiation missions were carried out by a 'Taimoortash' (First Minister of Court) on behalf of the Iranian government with the commission's aim to negotiate for the renewal of conditions.[14] The insistence on the inclusion of specific terms in the contract leads to a stalemate. Meetings between both parties continued for several years until 1931, when the situation became even more critical for Iran. Proceeds from oil dropped to £300,000 pounds, merely a quarter of its oil revenue of £1.28 million pounds in the previous year.[15]

8 Ronald W Ferrier, *The History of the British Petroleum Company* (Cambridge, 1982) 163.

9 Ibid. 167.

10 Thomas Anthony Buchanan Corley, *A History of the Burmah Oil Company* (London, 1983) 87.

11 Randy Alfred, 'May 26, 1908: Mideast Oil Discovered – There Will Be Blood' (21 March 2012) <http://www.wired.com/2008/05/dayintech-0526/>.

12 Homayoun Mafi, 'Iran's Concession Agreements and the Role of the National Iranian Oil Company: Economic Development and Sovereign Immunity' (2008) 48 *Natural Resources Journal* 409.

13 Nasrollahi Shahri, above n 6, 114.

14 As conditions for renewing the concession agreement, the Taimoortash requested amendments to the old concession contract. These were two shillings/ton royalty on oil produced; the return of three quarters of the concession area to the Government of Iran; an Iranian Government holding of 25 percent in the Anglo-Persian Oil Company (APOC); payment of tax in line with Iranian Taxation Law and finally, the complete transfer of all the company's operations to the government of Iran after the termination of the contract. Mohammad Malek, 'Oil in Iran between the Two World Wars' (9 March 2016) Iran Chamber Society <http://www.iranchamber.com/history/articles/oil_iran_between_world_wars.php>.

15 Ibid.

Although the world recession undoubtedly caused this disastrous drop in revenues, the government of Iran saw this as directly attributable to Anglo-Persian's intractable approach. The result was a decision from Reza Shah to end the concession, supported by the Iranian Majlis (Parliament). The British government protested the Iranian decision by sending several warships to the Persian Gulf, and ultimately the intervention of the League of Nation was required to resolve the dispute through diplomatic channels.[16]

Before the ruling from the International Court, the AIOC and the Iranian government agreed to the key specifications of the 1933 concession as follows:

a Payment of 750,000 pounds annually (a minimum guaranteed) plus a royalty (4s gold per ton) of oil produced
b Payment of tax to Iran (4 percent with a minimum guaranteed tax of 230,000 pounds annually)
c Iran's representation on the board
d Payment of one million pounds (by APOC) as settlement of all past claims
e Reduce the allowable area of exploration to 100,000 square miles
f Full cancellation of the exclusive right for the transportation of oil, 20 percent of the share to Iran
g Cheaper oil for Iranians[17]

With the implementation of the 1933 agreement, the royalties for 1931 and 1932 were recalculated on the new basis, with the result that 1,339,132 pounds sterling (US$5,758,267) was eventually paid for 1931, in lieu of the amount of 306,872 pounds sterling (US$1,319,549) that had caused so much vexation. The Iranian government's revenues from oil sold inside and outside the country increased from an average of 12.3 US cents a barrel during 1913–1932 to an average of 21.5 US cents in the period 1933 to June 1951. Total revenues rose from US$5.7 million in 1929 to US$10.3 million in 1936 and US$44.8 million in 1950. Oil production also rose from 116,000 barrels per day to 171,000 and 664,000, respectively, during the corresponding period.[18]

2.2.2 *From nationalisation to revolution (1951–1979)*

Government used to play a passive role in the oil industry prior to the nationalisation of the oil in 1951. However, the government's role became totally

16 Waniss A Otman, 'The Iranian Petroleum Contract: Past, Present and Future Perspectives' (2007) 44(5) *Oil, Gas & Energy Law Intelligence* 11.

17 Malek, above n 14.

18 Mohammad Yeganeh, Farokh Najmabadi, and Parviz Mina, 'The Development of The Iranian Oil Industry' (Proceedings of the Conference held at the School of Oriental Studies London in March 1990, Published by Society for Contemporary Iranian Studies, Middle East Center, University of London, 1991) 52–53.

different in petroleum operations after the nationalisation of the oil industry. According to Ramazani,

> After the passage of the Nationalisation Law (1951), the Iranian government went to the other extreme by controlling all exploration, extraction and exploitation operations. The grave economic and political conditions that ensued in the subsequent years revealed that realism demanded modernisation. Thus, it was decided to encourage the flow of foreign investment in oil, but at the same time provide for Iran's participation through some kind of partnership with foreign oil concerns.[19]

2.2.2.1 Nationalisation

The first anti-concession proposals were written and submitted to the Iranian parliament by the leader of the National Front of Iran's party, Dr Mohammad Mosaddegh, in December 1944. However, due to the Second World War and many complex security issues relating to Iran and its allies, issues related to nationalisation were put on hold until after the war.

After the Second World War, Iranian dissatisfaction with the level of oil revenues was greatly aggravated by its growing annoyance at the fact that the British government was extracting more income from APOC through taxation than the Iranian government was obtaining from the exploitation of Iran's national resources. For example, from 1945 to 1947, Iran's oil revenue including royalties and taxes amounted from 5.62 to 7.10 million pounds, whereas, British government taxation rocketed from 15.63 to 16.82 million pounds, over the same period.[20]

Financial injustice, pervading poverty and other reasons in Iran were catalyst to the nationalistic movement in Iran which was led by Mosaddegh. The movement resulted in the nationalisation of the Iranian oil industry in 1951. During this time, Dr Mosaddegh was appointed as the Iranian Prime Minister (1951) and he cemented the link between Iranian oil and Iranian nationalism by transforming oil from a fungible commodity to a political symbol. Mosaddegh immediately submitted the draft of the new Petroleum Law to the Majlis, incorporating much of his previous ideas and policies on nationalisation.[21]

The Petroleum Law was passed on 29 April 1951 and was applied with immediate effect. Within a month the NIOC was established, and the nationalisation of the Iranian oil industry was initiated.[22]

19 Rouhollah K Ramazani, 'Choice-of-Law Problems and International Oil Contracts: A Case Study' (1962) 11(2) *The International and Comparative Law Quarterly* 57.

20 John H Bamberg, *The History of the British Petroleum Company* (Cambridge University Press, 1994) 58.

21 Jerrold L Walden, 'The International Cartel in Iran: Private Power and the Public Interest' (1962) 11 *Journal of Public Law* 23.

22 Otman, above n 16, 5–6.

The nationalisation of Iran's oil industry generated much domestic and foreign argument as to the reasons why the Iranian parliament decided to revise the structure of the oil concession framework. This book argues it was due to Iran's recent independence, its desire to earn higher oil and gas revenues and the wish for more direct participation by the national government. This placed heavier financial burdens and greater risks on the international companies.[23]

In the end, it could also be said that the nine-point law provided for the implementation of nationalisation, covering inter alia provisions for expropriation of assets of the AIOC, the settlement of claims and counter claims of the two parties, the establishment of the NIOC for the operation of the Iranian oil industry and arrangements for the uninterrupted sale of oil to the former AIOC customers.[24] The nationalisation of Iranian oil had some purposes: creating domination for Iranian government, ownership and giving the control of the oil resources to Iranian government. Furthermore, British influence whether in the form of politics or economy was eliminated, so they did not have any control over Iranian rich oil resources anymore. Moreover, the Iranian government had freedom to make use of oil throughout exploration, extraction and exploitation.[25]

Nationalisation had both dramatic and enduring consequences because Britain and America thought Dr Mosaddegh was a threat to their nation's economic interests. The confrontation between Iran and Britain resulted in a worldwide purchase boycott of Iranian oil, and to temporary political and financial chaos. In the summer of 1953, a coup (*TPAJAX*) orchestrated by the Central Intelligence Agency (CIA) and British intelligence.[26] The coup ended in the downfall of Mosaddegh and restored the Shah to power.[27]

2.2.2.2 The 1954 Consortium Oil Agreement

After the 1953 coup and the return of Shah to Iran, it was set to produce more oil and sell at the global markets. It could be done by AIOC while the America wanted to reach Iranian oil in some ways. Therefore, US was seeking whether a new consortium of oil companies could be created to take up the AIOC's interests. Consequently, the Anglo-American inter-company talks led to signing of a memorandum of understanding in 1954.[28]

The consortium agreed that the shares would be as follows: 40 percent for BP (AIOC in that time), 14 percent for Royal Dutch-Shell, 8 percent each for

23 Mafi, above n 12, 410.

24 Mostafa Elm, *Oil, Power, and Principle: Iran's Oil Nationalisation and Its Aftermath* (Syracuse, 1992).

25 Ibid. 81–90.

26 On 19 August 1953 Iranian coup d'état, known in Iran as the 28 Mordad coup, was the overthrow of Prime Minister, Mohammad Mosaddegh, and his cabinet, orchestrated by the UK (under the name 'Operation Boot') and the US (under the name *TPAJAX* Project). Mark Gasiorowski, *Mohammad Mosaddeq and the 1953 Coup in Iran* (Syracuse University Press, 2004) 137.

27 Otman, above n 16, 5–6.

28 Mahmoud Toloui, *Powergame, Oil War in the Middle East* (Elm Publication, 1993) 127.

the five US companies (Standard Oil [NJ], Socony, Socal, Texas and Gulf) and 6 percent for Compagnie Française des Pétroles (CFP). This arrangement was later modified in April 1955 when each of the US major companies gave up 1 percent of its holding so that a 5 percent share could be made available for nine smaller independent US oil companies to hold through a joint organisation, the IRICON Agency, which they formed for this purpose.[29]

On the formation of the consortium, and for the future operation of the Iranian oil industry, the negotiations moved to Tehran after the agreement had been reached in London. The Standard Oil representative was head of the consortium negotiating team, and the Iranian delegation was led by the Finance Minister. The oil agreement was finally signed in Iran in 1954 after four months of intensive negotiations, at that time the Iranian Finance Minister submitted the agreement to the Iranian parliament. The parliament approves the agreement and the Shah signed the royal assent to create the Amini-Page contract.[30]

The agreement was declared that the oil profits should be divided equally between the consortium and the Iranian government, preserving the principle of 50/50 profit sharing according to the Middle East norm. This contract had a basic 25-year term, with a provision for automatic renewal for 15 years. The contract also required the consortium to relinquish exclusive exploitation rights to 20 percent of the area it controlled after each five-year extension period.[31]

While this agreement was an improvement over the 1933 concession, it again failed to live up to Mossadegh's promise that securing control of Iran's own oil would mean controlling its own destiny. It was obvious that the NIOC still did not have total control over output or marketing[32] and that the Iranian government was an owner with no rights.[33] The long reviled British and newly despised Americans were still meddling in Iran's domestic politics. Most importantly, the fact that the agreement was accepted by an increasingly autocratic and unpopular Shah, rather than Mossadegh, meant that what could have been considered a triumph for Iran was perceived rather as a humiliation.[34] Finally, the fact cannot be denied that the 1954 agreement failed to meet the main target of 1951 oil nationalisation.

29 'Oil Agreements in Iran' (20 July 2004) Encyclopaedia Iranica 15 <http://www.iranicaonline.org/articles/oil-agreements-in-iran>.

30 Ibid. 15.

31 Otman, above n 16, 6.

32 Daniel Brumberg, 'The National Iranian Oil Company in Iranian Politics' (Prepared in Conjunction with an Energy Study Sponsored by Japan Petroleum Centre and the James A. Baker III Institute for Public Policy, Rice University, 2007) 14.

33 Harvey O'Connor, 'How the International Oil Cartel Carved Up the Oil Resources of Iran after the Overthrow of Mossadegh; A Full Account of a Little-Known Story by an Expert in the Oil-Industry Field: The Iranian Oil Grab' (2010) 12 <http://www.marxists.org/history/etol/newspape/amersocialist/amersoc_5504-a.htm>.

34 Brumberg, above n 32, 14. Also See Mary Ann Heiss, *Empire and Nationhood: The United States, Great Britain, and Iranian Oil 1950–1954* (Columbia University Press, 1997) 209–221.

2.2.2.3 *The 1957 Petroleum Act*

The first Petroleum Law in Iran was enacted in 1957 in the years immediately following the signing of the 1954 Consortium Agreement. Three years after the consortium was established, and while negotiations were being conducted between the NIOC and Azinda General Italiana Petrole (AGIP) Mineraria (the upstream arm of the Italian State Oil Company (ENI), the first Petroleum Act was drafted and submitted to the Iranian parliament. It was then ratified in 1957.[35]

The discovery of some oil and gas fields[36] by the Iran Oil Company was the result of action by the fledgling national Iranian oil and gas industry. The company set up during the First Plan to explore and exploit petroleum not only proved Iran's growing technical capacity but also helped to give Iran a prestige not hitherto enjoyed by any other oil producing and exporting country. Against this background, it is therefore hardly surprising that renowned IOCs such as ENI decided to look for oil supplies in the Middle East by offering new contractual terms. Since access to crude oil resources was of utmost importance for Italy and ENI, a way had to be found for entry into the Middle East oil scene. The NIOC and ENI thus pioneered a new form of contractual relationship, thereafter known as 75/25 profit sharing, or better known today as Production Sharing Contract (PSC). This broke the hallowed 50-50 arrangement and heralded a new era in international oil agreements.[37]

However, a basic and important question is, what had prompted Iran's governors to enact the 1957 Petroleum law? Moreover, what was its aim? To encourage private investment in oil, the Iranian parliament passed the new Petroleum Law in July 1957. It aimed to provide a different basis for Iranian oil operations, a middle way between the concession system where the Iranian government had to assume the role of bystander and rent collector with no control over the management or direction of this most strategic industry, and the opposite extreme epitomised by the Nationalisation Law of 1951. The severe economic consequences following the 1951 Nationalisation Law demonstrated that a more pragmatic approach was required to attract and retain investment in Iran's crucial oil sector, while also enabling the government's active involvement in this key industry through partnership with foreign concerns with the expertise and capital to undertake the risky and invariably long-term investments that characterised it.[38]

Furthermore, swift exploration and extraction of petroleum started by the Petroleum Act in all spots of the country and the continental shelf (excluding the consortium area). Moreover, some processes like refining, transportation and sale of petroleum were resulted.[39] Doing so, the NIOC got the permission to

35 E H Wall, 'The Iranian-Italian Oil Agreement of 1957' (1958) 7(4) *The International and Comparative Law Quarterly* 786.

36 Alborz oilfield and the Sarājeh gas field.

37 'Oil Agreements in Iran', above n 29, 19.

38 Otman, above n 16, 7.

39 Wall, above n 35, 792.

enter into contractual relationships with persons, Iranian or foreign, possessing the requisite technical and financial competence, in order to develop the hydrocarbon resources of Iran.[40]

One important feature of this law was the permission granted to joint ventures with government participation. The minimum share to the NIOC for its participation in any such ventures was 30 percent,[41] which was a principle not always adhered to. As was the case with the 1953 Consortium, contracts were to be agreed for a period of 25 years[42] with compulsory relinquishment requirements starting after 10 years[43] not leaving the IOC with more than 1,000 square kilometres.[44]

The oil contracts conducted between the NIOC and IOC after the passing of the 1957 law are as follows.

The first, in 1957, was with the Italian Government-owned AGIP Mineria, which provided for the formation of the Iranian company, Société Irano-Italienne des Pétroles (SIRIP).[45]

A second oil contract was signed with Pan American Petroleum Corporation and led to the formation in 1958 of the Iran Pan American Corporation, or IPAC.[46] The fiscal terms were also a significant aspect of these contracts in that

40 'Oil Agreements in Iran', above n 29, 19.

41 *The Law Regarding Exploration, Discovery and Extraction of Oil in all Regions of the Country and Continental Shelf* (Iran) National Parliament of Iran 1957 art 6.

42 Ibid. art 7, paragraph 4.

43 Ibid. art 7, paragraph 3.

44 Ibid. art 8, paragraph 6.

45 This agreement was shaped and formed on the basis of a mixed organisation model in which the NIOC and AGIP Mineraria established a new juridical entity; the SIRIP (Société Irano-Italienne des Pétroles) was created with equal shareholding by the NIOC and AGIP Mineraria. The agreement covered three distinct zones: a zone of the continental shelf located in the northern part of the Persian Gulf, a continental zone located in the eastern slopes of the central Zagros Mountains and finally a zone along the coast of the Gulf of Oman. The total agreement area of some 23,000 square kilometres was to be reduced by 25 percent at the end of the fifth year from the beginning of exploration. In addition, an amount of, followed by a further reduction of 25 percent was reduced at the end of the ninth year. At the end of 12th year, In any case, the SIRIP could only hold terrain in which commercial fields had been discovered. 'Oil Agreements in Iran', above n 29, 20–21. Also See Marius S Vassiliou, *The A to Z of the Petroleum Industry* (Scarecrow Press, 2009).

46 This Agreement was negotiated and concluded between the NIOC and the Pan American Petroleum Corporation (owned by the Standard Oil Company of Indiana) in conformity with the bidding procedures as envisaged in the Petroleum Act. Although the vehicle chosen was the joint structure type operator, the major clauses were like those embodied in the SIRIP Agreement, with some innovations. In general, the agreement was a better-organised and more lucid document. The area under the Agreement was fixed at 16,000 square kilometres of the continental shelf in the Persian Gulf. The entity formed, the Iran Pan American Oil Company (IPAC), merely acted as an agent of its principals, except that in carrying out and performing the exploration obligations of the second party, the IPAC acted as the agent of Pan American Petroleum Corporation. Under this agreement, Pan American not only undertook a very significant exploration obligation by the standards of the day, amounting to a minimum of $82 million, it also offered to pay a large signature bonus of $25 million. Both these facets of the agreement

they appeared to give the NIOC 75 percent of net profits realised from the investment. These were fiscal terms unheard-of in petroleum investments at this time. In fact, the new contracts were participation agreements in which the Second Party (IOC) shared risks and rewards equally with the NIOC. Because the second party had to pay 50 percent of its share of profits as tax to the government of Iran, however, it effectively meant that 75 percent of profit share went to Iran and 25 percent to the second party. However, the second party still received 50 percent of the profits realised from its actual investment.[47]

Based on the success and experience gained by the NIOC with the implementation of the SIRIP and IPAC agreements, and given the ambitious nature of the government's development plans and economic growth objectives, a decision was taken to open a part of the continental shelf of the Persian Gulf for international bidding. However, this time round, the NIOC decided to carry out, at the expense of those interested in bidding, a marine seismic programme on the area in question and to make the information so obtained available to bidders as a part of the technical file. This approach proved to be an enormous success. Not only did this 'Iranian first' concept set a trend to be widely followed by other countries, it also resulted in the payment of more than $180 million in cash bonuses by five groups of oil companies who concluded joint structure agreements with the NIOC in 1965. The significance of this round of bidding went well beyond the figures associated with bonuses and exploration obligations. A major oil company, Shell, had broken ranks with the other major companies and accepted the concept of participation. This, too, proved to be the forerunner of many new agreements leading eventually to OPEC's Resolution and Participation in 1971.[48]

NIOC once again pioneered an Agency Agreement (a new type of contractual relationship), where the operator, Entreprise de Rechereche et d'Activités Pétrolières (ERAP) which is a French State Oil Company, carried the status of a contractor without any ownership rights to production.[49] The main features of this agreement were the following:

a Technical, financial and commercial services were undertaken by ERAP.
b The NIOC has financial responsibility for the agreement which covered operations, with it understood that all funds required for exploration, appraisal and development operations were to be supplied by ERAP until the cash flow accruing to the NIOC because of the operations would be sufficient to enable it to provide the financing for appraisal and development.

were considered outside of the norms and were widely commented on in the petroleum literature. Mohammad Yeganeh, Farokh Najmabadi, and Parviz Mina, 'The Development of The Iranian Oil Industry' (Proceedings of the Conference held at the School of Oriental Studies London in March 1990, Published by Society for Contemporary Iranian Studies, Middle East Center, University of London, 1991) 80–90.

47 Otman, above n 16, 7.

48 'Oil Agreements in Iran', above n 29, 21.

49 Yeganeh et al, above n 46, 91–93.

c If a commercial field was discovered and commercial production commenced, the NIOC was liable for the repayment of all funds advanced by ERAP.
d The NIOC was fully owner of oil produced at well-head.
e In the case of commercial discovery, ERAP was to be reimbursed out of part of production for the loans extended to the NIOC, while it was also entitled to purchase a certain quantity of production at a discounted price as remuneration for services rendered, in the case of commercial discovery.
f The NIOC was the owner of all the assets created or used regarding the operation.
g The tax status of ERAP was that of a purchaser of oil, making no profit in Iran.[50]

2.2.2.4 The 1974 Petroleum Act

The philosophy underpinning any law could be affected by social situation, economic issues, domestic or international conditions or a long history. Prior to the 1974 Petroleum Act, the global oil price has remained low until the late 1960s. However, there was an almost three-fold increase in crude oil prices from 1970 to 1974, from US$3.39 to US$9.35/bbl. This led to excessive profits for the oil companies, and an approach was made to change the substance of petroleum contract.

This situation caused two occurrences. First, in early 1973 the NIOC issued an ultimatum to the oil consortiums that unless a new arrangement was agreed upon, Iran would not extend the 1954 oil agreement beyond 1979 (the original 25 years), and that the consortium members would then be treated as ordinary buyers of Iranian oil. In these circumstances, the consortium members opted for a new arrangement to become privileged customers of the Iranian oil in return for giving up the management and control of the oil industry in the agreement area. Consequently, a 20-year Sale and Purchase Agreement was signed between the parties on 19 July 1973 (with retroactive effect from 21 March 1973), replacing the 1954 Oil Agreement. Second, the situation turned out to be one of the major factors that gave birth to new types of petroleum agreements with many host countries introducing PSCs and other services contracts, while some amended existing participation agreements.[51]

To further enhance its control and management of the petroleum operation carried out on its behalf by qualified operators, the NIOC drafted a new and innovative Petroleum Act in 1974. This was approved by the Council of Ministers and enacted by the Parliament. In 1974, Iranian oil production reached its historical peak at 6.021.6 mm b/d.[52]

50 Ibid.
51 Otman, above n 16, 7.
52 OPEC, 'Annual Statistical Bulletin' (2012) <http://www.opec.org/opec_web/static_files_project/media/downloads/publications/ASB2012.pdf>.

It was also the year in which a new Iranian Oil Act, which amended the 1957 Petroleum Law, came into force. This new law stated that exploration and production agreements with foreign oil companies could only be concluded based on "Risk Service Contracts". These contracts restricted the contractor's ownership right to any reserves discovered or to the production from the agreement area. In a telling clause, Section 1 of Article 3 stipulated that "the petroleum resources and the petroleum industry of Iran belong to the nation. The exercise of the Iranian nation over the petroleum resources of Iran with respect to the exploration, development, production, exploitation and distribution of petroleum throughout the country and its continental shelf is entrusted exclusively to the National Iranian Oil Company who shall act thereupon directly, or through its agents and contractors".[53]

As mentioned above, this Act first introduced the Risk Service Contract concept in Article 3. In this contract, the contractor (IOC) had to conduct upstream exploration entirely at its own risk and had no rights to the reserves discovered or to the production from any field developed. If exploration led to a commercial discovery, the IOC had to develop the oil field under the supervision of the NIOC. Thereafter, for a stipulated period not exceeding 15 years, the NIOC would sell 50 percent of the production to the IOC at a discounted price, enabling it to recover its original investment plus a reasonable return on investment.[54]

The 1974 Petroleum Law prohibited the IOCs from ownership of hydrocarbon resources and stipulated terms restricted solely to the NIOC. The terms of all the Participation Contracts made under the 1957 Law were also completely amended in line with Article 19 of this law. The fiscal changes brought about by the new law increased tax payments from 50 percent to 80 percent and royalty payments from 12.5 percent to 20 percent. Oil prices were henceforth determined by OPEC, in line with specific crude oil types. These moves severely impacted the profitability of the IOC's operating in Iran, although production was sustained at an average of 5.534 b/d for the years 1975–1978 inclusive.[55]

Thus, during the period following the nationalisation of the Iranian oil industry, Iran moved from individually negotiated agreements to nationalisation, experiencing three sorts of oil and gas contracts: concession contracts, product sharing agreements and service contracts. The concession agreement was specific to the period from Iran's oil discovery up to nationalisation; whereas, the other two oil and gas contracts were approved in the 1957 Petroleum Law (product sharing agreement) and in the 1974 Petroleum Law (service contract).

2.2.3 From 1979 Islamic Republic of Iran's revolution to the present day

The consortium agreement and all other contracts that had been conducted were terminated unilaterally following the 1979 Islamic Revolution. At this time,

53 The text of the Act was published by Public Relations Affairs, Iranian Oil Industry in 1974.
54 *Petroleum Law 1974* (Iran) National Iranian Parliament, Iran Senate 1974, art 3.
55 Otman, above n 16, 8.

Iran's oil and gas industry opened a new era of petroleum legal regime whereby the discretion of the state as to what type of contractual regime it could engage in was completely confined within the legislative framework.[56]

2.2.3.1 The Constitution of 1979

The Iranian Constitution prohibited the granting of petroleum rights[57] on a concessionary basis or holdings of direct equity stakes in petroleum ventures to foreign companies or individuals. There were three main articles dealing with matters related to the hydrocarbon industry: Article 44 (Sectors), Article 45 (Public Wealth) and Article 81 (Foreign Business).[58]

ARTICLE 44 – NATIONALISATION OF MAJOR INDUSTRIES[59]

Article 44 dealt with economic activities in the new state, which were divided into three categories: state, cooperative and private. In this article, the hydrocarbon industry falls under 'large scale and mother industries, and major minerals' which will 'be publicly owned and administered by the State'. The main point of this article is that private ownership in Iran's oil and gas industries is not permitted after the Islamic revolution by nationalisation of all major industries. However, privatisation of most mother industries became legally feasible later through legislation,[60] with the petroleum industry remaining an exception. Thus, even now the petroleum industry cannot be privatised in such a way as the electricity sector, for example. In fact, Article 44 of the Constitution

56 Nasrollahi Shahri, above n 6, 118.

57 Article 4: Islamic Principle: "All civil, penal financial, economic, administrative, cultural, military, political, and other laws and regulations must be based on Islamic criteria. This principle applies absolutely and generally to all articles of the Constitution as well as to all other laws and regulations, and the wise persons of the Guardian Council are judges in this matter".

58 *Iranian Constitution 1979* (Iran) (to view the constitution in English, this is accessible at: <http://www.iranonline.com/iran/iran-info/government/constitution.html> (accessed 18/02/2017)).

59 The economy of the Islamic Republic of Iran is to consist of three sectors: state, cooperative and private and is to be based on systematic and sound planning. The state sector is to include all large-scale and mother industries, foreign trade, major minerals, banking, insurance, power generation, dams, large-scale irrigation networks, radio and television, post, telegraph and telephone services, aviation, shipping, roads, railroads and the like. All these will be publicly owned and administered by the State. The cooperative sector is to include cooperative companies and enterprises concerned with production and distribution, in urban and rural areas, in accordance with Islamic criteria. The private sector consists of those activities concerned with agriculture, animal husbandry, industry, trade and services that supplement the economic activities of the state and cooperative sectors. Ownership in each of these three sectors is protected by the laws of the Islamic Republic, in so far as this ownership is in conformity with the other articles of this chapter, does not go beyond the bounds of Islamic law, contributes to the economic growth and progress of the country and does not harm society. The scope of each of these sectors, as well as the regulations and conditions governing their operation, will be specified by law.

60 General Policies of Article 44 of the Constitution of The Islamic Republic of Iran, Exigency Council.

not only forbids any form of private ownership, it prohibits private participation (i.e., investment), be it foreign or domestic given it uses the words, "owned and controlled by the state". Based on the 1987 Petroleum Act, foreign investment is illegal explicitly.

ARTICLE 45 – NATURAL RESOURCES AS "ANFAL"[61]

The mineral resources under Islamic law are considered as public wealth and property known as the "Anfal".[62]

According to the Holy Quran, God and the Prophet are owners of Anfal. After the revolution, all legislation is based on, and should accord with, Shi'a Islamic teachings.[63] According to these teachings, Anfal cannot be transferred or sold. This is therefore a serious barrier in negotiating any agreement that might give title to oil, either in place or at well-head, to a private party be it foreign or domestic.[64] Article 45 granted rights over all national resources to the government, with the hydrocarbon sector the main target.

ARTICLE 81 – ON FOREIGN BUSINESS

This article prohibited rights to, or ownership of, the country's resources by any foreign investor. This covered both the awarding of concession contracts based on taxation/royalty and equity or participation arrangements for the exploitation of hydrocarbons.[65] It states:

> The granting of concessions to foreigners or the formation of companies or institutions dealing with commerce, industry, agriculture, service, or mineral extraction, is absolutely forbidden.

"Absolutely forbidden" means that is even if it ratified by the parliament it would not be legitimate in the context of the Constitution. In other words, the government is the only authority which can legitimately deal with natural resources. Thus, the concession contract, PSA and joint venture or any other contractual regime is not allowed to involve foreign participation and control, ownership

61 Public wealth and property, such as uncultivated or abandoned land, mineral deposits, seas, lakes, rivers and other public waterways, mountains, valleys, forests, marshlands, natural forests, unenclosed pastures, legacies without heirs, property of undetermined ownership, and public property recovered from usurpers, shall be at the disposal of the Islamic government for it to utilise in accordance with the public interest. Law will specify detailed procedures for the utilisation of each of the foregoing items.

62 *The Quran*, Surah Anfal.

63 *Iranian Constitution 1979* (Iran) (to view the Constitution in English, go to: <http://www.iranonline.com/iran/iran-info/government/constitution.html> (accessed 18/02/2017)).

64 Nasrollahi Shahri, above n 6, 120.

65 Otman, above n 16, 9.

or the establishment of foreign companies, due to Articles 44, 45 and 81 of the Iranian Constitution.[66]

Despite the impact of these radical changes to Iran's oil industry, and the departure of expatriate staff and many key production Iranian personnel, the country's oil industry did not collapse as many had predicted.[67] Not only this, even the massive physical destruction inflicted on the industry in the 1980–1988 Iran-Iraq war did not halt production. However, these two events undoubtedly inflicted a body blow on the development of Iran's hydrocarbon industry, from which it has not yet recovered. As will be seen in the following sections, despite the constraints on Foreign Direct Investment (FDI) imposed by the 1979 Constitution, the Iranian government has struggled to implement a workable fiscal regime to attract the IOCs with their modern technology and financial muscle to re-build the hydrocarbon sector.[68] On 19 June 1980, the Ministry of Petroleum was established to grant all rights and responsibilities over the oil and gas industry.

2.2.3.2 The 1987 Petroleum Act and the move towards buy-back contracts

Due to events through 1970s and 1980s in Iran such as the Islamic revolution, the eight-year war (1980–1988) between Iran and Iraq and imposition of enormous political and economic sanctions against Iran from the West, there were profound changes in the Iranian economy. Regarding the hydrocarbon industry, the first Petroleum Law of Iran was ratified on first October of 1987. In this law, all of Iran's petroleum reserves were counted as public wealth,[69] all foreign investment in Iran's petroleum industry was cancelled[70] and all previous legislations were abolished.[71]

ARTICLE 1: DEFINITION AND CONTRACTUAL OBLIGATION OF PARTIES[72]

Article 1 outlines the contractual obligations (undertakings) concluded between the Ministry of Oil or an operational unit or any natural person or legal entity

66 Nasrollahi Shahri, above n 6, 121.

67 Manouchehr Takin, 'Case Study – Iran', in *Working with Sanctions, Trade Controls & Political Risk* (Simon Gore Consulting London, 5–6 November 2003).

68 Otman, above n 16, 9.

69 *The Petroleum Act of 1987* (Iran) (to view *The Petroleum Act of 1987*, art 2 in English, go to: <http://www.alaviandassociates.com/documents/petroleum.pdf> (accessed 18/02/2017)).

70 Ibid. art 6.

71 Ibid. art 12.

72 The following terms used anywhere in this Act shall have the meanings and the definitions described to them in this Article: Petroleum Resources: shall mean and comprise every one of the inland territorial divisions of land and waters and coastal and international waters and continental shelf where discovery of petroleum reserves is probable and petroleum reserves may be found, and their specific technical and geographical specifications have been determined by the Ministry of Oil.

for carrying out and fulfilling a part of the petroleum operations in conformity with the laws and regulations of the Government of the Islamic Republic of Iran and based on the provisions of this Act.

ARTICLE 2: PETROLEUM RESERVES ARE PUBLIC WEALTH AND UNDER THE AUSPICES OF MINISTRY OF OIL[73]

The main concept of this law is the restriction determined in the Constitution on oil and gas sectors. The wording in the 1987 law replaced the NIOC, which

---

Petroleum Operations: shall mean and comprise all the operations related to conservation, protection and exploitation of the petroleum resources such as research survey, geodesy, geological studies, exploration, drilling, operations, exploitation and production, acquisition of the required lands, preparation and execution of capital investment projects for erecting installations and industries, their development, expansion and renovation; custody, protection and safe-guarding of the units related to the oil industry. Also, production and processing operations for rendering crude oil, gas and other hydrocarbons (except coal) marketable; refining crude oil and production of petroleum derivatives and by-products; gathering, treatment and production of natural gas and associated products; utilisation of petroleum and gas derivatives and products for production of various petrochemical products; transportation, distribution, sale, and export of oil, gas and petrochemical products; commercial activities relating to the exports, imports and productions of oil, gas and petrochemical products; production and provision of industrial goods and materials used by the petroleum (oil) industry, establishment of the related incidental facilities and services for these operations and training and recruitment of the necessary expert personnel (workforce); provision of industrial safety and sanitation requirements and environment protection against pollution resulting from the operations by due observance of the criteria laid down by the organisations concerned; techno-economic reviews, design and planning activities, conclusion of construction, service and consultancy contracts in the fields of the above mentioned operations; carrying out scientific and technical studies, research and investigations for development and advancement of the technology and promotion of the level of technical and industrial know-how review of the innovations and inventions related to the oil industries and exchange of technical and scientific information and industrial experiences with the competent local and foreign institutes in the field of petroleum operations.

Where the scope of petroleum operations interferes with the lawful duties, plans and projects of other organisations and organs of the Islamic Republic of Iran, necessary decision shall be adopted through the by-laws to be prepared and made by the Ministry of Oil and approved by the Council of Ministers.

Operational Units: shall comprise any organisation, institute or company who assumes liability for and carries out certain basic and subsidiary specialised and general operations and related incidental petroleum services.

Contract: shall mean and comprise contractual obligations (undertakings) concluded between the Ministry of Oil or an operational unit, or any natural person or legal entity for carrying out and fulfilling a part of the petroleum operations in conformity with the laws and regulations of the Government of the Islamic Republic of Iran and on the basis of the provisions of this Act.

73 According to Article 45 of the Constitution (of the Islamic Republic of Iran), the petroleum resources of the country are part of the public domain (properties and assets) and wealth. As such, they are at the disposal and control of the Government of the Islamic Republic of Iran. Moreover, all installations, equipment, assets, property and capital investments which have been made or shall be made in future within the country and abroad by the Ministry of Oil and her affiliated companies will belong to the people of Iran and remain at the disposal and control of the government of the Islamic Republic of Iran. The authority to exercise sovereignty and ownership rights over the petroleum resources and installations is vested in the government of the Islamic

in all previous laws had been held as the sole authority over all petroleum industry activities, with the Ministry of Petroleum, which had been established after the 1979 revolution. However, the NIOC and all its subsidiaries continued to deal with all petroleum-related activities of Iran, under the nominal auspices of the Ministry of Petroleum.

ARTICLE 6: PROHIBITION OF FOREIGN INVESTMENT[74]

This article emphasised prohibition of Foreign Direct Investment (FDI) in Iran's petroleum sector and oil industry. The significance of the 1987 law was in outlawing foreign investment completely and rendering Iran's petroleum industry independent from any foreign assistance or participation. According to some observers, this can be traced to an intensely nationalist feeling after the revolution in Iran particularly, as well as during the Iran-Iraq War (1980–1988). The law was written in 1987 in the midst of the war, pursuant to the law, whereby only the government can be an investor in Iran's oil and gas industry and which will be predicted through the annual budget.

Since this was very difficult to achieve, the state entered into pure service contracts with international entities, through which the foreign companies provided services without investment, in return for a fixed remuneration generated by the sale of the extracted oil. In a pure service contract, all risk is borne by the state and is characterised by substantial capital from the state and the aim to seek outside expertise and technology.[75]

The government reaffirmed the 1987 Law through a series of far-reaching five-year-plans, the first of which was aimed primarily at post-war economic and infrastructure reconstruction. Thus, according to this law, no contract would lead to the granting of concessions to foreign or foreign investment in Iran's petroleum sector. Therefore, any FDI which led to ownership over petroleum resources, installations and equipment was prohibited and the only scheme permitted was the service contract.[76]

2.2.3.3 Buy-back contracts

The 1987 Law was determined in response to the dearth of funding, and for it to be implemented the government authorised the NIOC to obtain short- and

Republic of Iran which on the basis of the regulations, rights and powers prescribed in this Act shall be undertaken and executed by the Ministry of Petroleum in accordance with the general principles and policies of the country.

74 All capital investments shall be proposed through the Ministry of Oil based on the budget of the operational units and be included upon approval of the General Assembly, in the General State Budget. Foreign investment in these operations in any manner will not be allowed whatsoever.

75 Daniel Johnston, *International Petroleum Fiscal Systems and Production Sharing Contracts* (Pennwell, 1994).

76 Leila Zabbah, 'Investment Challenges in Iranian Oil & Gas Sectors – A Legal Approach' (2011) *Institute for International Energy Studies* 10.

medium-term loans from foreign financial institutions to finance five of its oil and gas project.[77] It also established a series of far-reaching five-year plans, the first of which was aimed primarily at post-war economic and infrastructure reconstruction. The law of the first five-year Economic, Social and Cultural Development (1989–1993/1994) plan in Note 29 permitted the government to resort to buy-back transactions as a means of meeting industrial and mineral needs.[78]

Basically, the Budget Act of 1994 introduced the buy-back contract as a legitimate means of attracting investment. A maximum of $3.5 billion of foreign investment was allowed, provided it did not create any commitment for the government or the state bank.[79] In addition, Note 22 of the law of the second five-year plan (1994/1995–1999/2000) granted the Iranian government to enter buy-back deals through Iran's banks. For buy-back transactions, executive rules were approved by the Council of Ministers and its relevant directive was issued by Iran's Central Bank.

This legislation permitted the IOC to invest in certain oil and gas projects under buy-back schemes. Therefore Article 6 of the Petroleum Act of 1987, which prohibits any foreign investment in oil and gas projects, was amended by implication. The authorisation to conclude buy-back contracts was restated in the second, third and fourth five-year Economic, Social and Cultural Development Plans, of 1994/1995–1999/2000, 2000/2001–2004/2005 and 2005/2006–2009/2010, respectively.[80]

2.3 Legal and comparative analysis

This section is devoted to comparative analyses of Iran's oil and gas legal frameworks as divided into two periods: the pre-nationalisation period of the D'Arcy Concession and the 1933 Concession Agreement; and the nationalisation to revolution period including all oil and gas contractual forms. The period after the revolution will be analysed in its own chapter (Chapter 6) due to the revolution's unique constitution and its specific rule and legislation.

The pre-nationalisation period (the D'Arcy Concession and 1933 Concession Agreement) emphasised the importance and exclusive privilege of these agreements from the perspectives of foreign participants. There were also attempts to renegotiate these unbalanced contracts due to lack of legislative framework and domestic public pressure. Therefore, any oil or gas agreement was subject to approval by the Shah of Iran (Iranian ruler) for lack of clear rule and legislation.

77 *The 1987 Petroleum Law*, above n 69, art 5.

78 Otman, above n 16, 9.

79 *Budget Act of 1994* (Iran), Islamic Parliament of the Islamic Republic of Iran, Iranian Official Gazette 1994 [No. 14313 dated 7/2/1373 (27 April 1994)].

80 The Economic, Social and Cultural Development Plans were approved by the parliament, inter alia, to advance the market orientation of the economy and to improve population living standards. Abdolhossein Shiravi and Seyed Nasrollah Ebrahimi, 'Exploration and Development of Iran's Oilfields through Buyback' (2006) 30(3) *Natural Sources Forum* 203–205.

However, in the period from nationalisation to revolution, Iran's oil and gas industry experienced different petroleum contractual regimes such as 'profit agreement' in 1954 consortium agreement, 'production sharing agreement' in 1957 Petroleum Law and 'risk service contract' in 1974 Petroleum Law. The comparative analyses of these contractual regimes give special focus on three fundamental issues regarding the legal framework: ownership, duration and income.

2.3.1 Ownership

According to the 1954 Consortium Agreement and the PSA (in 1957 Petroleum Law), once the petroleum reached well-head, its ownership was transferred to the consortium and IOC, respectively. In contrast, in an RSC (in 1974 Petroleum Law), the IOC is not entitled to any oil in the reservoir or at well-head.

2.3.2 Duration

Based on the 1954 Consortium Agreement, duration of the agreement was 25 years with the provision for automatic extension for up to 15 more years. In 1957 Petroleum Law, the contract period was 25 years with compulsory relinquishment requirements. However, the duration terms of the 1974 Petroleum Law differed in that they stipulated the contract terms were to be divided into exploration and exploitation operations, the former being extendable for another five-year period.

2.3.3 Income

The principle of 50/50 profit sharing between the Iranian government and the consortium was agreed in the 1954 Consortium Agreement. Iran's income from the sale of oil, including income taxes and the value of the 12.5 percent royalty, was calculated at posted prices. Based on the 1957 Petroleum Law, the PSA's financial terms were remarkable in that they appeared to give the NIOC 75 percent of net profit realised from the investment. In fact, participation agreements in Iran were based on a 50/50 ratio, where 50 percent of share was the property of the NIOC and the remaining 50 percent belonged to the IOC. The Iranian government acquired half of the IOC's share as tax. This effectively meant that Iran's income was 75 percent of the profit share, with only 25 percent going to the IOC. In addition, according to 1974 Petroleum Law, royalty payments to Iran increased from 12.5 percent to 20 percent and tax payments increased from 50 percent to 80 percent.

2.4 Conclusion

Chapter 2 reviewed the history of Iran's petroleum, oil and gas contractual framework from start of exploration to the present day. The review shows that Iran suffered tension and conflict over national interest and benefits in relation to the oil and gas industry.

To transition from individually negotiated agreements to nationalisation and from nationalisation to revolution was valuable but costly shift. The general types of oil and gas contracts are associated with three historical periods in Iran's oil and gas development. These contracts are for concession, product sharing agreements and service contracts. The concession agreement was specific to the period from Iran's oil discovery up to nationalisation. The other two oil and gas contractual frameworks were approved in the 1957 Petroleum Law (product sharing agreement) and in the 1974 Petroleum Law (risk service contract). Additionally, the Buy-back contract (a type of the service contract) was introduced into the global oil industry by Iran after the revolution.

It should be mentioned that regardless of the strengths and weaknesses of the contracts, each contractual framework was a turning point in that period regarding the opportunities and circumstances that occurred. Each of the petroleum contractual regimes was a step towards contractual framework evolution in Iran. For more understanding of the nature of international oil and gas contracts, an in-depth comparative discussion is provided in Chapters 3–5.

3 The nature and features of classic and new oil and gas concession contracts

3.1 Definition of concession agreement

The oil and gas agreements for this book are known as "concession agreements" which cover various types of contracts. Sometimes exploration and exploitation contracts are embodied into either a single document or separate documents. Also, the title will vary depending on whether the terms and conditions governing exploration and exploitation activities are found in the same document. The agreements that apply to exploration are often called "permits"; whereas, the titles issued for exploitation are "concessions" or "leases".

3.2 Classic concession contracts

The CCC was the most popular oil and gas contract form throughout the world when oil-rich countries still did not have an in-depth perception of the importance of oil and gas. In fact, oil-rich countries not only did not realise the value of oil and gas, but also they did not have the advanced equipment and technology required for oil and gas exploration. At this time, IOCs imposed their terms on host countries to explore for oil and gas and for further exploitation under the CCC form.

3.2.1 Definition

Concession contracts have undergone changes in form and concepts since they were first introduced over 100 years ago. The word 'concession' has been defined in the *Black's Law Dictionary* as:

> Grants, concession; the regular method by the common law of transferring the property of incorporeal hereditaments, or, such things whereof no livery can be had, for which reason all corporeal hereditaments, as lands and house are said to lie in livery: and the other advowsons, commons, rents, reversions, etc. to lie in grant … these thereof pass merely by the delivery of the deed …[1]

1 Henry Campbell, *Black's Law Dictionary* (MINN West, 4th ed, 1951) 361.

Also defined by *Macquarie Australian's National Dictionary* as "something conceded by a government or a controlling authority, as a grant of land, a privilege, or a franchise".[2]

Another definition of the concession, according to Professor A. Fatouros, is an instrument concluded between a state and a private person providing for the grant by the state to the individual of certain rights or powers which normally would belong to and be expected by the state.[3] The concession has also been defined by Professor Kenneth S. Carlston as:

> An agreement by a state to grant a privilege to conduct an enterprise of some sort for a defined period. This agreement may be made pursuant to constitutional or legislative authority, but such is the nature of the enterprise which is desired to be established that it becomes essential to function through contract as well as through general rules of law.[4]

Hence, the most comprehensive definition clarifies that a concession is a contract by which a government or a governmental organ hands over the administration of an organisation or a public service such as mines to natural or juridical persons to put into practice. The person must cover the costs and capital within a specified and limited time, against sums collected from users of public services. Payments should be made to the government under such titles as royalty in consideration of the benefits gained from the exploitation of public resources for a lengthy, but fixed period.[5] Under a concession, government submits the administration of an operation in exclusive or semi-exclusive form to the hands of a person or a private enterprise.[6]

Governments apply two methods to grant concessions: directly through sovereign organs such as the government, Prime Minister, the Ministry of Mines or the Ministry of Energy; or indirectly through national companies where 100 percent of the shares belong to the government.

3.2.2 The legal nature of oil and gas concession contracts

A concession contract is the granting of certain rights, such as mineral or mining rights, to an individual or an entity authorising him or it to explore for and, in the case of a discovery, to produce and exploit the mineral(s) object of the concession. Those rights entail ownership of the mineral(s) so found and, until recently, the discovery was the owner of the reserves of said mineral(s).

2 *Macquarie Australian's National Dictionary* (Macquarie Library Pty Ltd, 3rd ed, 1997), 230.

3 Arghyrios Fatouros, 'Government Guarantees to Foreign Investors' (1962) 63(3) *Colombia Law Review* 125.

4 Kenneth S Carlston, 'International Role of Concession Agreements' (1958) 52 *Northwestern University Law Review* 621.

5 Ezzatollah Taher Estakhti, *Concession on Tract and Its Legal Evolution* (Dissertation for LLM of Public Law, Shahid Beheshti Law Faculty, 1999) 22.

6 Karim Sanjabi, *Political Diary* (Zohreh Publication, 1963) Khaterat Siasi 1342, 76.

It remains the case in many countries such as the US that oil legislation closely follows traditional mining legislations. In most countries however – especially in Europe, the Middle East and developing nations – the reserves are considered to constitute inalienable natural resources, and the concessionaire acquires the ownership of the product at the well-head. In fact, through a subtle process, the mining rights are converted into a mere authorisation to explore and produce, with the minerals remaining the property of the State until produced. The counterpart of the rights granted to the holder of the concession consists of an obligation for the latter to pay to the granting authority (the host country) a royalty based on an agreed upon percentage of production.

Up to the 1950s, the concession contract was the traditional contractual framework for exploiting oil in Iran. The nature of economic concession has long been a controversial issue in international law.[7]

The question is whether oil concessions have the nature of public law or fall within the province of private law.[8] An oil concession has neither exclusive public nor private character, but a mixed public nor private character.[9] Some scholars have suggested that the economic development agreements have a public character because they involve vital interests of the developing country.[10] It seems, therefore, that the State can abrogate the concession by unilateral action in the public interest.[11] It might be argued that the matter is private because the concessionaire acquires privileges under the contract rights analogous to those in a contract of private law. Contracts concluded between a sovereign State and a foreign national are not governed by international law, but by the municipal law of the sovereign State.[12] The rationale is that the sovereignty cannot be surrendered by a sovereign to an unequal foreign party. In the *Serbian Brazilian Loan* cases,[13] the Permanent Court of International Justice (PCIJ) stated; "any

7 Muthucumaraswamy Sornarajah, *The Pursuit of Nationalized Property 79* (Ian Brownlie, 3rd ed, 1986) 547–551.

8 Ahmed Zaki El Chiati, *Protection of Investment in the Context of Petroleum Agreement* (1987) Brillonline Revise Works 204 Hague Recueil Des Cours <http://referenceworks.brillonline.com/entries/the-hague-academy-collected-courses/protection-of-investment-in-the-context-of-petroleum-agreements-volume-204-ej.9789024737420.009_170>.

9 Daniel Patrick O'Connell, 'A Critique of the Iranian Oil Litigation' (1957) 60(4) *The International and Comparative Law Quarterly* 267, 270 <https://www.jstor.org/journal/intecomplawquar>.

10 Rainer Geiger, 'The Unilateral Change of Economic Development Agreements' (1974) 23(1) *The International and Comparative Law Quarterly* 73 <https://www.cambridge.org/core/journals/international-and-comparative-law-quarterly/article/div-classtitlethe-unilateral-change-of-economic-development-agreementsdiv/C408F487C4BCA6DABAD-DE28109A14D8C>.

11 Derek William Bowett, 'State Contracts with Aliens: Contemporary Developments on Compensation for Termination or Breach' (1988) 59 *British Year Book of International Law* 49 <http://www.worldcat.org/title/state-contracts-with-aliens-contemporary-developments-on-compensation-for-termination-or-breach/oclc/83643737/editions?editionsView=true&referer=br>.

12 Frederick Alexander Mann, *Further Studies in International Law* (Oxford University Press, 1990) 178–179.

13 *Case Concerning the Payment in Gold of the Brazilian Federal Loans Issued in France (France v Brazil)* (Judgment) [1929] P.C.I.J (Ser. A) Nos. 20/21.

contract which is not a contract between States in their capacity as subjects of international law is based on the municipal law of some country."

Can an oil concession be termed an international treaty in nature or an agreement like a treaty? This view lacks merit as a concession is not analogous to a treaty if one of the parties is a foreign private company. According to Derek William Bowett, not only is an investment contract not a treaty, but also it cannot even be regarded as analogous to a treaty, for there is a world of difference between an agreement under international law between two equal, sovereign States and a contract between a State and a private party governed prima facie by the State's own law.[14]

Economic concessions are not agreements between subjects of international law. According to Angelo Piero Sereni,[15] the rules of international law do not lend themselves to the regulation of relations among parties which are not recognised as international subjects.

This view was accepted by the International Court of Justice (ICJ) in the Anglo-Iranian oil dispute of 1952.[16] On 22 July 1952, while declining its jurisdiction regarding the Anglo-Iranian oil dispute,[17] the Court authoritatively stated that the 1933 concession agreement "is nothing more than a concession agreement between a government and a foreign corporation. The UK Government is not a party to the contract; there is no private contract with the government of Iran and the Iranian government cannot claim from the UK any rights which it may claim from the Company, nor can it be called upon to perform towards the UK government any obligations which it is bound to perform towards the Company. The document bearing the signatures of the Iranian government and the Company has a single purpose: the purpose of regulating the relations between the government and the company regarding the concession. It does not regulate in any way the relations between the two governments".[18]

Thus, the concession contract cannot be categorised completely as private or administrative because in concessions, one side of the contract is the government, or an administrative body and the subject of the contract is the public affairs or services or the exploitation of public resources and wealth which ties the contract to public law. This results in room for discretion from the government about the cancellation of the contract, the interpretation of contract terms

14 Derek William Bowett, 'State Contracts with Aliens: Contemporary Developments on Compensation for Termination or Breach' (1988) 59(1) *British Year Book of International Law* 54.

15 Sereni argues that "an attempt at applying international law to private relations would be tantamount to seeking to apply the matrimonial laws of France or England to relations between cats or dogs." Angelo Piero Sereni, *International Economic Institutions and the Municipal Law of States* (Leyden Sijthoff, 1959) 210.

16 Greig argues that "it is possible for a State to enter into a contract with a corporation or an individual, but such an agreement will not be a treaty cognizable as such on the international Plane". Donald W Greig, *International Law* (Butterworths, 2nd ed, 1976) 458.

17 *Anglo-Iranian Oil Co. Case* (*U.K. v. Iran*) (Judgment) [1952] ICJ Rep. 501, 521.

18 Sunil Kanti Ghosh, *The Anglo-Iranian Oil Dispute: A Study of Problems of Nationalization of Foreign Investment and their Impact on International Law* (Master Thesis/Dissertation, Calcutta K. L. Mukhopadhyay, 1960) 46.

and nationalisation of the subject matter of concessions. However, a concession contract follows the rules of private law which are subject to the parties' will, and this characteristic leads us to call it a mixed contract.[19] According to commercial law principles, a concession contract should have as its goal to build economic-industrial infrastructure or natural resources exploitation by way of cooperation between private and public (governmental) capitals.[20]

The concession today is premised on transnational public-private partnerships.[21] A move away from the unequal traditional concession and towards more modern transnational public-private partnership-based contractual arrangements has occurred in the extractive sector.

The public-private partnership is a vehicle by which infrastructural and other public projects (such as the oil and gas industry) are implemented through the participation of private investment in such partnerships and by means of a financial contribution. The participation of the private sector in implementing various infrastructural projects became more important from the 1980s.[22] Therefore, the public-private partnership requires effective institutional and legal mechanisms which ensure the protection of rights and interests of the private sector and create a balance between the rights and interests of the private and public sector.[23]

3.2.3 Features

The classic concession system included the following simple characteristic features contained within some agreements.

3.2.3.1 Area

The area of the concession was very large; sometimes covering the entire national territory or, at least, the most promising part of that territory. This wide geographic area coverage was not reduced using relinquishment provisions for certain parts of the area, since few of the classic concessions included mandatory provisions of that kind. A typical example of this approach can be found in a 1937 concession agreement between the Sultanate of Muscat and Oman and an IOC (the 1937 Agreement)[24]:

19 Ezzatollah Taher Estakhti, above n 5, 16.

20 Rainer Geiger and Aril Seren, *Basic Elements of a Law on Concession Agreements* (Organization for Economic Co-Operation and Development (OECD), Multilateral Centre for Private Sector Development Istanbul, 2001), 7–9.

21 Michael B Likosky, *Law, Infrastructure, and Human Rights* (2006) 22.

22 UNCITRAL, *Legislative Guide on Privately Financed Infrastructure Projects* (2001).

23 UNCTAD, *Public Monopolies, Concessions, and Competition Law and Policies* (2009).

24 'Sultanate of Muscat and Oman' (Oil Concession Agreement 1937) Qatar national Library <https://www.qdl.qa/en/archive/81055/vdc_100000000833.0x00001b> and also See *Oil Concessions in Five Arab States 1911–1953: Kuwait, Bahrain, Qatar, Trucial States and Oman* (Cambridge University Press, 1989).

The area to which this agreement applies is the Sultanate of Muscat and Oman including all island and Territorial Waters appertaining thereto, but excluding Dhofar and Gwandur (hereinafter referred to as "the leased Area") and being all that territory within the boundaries of the Sultanate of Muscat and Oman.

3.2.3.2 Duration

The duration of the concession was very long; typically between 60 and 75 years, and sometimes up to 99 years (Kuwait). Thus, the following provision may be found in the 1937 Agreement:

> The period of this Agreement shall be 75 (Gregorian) Calendar years from the date of signature.[25]

3.2.3.3 Ownership

The IOC was the exclusive owner of the petroleum reserves found in the area covered by the concession; it was free to dispose of them as it saw fit. In that concession, the 1937 agreement provided:

> In consideration of the payments prescribed in Article 22 the Sultan hereby grants to the Company for the remainder of the per 100 of this Agreement the exclusive right to explore search for drill for produce, win, refine, transport, sell, export and otherwise deal with or dispose of the substances and to do all things necessary for all or any the above purposes within the leased area.[26]

3.2.3.4 Financial benefits

In concession contracts, financial and payment arrangements were designed under the following mechanisms:

- Payment of a sum as bonus to host state at the time of granting the concession
- Payment of a sum as land retention fee at the beginning of exploration phase
- Payment of a sum as royalty at the production phase[27]

Bonus is defined as a sum to be paid by the private party of the oil concession contract at the time of signing the contract, whether immediately or in instalments at fixed periods of time or subject to conditions.[28] In the other words, bonus is a kind of goodwill paid by the operating or investing company for quality areas.

25 Ibid. 1.
26 Ibid. 2.
27 George Lenczowski, 'Oil and State in Middle East' (1963) 14(3) *Middle East Journal* 87.
28 Mahmoud Mansouri Naraghi, *Legal Bases and General Terms of Middle East Oil Contracts* (Bita Publication, 1972) Osool –e- Hoghooghi va Sharayete 'omoomi Gharardadhaye Nafti Dar Khavar-e- Mianeh1350, 148.

As far as a land retention fee is concerned, it should be noted that in contracts designed for regions with limited area, a land retention fee was rather considerable. But, as to concessions on vast areas, a minor sum was demanded as land retention fee in proportion to every square kilometre or square mile.

The financial benefits accruing to the host country were limited and consisted primarily of payments based on volume of production – royalties – at a flat rate rather than a percentage of the value of the oil produced.[29] The following provision was included in the 1937 Agreement.

ARTICLE 8

During the option period of five years, the Company shall pay to the Sultan the sum of 5,000 rupees a month, making a sum of 300,000 rupees in all. The first payment shall be made within 30 days after the date of signature of this agreement, and subsequent payments on the first day of each calendar month thereafter.

In some contracts, royalty is calculated as a fixed sum for every ton of production and in others in the form of a percentage of the concessionaire's profits.[30]

3.2.3.5 Participation

All funds required for exploration and exploitation were provided by the IOC as a direct investment. There was no provision opening the way for the host country participation in the venture, be it at the exploration or exploitation stage.

3.2.3.6 Control

The concessioner retained control over virtually all aspects of the operation, including the rate of exploration, the decision to bring new fields into exploitation, the determination of production levels, the right to transport the hydrocarbons discovered, the hiring of personnel and the setting of prices. The host country participation in management – where it occurred at all – was limited to symbolic minority representation on the boards of a few concession-holding companies, but involved no effective influence on policy decisions. The following clauses included in the 1937 agreement are illustrative of this.

ARTICLE 12

The Company shall have the right to import water, the Substances, fuel, machinery, motor-cars and lorries, aircraft, equipment, plant, timber utensils,

29 See Chapter 2 Sections 2.1.1.1 and 2.1.1.2.

30 Foad Rouhani, *The History of OPEC* (Moanouchehr Roohani trans, 1975) Tarikhcheh E OPEC 1353, 291–292.

iron work, building materials, food supplies, medicines, medical supplies, office equipment and household furniture, and other materials, equipment and goods of whatsoever nature required by the Company and its employees for the purpose of its operations. Also, to export the Substances and articles previously imported by the Company free of customs or export duty and taxes or other charges. The Company, its personnel, its operations, income, profits and property including the Substances shall be exempt and free during the period of this agreement from all present or future harbour duties, imposts and charges of any kind whether state or local, tools and land surface rent of whatever nature.[31]

ARTICLE 13

For its operations, hereunder the Company shall have the right without hindrance to construct, maintain and operate power stations, refineries, pipelines and storage tanks, and any other facilities works which the Company may consider necessary, and for such purposes to use free of all payment any stone, sand, gravel, gypsum, lime, clay or similar material or water. The Company at its discretion may select the position of any such works. The Company shall likewise install and operate without hindrance all such means of transportation by land, air and water as may be necessary for the effective conduct of its operations hereunder.[32]

ARTICLE 14(B)

The Company shall have the right and be given the necessary facilities:

> To lay down pipelines, erect pumping station tanks and any other works and buildings over and on the territory of the Sultanate of Muscat and Oman for the transporting the Substances from any territory adjoining the Sultanate suitable for the refining or shipping of the Substances which the Company may select. No duties, taxes, charge or dues of any nature whatsoever shall be levied in respect of such import or transport.[33]

ARTICLE 16(B)

The company shall employ subjects of the Sultan for all works for which they are suited under the supervision of the Company's skilled employees, but if the local supply of labour should in the judgement of the Company be inadequate or unsuitable the Company shall have the right to import labour, preference being given to labourers from neighbouring Arab countries who will obey the local laws. The Company shall also have the right to import skilled and technical

31 'Sultanate of Muscat and Oman' (Oil Concession Agreement 1937), above n 166, art 12.
32 'Sultanate of Muscat and Oman' (Oil Concession Agreement 1937), above n 166, art 13.
33 'Sultanate of Muscat and Oman' (Oil Concession Agreement 1937), above n 166, art 14(b).

employees. This type of classic concession agreements did not provide for the possibility of renegotiation.[34]

For more clarification of the early or classic concessions framework, the general and common concession contract characteristics are enumerated as follows:

A Under a granted concession, the investing company enjoys an exclusive right to explore, extract, purify and export crude oil and natural gas in the region covered by the concession and assumes responsibility for all risks and costs.

B A maximum amount of time is fixed for the discovery and beginning of exploitation operations in an economical manner. The grantor is entitled to cancel the contract in such cases when the timetable is not met.

C The duration of concession typically lasted for 60 to 75 years and in some cases 99 years, as was the case of Kuwait.

D The geographical scope of the contract was vast as it sometimes covered the whole country or a significant portion of its territory and no mechanism was generally devised to decrease the regions covered by the contract.

E The oil company is deemed to be the owner of the reservoir and the produced product, and exerts comprehensive control over all operational dimensions and details including exploration speed, decisions as to explore new fields, determination of production rate, employment of personnel, price setting for oil and transportation of produced oil.

F For the good conduct of the operation, a set of rights are granted to the concessionaire. They are initially not directly related to the concession and are sometimes against the sovereign right of the host state, such as the right to construct road networks, railway, airports, radio, telephone, telegraph etc.

G The concession holding company was entitled to the right of ownership of land. If the land in question belonged to the State, it went under the control of the concessionaire free of charge. In cases where the land belonged to a private person, the owner was bound to submit it at a price within the range of prices of the adjacent pieces of land irrespective of the existence of oil deposit in it.

H No clause was inserted in the concession agreement regarding the participation of the host state in the investment and its involvement in the management of the project.

I Oil companies deliver a specified amount of oil and its products at a fixed price to the host state for the sole purpose of satisfying its domestic needs.

J For the good performance of the operation, the concession holding companies established subsidiaries, especially for transportation and marketing.

K Officially and prescribed in written form, the host state was entitled to supervision, inspection and auditing of the financial statements and revenues of the Company which practically faced obstacles on the way to their implementation.

34 'Sultanate of Muscat and Oman' (Oil Concession Agreement 1937), above n 166, art 16(b).

L In the early concession contracts, companies were not generally obliged to pay to the government any tax for their revenues and subject to concession contracts. Concessionaire companies were exempt from paying excise duty for the importation of tools and machinery used in their operation.
M In the event of a dispute between the company and host state, an arbitration mechanism was designed according to the scope of the substantive and procedural jurisdiction of the host state and relied on international custom or the civilised nations' law.
N In classical concessions, no rules were laid down for amending or revising the terms of the contract in consideration of the pass of time.[35]

Most countries which granted the first oil concessions lacked the required infrastructure to perform oil operations and deliver oil to domestic and international markets. Therefore, concession holders in addition to the oil concession obtained for the achievement of their goals such easements as the permit to construct road, railway, airport, port and quay from the host State.

It is expected that the construction of such installations will be welcomed in every country as a demonstration of signs of development. However, because of the pessimism surrounding the imperialistic goals of foreign companies and their national governments, the contract clauses related to such easements were evidence of the incompatibility of the concession system with national sovereignty. These sets of permits were viewed as a constituent component of the very nature of concession.

The stigma associated with the 'concession' term was so powerful that the English company also avoided using the word at the time the 1933 concession was in force. It was also indicated in the 1933 concession (1312 according to Persian calendar) under the title of Convention in its official correspondence and wording, and this word caught on as a rather established title for that contract in different political, legal and academic settings in the west.[36] With negative perceptions of concession left in the minds of companies, new titles were applied to the present-day contracts concluded that have the content of concession such as the concessionary contract or license.[37]

3.3 New concession contracts

New concession contracts concluded after the classical concession since 1960 include various contract types. Notably, the role of government gained more importance with the consolidation of the position of absolute sovereignty of

35 Keith W Blinn et al (eds), *International Petroleum Exploration & Exploitation Agreements: Legal, Economic, and Policy Aspects* (Barrows Company Inc, 2nd ed, 2009) 215–219.
36 William W Jr Bishop, 'The Anglo-Iranian Oil Company Case' (1951) 45(4) *The American Journal of International Law* 749.
37 Ezzatollah Taher Estakhti, above n 5, 228.

government over natural resources.[38] NCCs also had significant effect on the development and progress of concession agreements. Hence, the NCC is likely to be labelled a "license", and the terms will hereafter be used interchangeably. At a more basic level, however, the fundamental concept remains unchanged.

The NCC provided the host country with a more active role and a corresponding decrease in the responsibilities and rights of the IOC.[39] Such modifications however did not alter the legal nature of the concession agreement. The terms were very different from those under the classic concession system with the result that the features most disadvantageous for the host country were progressively eliminated. Thus, the basic terms of the agreements are similar although many differences remain. The following section examines the NCC with consideration to the elements that characterised the classic concession.

3.3.1 Features

The main features of the NCC are like others, irrespective of the type of contract concerned. In turn, the NCC's characteristics can be summed up as follows.

3.3.1.1 Parties

Although the sovereignty of the country as fundamental grantor remains, parties in the NCC are different to those in the classic concession. In the NCC, the usual practice is to authorise the delegated party such as the Ministry or national oil company to negotiate with the IOC on implementing the concession contract on behalf of the government. The Head of government is not likely to deal with IOC. Hence, representatives of the government as part of the concession agreement are responsible for administering the relevant legislation and for supervising all operation phases carried out by concessionaries as other part of concession agreement.

3.3.1.2 Method of awarding a concession

The methods of awarding a concession are as follows:

A Indirect negotiation

In indirect negotiations, the NOC awards a concession to the IOC on behalf of the government. The government typically does not allow direct negotiation to avoid possible corruption. So, the negotiation is conducted indirectly through a state-owned oil company.[40]

38 Bevan Berittan, 'The New Concession Contracts Regulations and Utilities Contracts Regulations Come into Force Today' (2016) <http://www.legislation.gov.uk/uksi/2016/273/contents/made>.

39 Gao Zhiguo, *International Petroleum Contracts* (Graham and Tortman Ltd, 1994) 12.

40 Ibid. 28.

B Auctioning

The most common method of awarding concessions is competitive bidding or auctioning. All provisions of the agreement, other than the term to be bid, are established in advance. Applicants may be required to meet certain minimum financial and experience requirements to participate in the bidding process, but the licenses on specific blocks are awarded based solely on competitive sealed bids.[41]

C Tender

The tender is an alternative to both the auctioning process and indirect negotiation and allows the sovereign nation to take a variety of factors, other than the high bid, into account in making an award. Most North Sea countries use this system.[42]

3.3.1.3 Scope of rights granted

In the NCC, the scope of rights is granted to defined areas commonly termed "block". A limited number of block(s) is often granted for concession operations. Depending upon the country, the type of license granted, the type of area covered and the size of the block offered for a concession will vary considerably.[43]

Nonetheless, the block(s) should be large enough to make it reasonably likely that exploration and production will be profitable. A good illustration of this new modern approach is found in a new form of concession agreement entered into in 1967 between the Sultanate of Muscat and Oman and an IOC (the 1967 Agreement).

ARTICLE 5

"The Company may at any time on giving to the Sultan 60 days written notice in advance relinquish such part or parts of the Leased Area as it may select and must so relinquish sufficient part or parts as shall reduce the Leased Area at each of the dates set out in the table appearing below to no more than the number of square miles set opposite the respective date:

Date	*Square miles*
1st January, 1970	60,000
1st January, 1980	40,000
1st January, 1990	20,000

Areas relinquished on or before 1st January 1970 shall consist of blocks of not less than 1,000 square miles each and areas relinquished after 1st January. 1970 shall consist of blocks of not less than 500 square miles each. Each block shall

41 Geiger and Seren, above n 20, 19–21.

42 Peter Cameron, 'North Sea Oil Licensing: Comparisons and Contrasts' (1985) 4 *Oil & Gas and Law Taxation Review* 29.

43 Zhiguo, above n 39, 26.

consist of units bounded by 5-minute parallels of latitude and 5-minute meridians of longitude. The greatest length of any block shall not exceed six times its average width".[44]

3.3.1.4 Duration

The duration of the modem concession is usually in the 35 to 40-year range with the possibility of extension if oil is still being produced in commercial quantities at the end of the period. For example, the 1980 Abu Dhabi concession provides for a 35-year term.

ARTICLE 3

The terms of this agreement shall be a period of 35 years, from and after the effective date.[45]

The "two-term" technique exemplified licenses served in (concession) oil and gas new concession contracts. An initial, relatively short period is granted to permit the licensee (concessionaire) to conduct exploratory testing and begin the work programme. The license is then continued into a further term only if the initial work conditions have been met. For instance, the Turkish petroleum code, Article 65, specifies that a license is to be granted for 20 years with the possibility of two extensions for no more than ten years each if certain conditions have been met. Also, licenses granted by Norway during the licensing rounds of the 1980s provided for a six-year term with a "period of prolongation" of 30 years.[46] Most UK licenses during this decade were for the same length.[47]

3.3.1.5 Government revenue

The NCC's provision for compensation to the host country are considerably sophisticated and very widely.[48]

Basically, government revenue – in other words, compensation to the host country – is acquired through the following mechanisms:

A Bonus

Many concession agreements include bonuses payable on signature of the agreement, on discovery of the petroleum field or on reaching certain levels of production. For instance, the Abu Dhabi concession case provides for a

44 Blinn et al, above n 35, 62.

45 *Abu Dhabi Concession Contract* 1980 (The United Arab Emirates UAE) art 9. The concession can be found in: Detlev F Vagts, *Transnational Business Problem* (Foundation Press, 1986).

46 Cameron, above n 42, 42.

47 Terence Daintith et al (ed), *United Kingdom Oil & Gas Law* (Sweet & Maxwell, 2nd ed, 1984) 5357.

48 Zhiguo, above n 39, 36.

bonus payment at the beginning of the concession and later upon attaining certain levels of production.[49]

B Annual rent

The concession providence for annual rental payment based upon certain level of production.[50] It is calculated from the amount of crude oil sold during the year. Therefore, some oil-rich countries announce the schedule of annual rent every year which depends on the level of production in that year. Thailand's NCC is a good sample.

C Royalty

Royalty is a payment expressed as a percentage of the oil and/or natural gas volumes produced by the licensee in a concession contract. It is payable in cash or kind (as government prefers) to the owner of the petroleum in situ, to both onshore and offshore production.[51] The most common type of payment to the State made under the concession framework is a royalty, to the extent that the financial framework of a concession contract generally includes a royalty. In fact, a royalty was initially the sole payment.

The royalty is calculated based on the produced product rather than the profits made by the company. This is unpleasant for oil companies, especially in areas where production costs are high. Thus, companies tend to pay only part of the host State revenues in the form of a royalty so that it will not be the sole mechanism of the host state's income.

However, after the social and economic development of oil-rich countries, the enactment of tax statutes and improvement to tax levying bodies, a royalty is seen in practice as losing its significance in the financial arrangements of the contract. Apart from tradition and custom, the sole factor keeping royalty payments in contracts is that it guarantees a minimum payment to host State irrespective of the profitability or non-profitability of the project.[52] It is for this reason that the royalty demonstrates its real importance and function at a time when the total income decreases dramatically.

A royalty primarily constitutes between 10 percent and 15 percent of the product. Oil-rich countries, however, design various royalties, paying attention to different strategies for the development of oil fields and established financial systems in the country. For instance, in the US, oil field owners sometimes submit the fields at auction with a rate of up to 50 percent. In New Guinea (situated in Oceania), however, the rate of royalty is 1.25 percent.[53]

The royalty will be more profitable using a sliding scale based on level of production. A good example is the UK where onshore licenses granted

49 Zhiguo, above n 39, 37.

50 *Abu Dhabi Concession Contract* 1980 (The United Arab Emirates UAE), above n 187, art 10–11.

51 Daniel Johnston, *International Petroleum Fiscal Systems and Production Sharing Contracts* (Pennwell, 1994) 3.

52 Blinn et al, above n 35, 227–231.

53 Blinn et al, above n 35, 228.

before the effective date of the Petroleum (Production) Regulations of 1982 were payable under the following scale:

# Of tones produced & saved	*Royalty rate (%)*
First 100,000	5
Next 50,000	7.5
Next 50,000	10
Thereafter	12.5[54]

Alternatively, the scale is much higher and all other portions of government revenue are much greater where oil company interests in development are great and where profitable production appears assured. For example, the 1980 Abu Dhabi concession combines a rather "classic" concession format with government revenue based on payments analogous to the bonus, delay rental, and royalty payments found in the standard US oil and gas leases.[55] It is entered into at a time when oil prices are near their peak and uses a more sophisticated method for determining royalty payments than is found in most modern US leases. The relevant provision is as follows.

ARTICLE 13

The Company shall pay to the government a (fully expensed) royalty equal to 12.5 percent of the posted price of crude oil produced and saved in the concession area each year. This excludes crude oil used by the Company in its operation hereunder, as gauged at the point of export after deducting the basic sediments and water. If the production of crude oil during a calendar year shall reach an average rate of 100,000 barrels per day, the Company shall pay a (fully expensed) royalty of 16 percent of the posted price. If the production of crude oil during a calendar year shall reach an average rate of 200,000 barrels per day, the Company shall pay a fully expensed royalty of 20 percent of the posted price.

The royalty herein provided shall be paid in whole or in part, in kind or in cash, at the discretion of the government. The government's decision to take its royalty wholly or partly in kind shall be given by notice in writing to the Company not less than three calendar months prior to the beginning of the calendar year to which such notice applies and shall cover a minimum period of one calendar year. Deliveries in kind hereunder shall be credited against royalties at the prevailing posted price.[56]

Sliding scales can also be based on factors other than levels of production. The Algerian mineral law regime fixes a base royalty rate of 20 percent, but reduces the percentage to 16.25 and 12.5 in areas which present exceptional difficulties for exploration and development. Recently, variable royalties have become more popular than fixed royalties.[57]

54 Daintith et al, above n 47, 1-1194.

55 Vagts, above n 45, 448–465.

56 *Abu Dhabi Concession Contract* 1980 (The United Arab Emirates UAE) art 13.

57 Nour E Terki, 'Comment, "The Algerian Act of 1986 and the Encouragement of Foreign Investment in the Area of Hydrocarbons"' (1987–88) 3(80) *Oil & Gas Law Tax.*

3.3.1.6 Tax

Another significant element of the government concession is tax. The evolution of the taxation payment illustrates the extent to which it is complicated. In the NCC, the concessionaire pays to the host country a specific amount of tax on the income earned in the country.[58]

Since the 1970s, the trend has been to devise more and more complex tax regimes because of the oil crisis. For example, the introduction of special taxes designed to increase government revenue in relation to the profitability of petroleum operations. The various "windfall profits" taxes provide for a supplementary taxation in cases where profit accruing by the IOCs exceeds certain limits are a good illustration of this trend. A more recent design is the introduction of the Rate of Return (ROR) taxation system which calls for adjustment of the government "take" as a function of the IOC's Discounted Cash Flow (DCF) rate of return. Indeed, valuation of oil is necessary not just for determining in-cash royalty, but also for assessing taxes.

The tax rate is mostly established in legislation which may even be distinct from the relevant petroleum code, even though taxes frequently constitute the greatest source of government revenue on a profitable operation. Indeed, in the UK, the Petroleum Royalties (Relief) Act of 1983 eliminated royalty payments on petroleum from most new offshore fields. Excepting licensing fees and other bonus-like payments, taxes were almost the sole source of government revenue.[59]

3.3.1.7 Ownership

Although the foreign contractor is granted rights to explore and sometimes develop the oil field, ownership of resources is different. Based on the NCC, ownership of resources remains with the government. It should be noted that ownership of petroleum existing on or below the surface belongs to government. However, the government can grant ownership to a foreign company in a well-head or in a sale point. Thus, oil resources are owned by the government, but petroleum is owned by the concessionaire at well-head subject to government approval.

3.3.1.8 Training and employment

In the NCC, the government typically seeks to exercise some measure of control over the work-force brought into the country. Hence, the IOC is required to

58 In the classic concession, it was unclear whether the multinational had to pay tax on the income, because the government had already been paid a royalty. In later years, companies fought to impose an income tax. However, given the foreign tax credit given on US income tax for taxes paid to foreign government, US corporations preferred to pay foreign taxes in lieu of royalties. Most modern concessions contain both royalty and tax provisions for compensation. Note that countries have a right to be paid both for their resource in the ground, through a royalty, and for the income earned within their borders, through an income tax.

59 Daintith et al (eds), above n 47, 4-001 to 4-253 (regarding the relevant tax provisions in the UK).

employ nationals of the host country to the extent practicable. For example, the 1967 agreement states:

> The Company shall train and employ subjects of the Sultan as far as practicable for all work in the management and conduct of its operations hereunder for which they are suited.
>
> If the local supply of unskilled, skilled or technical employees should in the judgement of the Company be inadequate or unsuitable, the Company shall have the right to recruit other employees from outside the Sultanate, except from sources not approved by the Sultan, and bring them into the Sultanate.[60]

3.3.1.9 Participation

The licensee or concessionaire's discretion is further limited by the requirement that the host country's state oil company participate in the license. Although the state company is not likely to be the operator, it is a party to the joint operating agreement covering the licensed area and participates in operational and developmental decisions.

3.3.1.10 Report of operation

According to the NCC, the IOC is required to report all project operations to the government.

In some countries where the NCC is used as a legal framework for the oil industry, some details about the phases of operation are required by the government. Furthermore, language to that effect is included in the agreement. For better understanding, there are two clauses in the 1967 agreement as follows:

ARTICLE 9

a The Company shall present to the Sultan within three months of the end of each year a report of its operations within the Sultanate including geological data, drilling operations carried out, employee statistics and such other data as may be required by the Sultan.

b The Company shall present to the Sultan at least two months before the commencement of each year a statement of its intended operations in the Sultanate including a description of the nature and extent of the geological and geophysical exploration and drilling operations planned to be carried out in that year in the leased area.[61]

60 Blinn et al, above n 35, 63–64.

61 Blinn et al, above n 35, 92.

3.4 Distinguishing between the classic concession and the new concession contract

This section explores the following distinguishing characteristics between the CCC and the NCC.

3.4.1 Party

In the CCC, the party granted the concession is a natural person or a juridical person like an IOC or consortium; whereas in the NCC the party is granted the concession by law or relevant legislation.

3.4.2 Method of awarding

One of the most evident types of CCC is direct negotiation. As mentioned previously, all concession was awarded based on individual negotiations with no pre-conditions. Thus, concessions were signed between the King and foreign individuals or companies; whereas, a concession in an NCC is awarded through competitive bidding or auctioning. In this method, the negotiation is conducted indirectly through a state-owned oil company authorised on behalf of the government. This system, unlike the classic concession, is not exposed to corruption.

3.4.3 Area of concession

The geographical scope of the CCC was so vast that it covered the whole or a significant part of territory, and no mechanism was generally devised to decrease the regions covered by contract. Compared to the classic concession, the area granted by the NCC is quite limited. As stated, the country follows the NCC contractual system whereby licenses are issued for defined areas as block(s). In fact, the most obvious factor distinguishing the new type of concession from classic type is the reduction in geographical areas covered by the concession. Some authors believe this is incompatible with the national sovereignty of states.

3.4.4 Duration

The duration of the CCC was typically not less than six or seven decades, and in some case up to 99 years (e.g. the Kuwait case). In contrast, the NCC duration is usually 35 to 40 years. However, there is the possibility for an extension for 10 years or more.

3.4.5 Ownership

There is a big difference in ownership between CCC and NCC. In the CCC, the IOC was owner of the reservoir and had exclusive right to the oil produced. In fact, the petroleum and its resources, and rights to the exploration, development and export of the petroleum was granted to the foreign company, exclusively. In contrast, in the NCC the oil resource belongs to the government and only the petroleum in the well-head owned by the concessionaire. The concessionaire's ownership to the petroleum in the well-head is also subject to government approval.

3.4.6 Government revenue

Government revenue in the CCC was limited, comprising a bonus, land retention and fixed royalty. Thereafter, government revenue was less than what it should be. In the NCC however, government revenue can vary widely. The structure of some fixed payments has changed to provide more benefits to the government such as types of bonuses, annual rent and royalty payments, as well as new financial frameworks to take more revenue from oil income such as sliding scales, a variety of royalty types, windfall benefits and taxes.

3.4.7 Taxation

In CCCs, companies were not generally obliged to pay the government a tax for their revenues and were subject to concession contracts. Concessionaire companies were exempt from paying excise duty for the importation of tools and machinery used in their operation. In NCCs, the complicated taxation mechanism levied on the IOC considers the level of oil production, oil income and amount of extraction.

3.4.8 Participation

According to the initial concession, the IOC as a direct investor provided all funds required for exploration and exploitation. In other words, no clause was inserted in a classic concession agreement regarding participation of the host country in the investment and its involvement in the management of the project. So, there was no provision for government participation in the venture. In contrast, participation has major role in the NCC. In NCCs, the government is a party to the joint operation agreement and can participate in management, board and operational and developmental decisions.

3.4.9 Control

The government can control the oil operation phases to the extent that it takes part in the project. Participation will enable the government to control the oil project. In fact, in CCCs the IOC exerted comprehensive control over the entire operations including exploration speed, decisions as to explore new fields, determination of production rate, employment of personnel, price setting for oil and transportation of produced oil. In the NCC however, unlike the CCC and the exercise of sovereignty, host countries are given authority to control the IOC's decisions, although the extent of this control depends on the terms of the NCC, with management and control mostly in the hands of the concessionaire.

3.4.10 Renegotiation

In CCCs, no rules were laid down for renegotiation of the contract's terms in consideration of the passing of time. In NCCs, the parties insert the renegotiation terms in the agreement to amend or revise the terms of agreement in response to new situations and unexpected conditions.

3.4.11 Settlement of dispute

In the CCC, in the event of a possible dispute between the company and host country, an arbitration mechanism was designed according to the substantive and procedural jurisdiction of the host country and relied on international custom or the civilised nation's law. Whereas in the NCC, an attempt to resolve any dispute shall first be made through mutual settlement. If this fails, an ad hoc arbitration is undertaken. Also, interpreting an award is accomplished according to the host country's law and applicable principles of international law.

3.5 Conclusion

Although the CCC has been used around the world for oil and gas contracts, it has almost disappeared as industrial practice.

Section 3.4 of this chapter analysed the key advantages of the NCC as a contractual form for contemporary oil and gas resource development. These advantages can be summarised as follows:

- In the NCC, the party is granted the concession by law or relevant legislation.
- The method of award in the NCC is through competitive bidding or auctioning.
- Area of concession in the NCC is quite limited and defined as a block.
- The duration of the NCC is shorter than the CCC.
- In the NCC, the oil resources belong to the government and only petroleum in the well-head is owned by the concessionaire.
- Government revenue sources in NCC are wide and various.
- A complicated taxation mechanism is applied to the IOC in an NCC.
- In the NCC, the government is given authority to control oil and gas operations.
- NCCs allow for the parties to renegotiate the terms of contract in response to new situation.
- In the NCC, attempts to resolve any dispute shall first be made through mutual settlement and then through ad hoc arbitration if a mutual settlement cannot be reached.

The NCC is a contract framework that has enough flexibility to be compatible with the different perspectives and interests of the contracting parties. To further our understanding of the role of the NCC in the development of the oil and gas industry, an examination of some countries which currently use or have previously used the NCC as a contractual framework is provided in the next chapter.

4 New concession contract

Comparative national framework

4.1 Brazil

The concession regime was the first system adopted to regulate the petroleum industry and is still the most widely used system throughout the world.[1] Basically, a concession is an arrangement whereby the IOC is granted the right to explore and exploit oil and gas in exchange for the payment of all costs, and also specific taxes related to the operation.[2] Under a concession arrangement, the host country government typically grants the contract holder exclusive exploration rights (exploration licence), as well as exclusive development and production rights (lease or Concession) for each commercial discovery.

The 1997 Oil Act provides that exploration and production of oil and gas in Brazil should be carried out under the concession regime.[3] Because the Brazilian federal government is the original holder of hydrocarbon rights, after a bidding process it grants exclusivity to the winning oil company to explore and produce hydrocarbons within a determined area.[4] The oil companies may participate in the bidding process individually or as an organised consortium, usually comprised of both operating and non-operating members. Petrobras has been a major participant, but is subject to the same retaining conditions as private companies.

The concession agreement is signed by the National Petroleum Agency (NPA) and the oil company. The oil company may enter the agreement individually

1 Pedro Van Meuers, 'Financial and Fiscal Arrangements for Petroleum Development on Economic Analysis' in Nicky Beredjick and Thomas Walde (eds), *Petroleum Investment Policies in Developing Countries* (Graham & Trotman 1988) 5.

2 Keith W Blinn et al (eds), *International Petroleum Exploration & Exploitation Agreements: Legal, Economic, and Policy Aspects* (Barrows Company Inc, 2nd ed, 2009) 47.

3 Originally, the *Oil Act* did not contemplate the PSA. It was only in 2010 that Lei No. 12,351 introduced the PSA regime into the legal framework. Lei No. 12,351 amended the *Oil Act*, but it did not end the Concession regime. Each regime is applicable according to the reserve location.

4 Bain & Company, 'Studies of Regulatory, Corporate and Financial Alternatives for the Exploration and Production of Oil and Gas and the Industrial Development of the Oil and Gas Production Chain in Brazil' (2009) DOC Player <http://docplayer.net/8345768-Studies-of-regulatory-corporate-and-financial-alternatives-for-the-exploration-and-production-of-oil-and-gas-and-the-industrial-developmentof-the.html#show_full_text>.

or in a consortium, according to the rules and limitations provided by the invitations to bid. The agreement usually lasts for up to 35 years and includes an exploration phase and a production phase.[5]

The duration of the exploration phase is typically between three and eight years. A period during which the concessionaire must submit a 'Minimum Exploration Plan' (MEP) for NPA approval.[6] The MEP is the bidder's commitment to develop definite exploratory activities (measured in work units). As the development of the MEP reveals, the concessionaire must gradually return the areas it is not interested in developing to the NPA. This can be compared to the production phase with duration of up to 27 years. During this time, the concessionaire chooses geographic areas it deems commercially viable and prepares a development plan. The NPA is responsible for supervising the performance of the concessionaire's development plan.

The exploration, development, production and decommissioning activities are conducted at the concessionaire's sole costs and risk. In return, the concessionaire becomes the owner of the hydrocarbons extracted and can dispose of the resources pursuant to the concession agreement and the law. Finally, the government's financial return typically consists of a signature bonus, royalties, special participation, occupation and land retention fee and general taxes (i.e. income, profit and social security). The following section details the grant process for oil and gas exploration and production rights in Brazil – the so-called 'Brazilian Rounds'.

4.1.1 *Brazilian rounds: granting of exploration and production rights*

The bidding process is referred to as the Brazilian Rounds and is conducted by the NPA through public tenders. From 1999 to 2013, the NPA has conducted 12 rounds and almost 800 areas were under concession.[7]

There are three criteria for selecting:

i A signature bonus
ii Local content
iii Analysis of the MEP

5 A good example is the "Libra Project" in Libra Field. In Libra Field, a five-company consortium including Brazil's Petrobras (operator, 40 percent stake), UK's Shell (20 percent), France's Total (20 percent), and China's CNPC (10 percent) and Cnooc (10 percent) won the auction and signed a thirty-five-year contract. *Narrative Report, Libra Project, Brazil* (September 2014) Open Oil <http://openoil.net/wp/wp-content/uploads/2014/09/OO_br_Libra_narrative_1.0_161104.pdf>.

6 *DIARIO OFICIAL DA UNIAO* (Brazil) [Lei No. 9,478, art 44, 111, de 6 de Agosto de 1997, de 7.8.1997 Brazil] <http://www.planalto.gov.br/ccivil_03/leis/19478.htm>.

7 *AGENCIA NACIONAL DO PETROLEO, GAS NATURAL E BIOCOMBUSTIVEIS 2012* (Brazil) art 57 available at <http://www.anp.gov.br/?pg=62402&m=&t1=&t2=&t3=&t4=&ar=&ps=&cachebust=1363716523347>.

A signature bonus is the amount of money offered by the bidder to explore and produce the field. It is paid when the concession agreement is signed. The local content represents the bidder's commitment to contract a minimum percentage of goods and services with Brazilian companies.

In fact, each round must be initially authorised by the National Energy Policy Council (NEPC), with the field to be tendered in the proceeding then determined by the NPA. Once the tendering fields are defined, the round is publicly announced and the invitation to bid and a draft of the concession agreement are published for public analysis. The period then starts for bidders to file their qualification documents. At the end, bidders (individually or organised in consortiums) present their offers and the NPA conducts the bid auction.

4.1.2 Main contractual terms

4.1.2.1 Ownership

Based on the Brazilian concession contract, the hydrocarbons generally belong to the federal government until they are extracted from the oil field. Once the hydrocarbons are extracted, they become the possession of the IOC. In other words, when the petroleum is explored it belongs to the state, but when it is under production it belongs to the IOC. Thus, the contract holder becomes the owner of all the hydrocarbons produced, subject to payment of a royalty in the form of oil and natural gas or in cash.[8]

4.1.2.2 Manifestation of interest

The IOC will find it more attractive if the concession process initiates with an interested manifestation. The IOCs that desire to participate in the auction rounds promoted by the ANP must acquire all necessary information. In addition, there are technical, legal and financial qualification requirements that must be respected for the IOC to acquire the right to explore.[9]

4.1.2.3 Parties and their responsibilities

One of the main regulatory bodies in oil and gas activities in Brazil is the ANP. The ANP, as represented by the Brazilian government, oversees granting the concession rights. The other party is the concessionaire and may be the operating company or possibly a consortium of companies. To grant the contract under the concession regime, certain requirements need to be met in the exploitation phase.

8 *Brazil's Constitution of 1988 with Amendments through 2014* (Brazil) Article 20 (to view English translate is accessible in <https://www.constituteproject.org/constitution/Brazil_2014.pdf> (accessed 29/08/2017)).

9 Marilda Rosaldo Sa Reberio, 'The New Oil and Gas Industry in Brazil: An Overview of the Main Legal Aspects' (2001) 36(14) *Texas International Law Journal* 145.

The IOC must submit a plan called the 'Plano Exploratorio Minimo' (PEM). The PEM must be approved by the ANP and the IOC must perform the work in accordance with the PEM. This is the basis of the contractual arrangements.

Also, the IOC has the obligation to deliver a statement of marketability to the ANP. The IOC is obliged to fulfil the statement once it is approved in the production phase. In case of auction, during the auction process all auctioneers are required to submit a Plan of Development to the ANP. The ANP is then required to ensure that the IOC follows up with the Plan of Development submitted during the auction process. The IOC must also plan and act according to the PEM. Any losses and damages derived from the concessionaire's activities will make it liable to the ANP, the government and third parties.[10]

4.1.2.4 Costs and risks

Based on the Brazilian concession agreement, the IOC must always assume all costs and risks associated with the operations and its consequences. In addition, it must bear all losses incurred without being entitled to any payment, reimbursement or indemnification.[11]

4.1.2.5 Main revenues

The criteria for the collection of wealth generated through exploration have undergone several alterations. According to the concession contract in Brazil, the IOC must pay contributions such as a signature bonus, royalties, a special participation fee and payment for the occupation and retention of the area. The most important revenues and their main aspects are discussed in the following section.[12]

A Signature bonus

The signature bonus is the amount offered by the winning bidder for the concession of crude oil and natural gas. It is paid to the ANP on the date the concession agreement is executed. The signature bonus is the value paid by the company that wins the auction for the determined concession area. In Brazil, the minimum value of the signature bonus is established in the announcement and corresponds to the payment offered in the proposal for obtaining the concession. The bonus is to be paid when signing the contract in one single payment.[13]

B Royalties

Royalties refer to the financial compensation paid monthly by the concessionaires operating each field. The payments start in the month of the

10 Ibid. 155.

11 *Production Sharing Contracts and Concession in the Brazilian Subsalt Region* (University of Oslo, 2010) 17.

12 Ibid. 18.

13 Ibid. 18.

respective start-up production date, without allowance of any deductions. Royalties generally range from 5 percent to 15 percent of the reference prices for oil or natural gas as established in the relevant bidding guidelines and concession contract. All fields in production currently pay the maximum 10 percent rate in the concession contract in Brazil.[14]

One of the important issues for consideration when determining the royalty applicable is, among other factors, the geological risks involved and the production levels expected.

C Special participation fee

The government's other main revenue through the concession contract is a special participation fee. This fee constitutes an extraordinary financial compensation payment by the concessionaires to the government in the event there is a large volume of production or high earnings. Each determined concession area has its own determined rate and the main purpose of the special participation fee is to capture the extraordinary profits. To assess the special participation over the crude oil and natural gas production, progressive rates ranging from 0 percent to 40 percent are applied on the production net revenue for each field on a quarterly basis. This depends on volume of production, whether the block is onshore or offshore, and if offshore, whether it is in shallow or deep water.[15]

D Payment for the occupation and retention of the area

The payment amount for the occupation and retention of all areas in Brazil is determined by law. The payment is typically referred to as a rental fee and is widely practiced in several oil-producing countries.[16]

In Brazil, the payment for site occupation and retention is made annually and is determined by the size of the block. It is assessed every calendar year from the signing of the contract of concession. Calculation of the payment amount considers the number of days for which the contract is valid in each year. Also, when the site is on land the concession contract should include a clause that determines the payment amount to the holders of the land. The payment is decided by the ANP, but is restricted to between 0.5 percent and 1 percent of the output of oil or natural gas. This payment should reflect the fraction of land for each land holder and should be paid in local currency.

14 Usually 10 percent as provided by the *Oil Act*. According to the *Oil Act*, this amount may be reduced to a minimum of 5 percent depending on the NPA assessment of the geological risk involved and production expectations. Ibid. art 47 § 1. Under the concession regime, the income from royalties is distributed among the federation under the following (simplified version of the) rule: The Union is entitled to 40 percent, while the states and municipalities hosting production (when offshore, the projection on their territories' limits towards the ocean is considered) retain 22.5 percent and 30 percent of the royalties, respectively. The remaining 7.5 percent is distributed equally among all other states and municipalities. *Id.* art 49. This rule has recently (2012) been partially revoked by the *Federal Act*.

15 Daniel Johnston, *International Petroleum Fiscal Systems and Production Sharing Contracts* (Pennwell, 1994) 33.

16 Ibid. 38.

4.1.2.6 Remuneration of the IOC

According to the Brazilian concession contract, the hydrocarbons belong to the IOC after they have been extracted and the income of the IOC is the result of the commercialisation of the petroleum. The IOC is the rightful owner of the produced oil after extraction as remuneration for undertaking the costs and risks including oscillating market prices, something that directly affects the return on investment.[17]

4.1.2.7 Local content

'Local content' obligates the IOC to utilise the local industry so that, in addition to the direct financial compensation given to the host country, the oil-producing country can develop its industry and produce jobs in the sector. IOCs fulfil this requirement by providing contracts to local industry players. This actively supports them to overcome their lack of industry expertise and to educate highly trained technical personnel.

The main purpose of the local content obligation is to encourage technological development, training and to educate human resources. This condition means that the creation of jobs and generation of salaries in the respective segments make an important contribution to the wealth of the State. Furthermore, the concessionaires must assure preference to Brazilian producers whenever the suppliers offer competitive prices, production time and higher quality outcomes compared to other competing international companies.[18]

It is concluded that the NCC in Brazil is based on the government granting exclusive rights to a concessionaire to explore and produce oil and gas in each area of land for a certain period. In exchange, royalty and tax payments must be made (hydrocarbons belong to the government if they are not extracted). Companies interested in becoming a concessionaire must take part in a bidding round promoted by the ANP. The bidding criteria are transparent and constitute a system whereby each bidder is allocated points subject to the proposed signature bonus, the minimum work programme and local content percentage. In addition, the concession contract in Brazil is attractive to the IOC in terms of remuneration. However, one of the important features of the concession contract in Brazil is that it is utilised in high-risk geological areas.

4.2 Thailand

Generally, the concession systems have evolved in Thailand under the "Old Terms" (1971–1988) or the "New Terms" (1989 onwards).[19] The first concessions system was characterised by larger concession areas, longer duration

17 *Production Sharing Contracts and Concession in the Brazilian Subsalt Region*, above n 11, 20.

18 *Production Sharing Contracts and Concession in the Brazilian Subsalt Region*, above n 11, 21.

19 For a general description, See Albert T Chandler, 'Evolution of the Thai Petroleum Concession' (1987/88) 10 *OGLTR* 287–297; and Albert T Chandler, 'The Thai Petroleum Concession' (1984) 2 *Journal of Energy and Natural Resources* 48–54.

and a fixed royalty. However, the second concessions system, called the Modern Concession Contract (MCC), was concluded in accordance with the New Terms. It featured reduced concession area and terms, a sliding-scale royalty and a flexible policy framework. The instrument has several synonyms such as permit, license or lease.

4.2.1 Parties to the contract

The Thai MCC delegated the Minister of Industry to sign and award petroleum concessions and renewals with the approval of the Council of Ministers. It is the Department of Mineral Resources (DMR) within the Ministry of Industry however which is authorised to negotiate for and execute the petroleum concession between the government and the IOC.[20]

4.2.2 Reserve ownership in Thailand

Although the title to petroleum under a concession contract passes to the concessionaire at the well-head, the concession system does not mention when the petroleum title transfer takes place. It appears that the petroleum resources and the petroleum belong to the government for as long as it is not extracted.

4.2.3 Main contractual terms

Below is a summary and examination of the main terms and conditions of the MCC in Thailand.[21]

4.2.3.1 Area

According to Thai MCCs, a limited concession area (block) is granted to the IOC. Unlike the old term that has restrictions applied to offshore areas where the water is more than 200 m deep, the new terms abolished the maximum area restriction for offshore concession areas designated by the DMR as deep-water blocks.[22]

20 Gao Zhiguo, *International Petroleum Contracts* (Graham and Tortman Ltd, 1994) 31.
21 Documents and concession contracts used to make the following observation include, inter alia;

1. *Petroleum Act* [B.E. 2514 of 1971] and *Petroleum Income Tax Act* [B.E. 2514 of 1971]
2. *Ministerial Regulation* [No. 4 B.E 2514 of 1971] (model concession contract), and *Ministerial Regulation* [No. 17] (revised model concession contract)
3. *Triton Oil and Gas Corp Concession* [No. 8/2512/12] covering offshore exploration blocks 18 and 19 dated 12 October 1972, in Barrows Company, Asia Contracts, 1973, Thailand A 1–13
4. *Gopher Oil Ltd. Petroleum Concession* [No. 4/2528/29 dated 21 November 1985], 1986, 77–89.

Hereafter the above contracts will be collectively cited as 'the model and individual MCCs'.

22 Zhiguo, above n 20, 32.

4.2.3.2 Duration

Table 4.1 summarises the terms of the concessions allowed under both the old and new terms.[23]

4.2.3.3 Grant of rights

Based on the Thai MCC, the granted right includes the right to own and use of the land for the purposes of petroleum operations both within and beyond the concession area, but excludes refining. Where such land is in the public domain and not being used by the public, the concessionaire shall be entitled to enter upon or pass through it and to erect upon it any structure without applying for permission and without payment of compensation. Such an exclusive and extensive grant is not dissimilar to that under a traditional concession agreement.[24]

The right to refine and transfer crude oil from a concession area, effective only upon the date the concessionaire received approval in writing from the government, is reserved exclusively for the state.[25]

4.2.3.4 Obligations to concessionaire

A Minimum expenditure and work obligation

In Thai MCCs, both minimum expenditure and the physical work required are considered the obligations of the concessionaire.[26] Failure to fulfil the exploration work commitments is regarded as a serious breach of contract and may result in legal action by the DMR if negotiation for a

Table 4.1 Duration of Thai modern concession contracts

	Duration (years)	
Particular	*Old terms*	*New terms*
Exploration	8	6
Renewal	4	3
Production	30	20
Renewal	10	10
Total duration		
Original	38	26
Extension	52	39

Sources: Secs. 25 and 26 of the *Petroleum Act* B.E 2514 of 1971, and sec. 7 of the *Petroleum Act* No. 4 of 1989.

23 Zhiguo, above n 20, 33.

24 Zhiguo, above n 20, 32.

25 Department of Mineral Resources (DMR), 'Development of offshore mining and petroleum in Thailand' (unpublished document 1989), Bangkok, Thailand, 18.

26 The physical work obligation commonly comprises seismic surveys of an agreed number of kilometres, a study of the available geological and geophysical data, and drilling of exploratory wells.

settlement between the two parties fails.[27] The expenditure amount and the level of work are proposed by the concessionaire in its bid for petroleum rights and are agreed upon in each individual contract.[28]

B Progress reports of petroleum operation

The concessionaire is also obliged to submit its petroleum operation progress report to the government.

Since the introduction of the new terms in 1989, the submission requirement has expanded to include the results of the petroleum operation report and a detailed production plan prior to production. The results of a review of the production plan are reported in writing annually to the government.[29]

C Obligation to the produce

The concessionaire has two production obligations. The first is the obligation-to-produce clause which provides that "the concessionaire shall commence petroleum production within four years" from the date on which the concurrence is granted.

The production period is deemed to have expired if petroleum production fails to commence within the said period. However, the concessionaire is entitled to apply for an extension to the period; two extensions of two years each are permitted.

The second obligation is the "sole risk" clause whereby the government has the right to require the concessionaire to expedite the production in its reserved area should the country have a need for petroleum to foster its economic development. If the concessionaire fails to come to terms with the government within 12 months following such a request, the government shall then be entitled to exercise – by serving a written notice to the concessionaire – its right to undertake petroleum operations in that area at its sole risk.[30]

In these circumstances, the concessionaire's rights in the said area are terminated, and the government may appoint an agency or individual to carry out operations. In return, the concessionaire will be reimbursed for the costs incurred, if the government's operation yields a profit. Furthermore, the concessionaire is entitled to seek co-venture with the government if it falls within the first three years of the sole risk option. If the government fails to commence production within two years from its takeover, the concessionaire is further entitled to ask for the return of the concession area.

27 The Bass Strait Oil & Gas (holding) Company spent only $1.14 million out of its $8.65 million minimum expenditure in its block covering 5,560 km during a three-year period beginning November 1985. After failing to negotiate a settlement, the DMR took legal action and sued the company for more than $7.5 million and 7.5 percent in the stipulated amount for allegedly breaching the terms of the concession. See 'Thailand Oil Prospects Brighten' (1992) *Oil& Gas Journal* 33.

28 *Triton and Gopher Concessions* (1987) Clause 4.

29 Zhiguo, above n 20, 33.

30 Ibid. 35.

In the event of a return, the original concession period will be extended accordingly and the government is entitled to receive a refund equal to the amount it has invested.[31]

4.2.3.5 *Fiscal regime and exclusive benefits*

A Fiscal regime

The fiscal regime of Thailand's MCC comprises a royalty, income tax, and the Special Remunerator Benefit (SRB).

- Royalty

  Broadly speaking, the royalty may be paid in cash or in kind depending on the government's preference. According to the Thai MCC, the royalty is calculated using a sliding-scale rate based on specified production rather than a fixed 12.5 percent.[32]

  In Table 4.2 the sliding-scale rate presented along with five specified production level in the deep-water royalty calculation[33]:

- Income tax

  The concessionaire in the Thai MCC is subject to payment of a petroleum income tax which has remained at a rate of 50 percent of net profits derived from the petroleum business, or 35 percent of profits plus a 23.08 percent remittance tax. The income tax rate is always negotiated and may play the significant role in attracting IOCs.
- Special Remunerator Benefit

  The Special Remunerator Benefit (SRB) is actually a form of tax introduced as a part of the 1989 package of legislative changes.[34] It is calculated on a block-by-block basis annually, subject to a ceiling of

Table 4.2 Sliding-scale royalties in Thailand

	Sliding – scale royalty (%)	
Production levels (b/m)	*Onshore*	*Offshore*
0–60,000	5.00	3.500
60,000–150,000	6.25	4.375
150,000–300,000	10.00	7.000
300,000–600,000	12.50	8.750
600,000+	15.00	10.500

Source: 'Schedule of royalty' Act No. 4 of 1989.

31 Ibid. 36.

32 Ibid. 41.

33 Ibid. 42.

34 From 1981 to 1987, to encourage and attract foreign investment, the Thai government made a deliberate effort to review its petroleum legislation in light of changed economic circumstances.

75 percent of petroleum profit for the year. In other words, the SRB is not payable except in the accounting year in which the petroleum operation in any block has yielded an 'annual petroleum profit' (i.e. a balance remains after recovery of petroleum costs for the current and/or past year).

In fact, the SRB is calculated by subtracting petroleum costs (operating costs) and the special reduction (or uplift) – an amount prescribed by the government from time to time in awarding concessions with a view to providing further incentives to induce investment for petroleum operations in Thailand – from the gross petroleum revenue. If the concessionaire has an 'annual petroleum profit' it is then subject to the SRB payment computed at a sliding-scale rate.[35]

In fact, Thailand's SRB is a unique – if not the first of its kind in world petroleum agreements in terms of its computation – 'windfall profit' tax. It provides for supplementary taxation in cases where profits accruing to foreign investors exceed certain limits. The objective of this tax diversification is to increase the host country's revenue in relation to the profitability of petroleum operations.[36]

B Exclusive benefit to government

The Exclusive Benefit to Government (EBG) (also known as a 'special advantages') can be an issue during negotiations because neither the *Petroleum Acts* nor the model contracts include a specific provision on the types and amount of these advantages.[37] The EBG in Thai MCC's include a signature bonus, annual bonus, annual benefit, domestic supply, Training employment and Thai participation. Those that can be implemented in Iran are the following:

- Signature bonus

  The signature bonus is an agreed amount of money that should be paid as a rule by the concessionaires to the government upon signing the contract. In Thai MCCs, the signature bonus was typically around $50,000 prior to the 1990s.
- Annual bonus

  The annual bonus must be paid (and escalates) when production reaches a certain level.[38] The payment is thus based on production levels and is more a royalty in cash than a bonus. In fact, it is treated by some as a 'graduated royalty'.[39]
- Annual benefit

35 *The Petroleum Act 1971* (Thailand) [Division 7 of No. 4].

36 Zhiguo, above n 20, 45.

37 *Triton and Gopher Concessions* (1987) Clause 6.

38 CCOP EPF, 'Thailand Exploration/Development History' (2002) <http://www.ccop.or.th/epf/thailand/thailand_explor.html>.

39 Albert T Chandler, 'Thailand: Oil and Gas Concessions Special Conditions' (1985) 3 *Journal of Energy and Natural Resources* 64.

Based on the Thai MCC, the annual benefit places an obligation on the concessionaire to refrain from claiming expenses exceeding 19 percent of the value of petroleum sold or disposed of, excluding royalties and agreed-upon bonuses, during any given year.[40]

If expenses are higher than the specified percentage, payment of an amount equivalent to the excess is required as an annual benefit. However, should the deductible costs claimed in each year be less than or exactly equal to 19 percent of the petroleum proceeds, no annual benefit is payable to the government.[41] This annual benefit is a cost control device as it penalises the concessionaire should it claim expenses higher than the stated percentage of the value of petroleum sold or disposed of in any given year. This mechanism is seldom employed in the international petroleum industry.[42]

It is of importance to note that the annual benefit has been abrogated since 1990. Those concessionaires holding onshore exploration blocks awarded between 1982 and 1989 will be released from their annual benefit and annual bonus obligations should they apply for conversion to the new terms.[43]

4.2.3.6 Settlement of dispute

According to Thai MCCs, an attempt to resolve all disputes between the government and the IOC should be made through mutual settlement at the outset. Failure in this attempt will result in an ad hoc arbitration. The arbitration procedure is governed by the relevant provisions of the rules of the International Court of Justice (ICJ) of 6 May 1946. Applicable laws in rendering an award are those of the Kingdom of Thailand and the principles of international law as applicable.[44]

4.2.3.7 Revocation

In Thai MCCs, the government has full entitlement to revoke the concession contract once the concessionaire violates the provisions of the transfer of petroleum rights, fails to meet the agreed terms and condition, or becomes bankrupt. Termination of the concession does not relieve the concessionaire from the financial and special advantage obligations not previously discharged.[45]

40 Albert T Chandler, 'Current Development in the Thai Petroleum Concession' (1988) *Oil and Gas Law and Taxation Review* 267–271.
41 Ibid. 289–292.
42 Zhiguo, above n 20, 38.
43 The terms released since 1990.
44 *The model and individual MCCs* (Thailand) Clause 13.
45 *Ministerial Regulation* [Nos. 4 and 17] Clause 15.

To conclude this section, the Thai MCC provides IOCs with adequate exploration incentives and has attracted much risk capital for petroleum development in the country. The MCC system has steadily incorporated new mechanisms to balance the needs of oil-producing countries and the IOC such as increased management control, more elaborate financial provisions and most importantly, obligations for concessionaires to benefit national economic development. As identified above, the royalty, petroleum tax and unique SRB system constitute the three main pillars in the government's revenue stream, and the supplementary role of the EBG is designed to serve Thailand's economic interests. Hence, the Thai MCC is a good example of the role played by the MCC in developing Thailand's oil and gas industry and in supporting profitability.

4.3 Australia

According to the International Energy Agency (IEA), Australia is one of the largest countries for energy resources including coal, oil, natural gas, oil shale and nuclear energy.[46] In this book, the focus is on oil and natural gas, particularly.

For companies to produce petroleum they first need access to the commodity. In most countries, access is controlled by the government as owner of the resource.[47] In Australia, access to petroleum is achieved through the Modern Licensing Regime (MLR) which is granted under the Offshore Petroleum and Greenhouse Gases Storage Act 2006 (OPGGSA).

The licensing system can be labelled as an NCC, permit or lease.

4.3.1 Ownership and accessibility

4.3.1.1 Ownership of minerals

Generally, countries have different rules in relation to ownership of minerals.

On the one hand, there are countries such as Australia, the UK, Norway and Iran which control the ownership of petroleum through a licensing or contract system. Ownership of the petroleum can be determined either when it is produced at the well-head or when it is still underground. However, the physical characteristic of petroleum is different to that of hard rock minerals such as gold and iron ore, in that petroleum is fluid in nature and will travel towards low pressure created by the petroleum well, irrespective of property lines on the surface. This is not such a problem for those countries which own the petroleum or control the ownership of petroleum through a licensing or contract system.

46 'Key World Energy Statistics' (2012) *International Energy Agency* <http://alofatuvalu.tv/FR/12_liens/12_articles_rapports/IEA_rpt_2012_us.pdf>.

47 There are few exceptions to government ownership of petroleum, the main one being private land in the US which also carries with it ownership of the underlying petroleum.

However, obtaining clear title to petroleum covered by licence or contract is going to be a significant issue for any oil company seeking to invest in another country.[48]

On the other hand, there are countries such as United State (US) in which the ownership of the petroleum belongs to landowner. In the early days of the petroleum industry in the US, (the first commercially successful well was drilled at Titusville, Pennsylvania in 1859), this created problems when, for instance, a well was drilled close to a property boundary on the surface, and the petroleum drained into a reservoir below the neighbour's land. Ownership of the surface also carried with it ownership of what lay beneath the surface, so the neighbour would own the petroleum under his land.[49] The main way of dealing with this was for the owner of the well to drill offset wells on his side of the boundary to protect his lines by extracting the petroleum before it could flow to the neighbour's wells.[50] This resulted in too many wells being drilled, often spaced too close together, and the rapid production of easily extracted petroleum instead of the full depletion of the reservoir.

To deal with the situation of wells close to property boundaries draining wells under adjoining properties, the US courts came up with the 'rule of capture'. This rule states that the owner of land acquires title to the oil and gas which is produced from wells drilled on his hand.[51] This ruling has been of critical importance to the early development of the oil industry in the US and has been applied in other countries.[52] First, it clarified title to the petroleum produced from a well. Second, it encouraged first movers to extract as much petroleum from a reservoir as quickly as possible, assisting the rapid development of the fledgling petroleum industry.

However, there was a downside to the rule of capture in that it also encouraged inefficient production, as this contributed to too many wells being drilled. The rule of capture became qualified in the US by the recognition of 'correlative rights',[53] meaning that land holders of a common reservoir has rights and duties depending on each other, so it would not be lawful to damage the reservoir by negligent drilling or wasting gas.[54]

The principle that the holder of the necessary licence obtains title to petroleum produced from wells in his licence area is also contained in Australian

48 Tina Hunter and John Chandler, *Petroleum Law in Australia* (Lexis Nexis, 2013).

49 In Australia law this is called the "accession" principle. The owner of the land owns everything above and beneath the surface. In Australia this is subject to two things: first, in some cases, minerals were reserved from the freehold title on its original grant; and second, legislation was passed later in some states giving the state ownership of petroleum.

50 *Elliff v Texon Drilling* (1948) 146 Tex 575.

51 *Brown v Humble Oil Co* (1935) 126 Tex 296 at 305; *Barnard v Monongahela Natural Gas Co* (1907) 216 Pa 65 A 810; and *Elliff v Texon Drilling* (1948) 146 Tex 575.

52 Terence Daintith, *Finders Keepers? How the Law of Capture Shaped the World Oil Industry* (RFF Press, 2010).

53 Hunter and Chandler, above n 48, 28.

54 *Ohio Oil Co v Indiana* (1990) US 190.

petroleum legislation. This can be viewed as a statutory from of the rule of capture. The impact of this rule has been lessened in Australian in modern times because there is no petroleum in ground in private ownership, and because of the regulation of its extraction by the government, which would not generally permit the drilling of multiple wells. However, it is certainly something which still affects the behaviour of petroleum companies seeking to protect their discoveries or get first-mover advantage in relation to a common reservoir. For instance, a company which has a well in production is going to think carefully about securing exploration acreage which becomes available next door in case the reservoir extends into that acreage and can be drained by an incomer. If on the other hand the company discovers a reservoir crossing a boundary, it may seek to get into production quickly as possible.[55]

4.3.1.2 Ownership of minerals and access to resources

According to common law, the owner of the land owns the airspace above the land and the minerals and resources under the land as well. Based on maxim *'cuius est solum eius est usque ad coelom et ad inferos'*,[56] which means 'to whomsoever the soil belongs, he owns also to the sky and to the depths'. Under this presumption all minerals whether on or beneath the land belonged to the landowner.[57] The source of this law possibly derives from an interpretation of Talmudic Law.[58] It is noteworthy that even in England in the case of *Bury v Pope* in 1586, such a presumption was maintained[59] and applied to the Royal Prerogative on Royal Metals (e.g. gold and silver). During the period from British settlement of Australia until the first mining law was enacted in 1851, the British Government controlled all minerals and other natural resources.[60]

In England, customs, privileges and immunities at common law were conferred on the Sovereign through his or her Royal Prerogative. Therefore, when colonial governments granted title to land prior to 1851, under common law, resources (including the minerals) were deemed to be the property of the grantee unless there were mitigating circumstances such as the presence of precious metals of gold and silver, which were vested in the crown.[61]

55 Hunter and Chandler, above n 48, 28.

56 Hossein Esmaeili, 'Boundaries of Land, Fixtures and Ownership of Minerals and Resources' in Hossein Esmaeili and Brendan Grigg (eds), *The Boundaries of Australian Property Law* (Cambridge University Press, 2016) 211.

57 Adrian Bradbrook, 'The Relevance of the Cuius est Solum Doctrine to the Surface Landowner's Claims to Natural Resources Located Above and Beneath His Lands' (1988)11 *Adelaide Law Review* 462.

58 Kevin Gray, 'Property in Thin Air' (1991) 50(2) *Cambridge Law Journal* 252–253, See also *Deuteronomy* [Correspondence] (1931) 47 *Law Quarterly Review* 14.

59 *Bury v Pope* (1586) Cr Eliz 118; 78 ER 375.

60 M Hunt, *Minerals and Petroleum Law* (1996) 8.

61 Ibid.8.

In Australia, economics played a major role in the drafting of legislation that determined who controlled the minerals. By the mid-19th century, changing legislation had the effect that in the case of a land holder who also owned minerals on his land, in the event of his transferring the land to a new land holder, transference of minerals no longer applied.[62]

Legislation covering the ownership of minerals, especially gold, varied from jurisdiction to jurisdiction. In New South Wales (NSW), for example, under the *1861 Crown Lands Alienation Act,* a person holding a land grant was entitled to certain types of gold on his property.[63] However, the gold deposit was found to be auriferous (gold in rock) the Crown had the right to compulsorily acquire the land with the land holder being compensated.[64]

In the mid-19th century, statutory provisions provided for reservations of minerals for the Crown[65] apart from the exceptions noted above. At present, in all Australian jurisdictions, legislation recognises Crown ownership.[66] The separation of ownership of minerals and land raises many issues, not least being the definition of minerals and under what conditions do mining companies have the right of access to private lands for exploration and mining taking into consideration the likely effects on the environment and Native Title interests.[67] While the *1993 Native Title Act* was watered down by the Howard Government allowing base metals mining to be authorised by State Governments without native title holder consent, nevertheless the National Native Title Tribunal and the Federal Court has facilitated vast tracts of land in Western Australia (WA) to be declared native title by consent of all parties. Some of these agreements involve Indigenous Land Use Agreements (ILUA) others involve shared use of Pastoral Leases.[68] Yet The High Court of Australia in 2002 held that extinguishment prevailed over certain pastoral holdings in WA removing any rights of the claimants, noting in a report covering over 400 pages that the case was difficult.[69] Of course mining and energy production has international implications. (Mining whether onshore or offshore, is subject to regulation by a large number of international instruments and treaties covering sustainable develop-

62 *Batten Pooll v Kennedy* [1907] 1 Ch 256 and *Eardley v Granville* (1876) 3 Ch d 826, 834.

63 Esmaeili and Grigg, above n 56, 112.

64 *Crown Lands Alienation Act 1961*, No. 26a, 3379.

65 For example, under the *Crown Lands Alienation Act 1861* (NSW), all grants by the Crown issued on or after 1858 were required to reserve minerals for the Crown, *Crown Lands Alienation Act 1861 (NSW) s 7.*

66 *Mining Act 1971 (SA)* s 16; *Crown Lands Act 1989* (NSW) s 171; *Mineral Resources Act 1989* (Qld), s 8; *Mine Resources (sustainable development) Act 1990* (Vic) s 9(1); *Mining Act 1978* (WA) ss 9(1), 8(1); *Mineral Resources Development Act 1995* (Tas) ss 3, 6; *Minerals (Acquisition) Act* (NT) s 3.

67 Rosemary Lyster and Adrian Bradbrook, *Energy Law and the Environmental* (Cambridge University Press, 2006).

68 See National Native Title Tribunal Report, 1994–2017; and Commonwealth Native Title Act 1993.

69 *Westen Australia v Ward* (2002) 213 CLR 1, 185 [382].

ment, climate change, the protection of marine environments and protection of world biodiversity.)[70]

Minerals such as hydrocarbons, petroleum, natural gas and other resources are defined by common law as 'every inorganic substance forming part of the crust of the earth, other than the layer of soil which sustains vegetable life'.[71] However, definitions are problematic and as the above quote demonstrates, most authorities try to bring all minerals under one umbrella and as Michael Crommelin puts it, statutory definition of title to land resources in Australia, '[has] long been a vexed issue'.[72] Generally, legislation relation to mineral resources vests all minerals in the Crown in various jurisdictions.[73] Minerals are defined in s 6 of *the Mining Act 1971* (SA) as 'any naturally occurring deposit of metal or metalliferous ore, precious stones or any other mineral (including sand, gravel, stone, shell, coal, oil shale, shale and clay)'.[74]

However, as defined by the Act, 'minerals' exclude any metal, metalliferous substance or mineral recoverable from the seas or water supplies. Also, 'minerals' exclude material that has been dumped or discarded in the course of mining operations. Also excluded are soil, petroleum or other substances that come under the *Petroleum and Geothermal Energy Act 2000* (SA). It should be noted, however, that s 75 of *the Mining Act 1971* (SA) provides that on freehold land, extractive minerals such as sand, gravel, stone, shell, shale and clay are owned by the freehold landowners who may mine these for themselves.[75] Conflicts arise where the Crown owns the minerals on freehold land and where mining companies in pursuit of their financial interests put pressure on the landholders and the relevant state government to gain access for exploration, and if such proves positive, for full-blown mining.[76]

This is especially an issue in Queensland where the Adani proposed mine is supported by some Indigenous landholders because it will provide jobs, yet opposed by other Indigenous stakeholders because matters of custodianship and culture override jobs and money. Generally, miners intending to enter land for the purpose of exploration must issue an appropriate 'notice of entry' before entering any private land for the purpose of mining activities. The landholder

70 Patricia Birnie and Alan Boyle, *International Law and the Environment* (Oxford University Press, 3rd ed, 2009).

71 *Lord Provost and Magistrates of Glasgow v Farie* (1888) 13 App Cas 657, 689.

72 Michael Crommelin, 'The Legal Character of Resource Titles' (1998) 17 *Australian Mining and Petroleum Law Journal* 57, 57.

73 For example, s 16 of *the Mining Act 1971* (SA) Provides: 'Notwithstanding the provisions of any other Act law, or of any land grant or other instrument, the property in all minerals is vested in the Crown. ... This section applies in respect of all mineral land and in respect of all other land (including reserved land) in the State or under coastal waters on the landward side of the baseline'.

74 Esmaeili and Grigg, above n 56, 112.

75 *The Minerals Resources Act 1989* (Qld) provides in s 6 that soil, sand, gravel, and rock are not classified as minerals for the purpose of the Act.

76 Esmaeili and Grigg, above n 56, 113.

may then issue a 'notice of objection' filed with the appropriate court[77] and if the parties cannot agree then the court may settle the dispute. The matter is complicated by the fact that legislation differs between jurisdictions.[78]

In South Australia, for example, for the landowner to prevent mining activity he must prove that any mining activity would be deleterious to the landowners' interests and that no amount of compensation could rectify this.[79] In *Bocardo SA v Star Energy Onshore Ltd* it should be noted that while the landowner of a property cannot prevent underground mining activity he can with the force of law prevent drilling activity affecting his land surface.[80] Also, current legislation makes it hard for landholder to gain access to exploration projects' Program for Environment Protection and Rehabilitation (PEPR), documents which outline the plan for the life of a mine.[81]

Ownership of petroleum resources in Australia is vested in the Crown as applied in each state and territory. Crown ownership of petroleum (except oil shale) in Tasmania is vested in the Crown unless it was held prior to the declaration of Crown Ownership.[82] Similarly, ownership of petroleum is vested in the Crown in Queensland. In New South Wales, ownership of petroleum existing in a natural state on or below the surface of any land in the state is the property of the Crown.[83] Moreover, petroleum found either on the surface or below the land is also owned by the state, whether alienated in fee simple.[84] Ownership of onshore petroleum resources on states and territories land is reserved for the Crown in right of the Commonwealth.[85]

The relevant government has the unlimited right as the owner of petroleum resources to award the rights to its petroleum resources to petroleum operations.[86] Thus, while ownership of mineral and petroleum resources is vested in the Crown in respect to the relevant state or territories, the Crown, pursuant to the relevant statute, grants various titles (also known as a lease, licence, tenement or permit) to a lessee (also known as a licensee or permittee). The granting of licences and the types of licences are discussed in the following section.

77 In some jurisdiction there are specialist courts and tribunes dealing with land, environment and resources issues. For example, South Australia has the Wardens Court and the Environment, Resources and Development. Court, NSW has the land and environment Court, and Queensland has the Planning and Environment Court. Tasmania has the Resource Management and Planning Appeal Tribunal.

78 Esmaeili and Grigg, above n 56, 113.

79 *South Australia Land Commission v Burton and Taylor* (1980) Warden's Court Reports 41; *Cross v Mason and CRA Exploration Pty Ltd* (1978) Warden's Court Report 22; and *Bush and Bush v Taylor* (1981) Warden's Court Report 1.

80 *Bocardo SA v Star Energy UK Onshore Ltd* [2009] 3 WLR 1010 [59] and [69].

81 See <https://www.abc.net.au/news/rural/2017-02-03/sach-mining-act-review/8239998>.

82 *Mineral Resources Development Act 1995* (Tas) s 6.

83 *Petroleum (Onshore) Act 1991* (NSW) s 6(1).

84 *Petroleum and Geothermal Energy Resources Act 1967* (WA) s 9.

85 *Atomic Energy Act 1953* (Cth); *Minerals Acquisition Act 1981* (NT) s 3.

86 United Nations Assembly Resolution, *Permanent Sovereignty over Natural Resource*, Article 1, 1803 (XVII) (14 December 1962, Adopted by General Assembly Resolution 1803 (XVII) of 14 December 1962).

4.3.2 Licence and modern licensing regime

A licence is a permission that licensor (e.g. government, state ...) grants to a licensee (e.g. NOC, IOC ...) to exploit a certain area (block/s) in return for a royalty or fee and taxation. Although the reservoirs in-ground belong to government, it can be booked, ownership of any extracted oil and gas transfers to the licensee at the well-head. Essentially the licensing regime is a regime that the licensee bears the risks however, it gains a certain share of benefits, and others rights or constrains which are considered by the terms and conditions of the licence.

In a number of cases a CCC has gradually shifted to a licensing system.[87] These more formal agreements can also introduce a competitive element, such as requiring bidding for exploration rights, as well as giving greater governmental control over operations. Licences have been categorised as concessions mainly for historical reasons. Conceptually, licences can be closer to concessions in cases which give the licensee a clear set of rights and entitlements, such as the ownership of petroleum. But in other cases, a licence is merely an authorisation allowing conduct that would otherwise be unlawful.[88] This is the case in Australia, in which licences are granted under the OPGGSA.

What is the MLR and why does Australia choose this contract form? The MLR has been described by Bunter as: "...the identification by government of potential (upstream) petroleum investment opportunities in the national territory, their subdivision into discrete contract areas of prospective size, their offering to the international oil companies by a suitable tendering process, and the establishment and negotiation of technical, financial and contractual terms and conditions (for award) consistent with their petroleum prospectively and with the national interest".[89]

The MLR is typically granted for the exploration and production of petroleum in specific areas and for a specific period. Exploration acreage is often offered in licensing rounds. These are discrete acts of licensing which take place on a regular sequential basis, often separated by several years, and which offer a certain defined area or acreage.[90] This system is designed to assist the state by broadening the market so that the largest number of oil companies can bid

87 Mike Roggenkamp, 'Energy Law in the Netherlands' in Mike Roggenkamp et al (eds), *Energy Law in Europe* (Oxford University Press, 2001) 639.

88 Greg Gordon, ' Petroleum Licensing' in Greg Gordon, John Paterson and Emek Usenmez (eds), *Oil and Gas Law Current Practice and emerging Trends* (Dundee University Press, 2001) 67; and Terence Daintith, Geoffrey Willoughby and Adrian Hill, *United Kingdom Oil and Gas Law* (Sweet & Maxwell, 3rd ed, 2000), Looseleaf [1-302].

89 Michael Bunter, *The Promotion and Licensing of Petroleum Prospective Acreage* (Kluwer Law International, 2002) xxii.

90 This is the system used in Australia, however in some states there may be an informal licensing system where the state does not define the specific area for licensing. Here, the oil company approaches the rights-holder informally, and a deal is made. This is sometimes called an "over the counter" system.

competitively for the acreage on offer. The bidding is divided into programme of work or cash amount, or both. In Australia, it is based on work programme to improve the overall petroleum resource through exploration.

Exploration licences are granted for a period which is usually up to 10 years, although this is discretionary in some states. Often licences can be renewed. It is usually a condition of exploration licences that at certain intervals part of the original licence area will be relinquished and returned to the state. This often coincides with renewal. The relinquished area is considered to be less productive and is generally required to be of a shape and size that is suitable for reoffering as exploration acreage. This gives other companies an opportunity to explore the area further, and assisted with new technologies, often finding what the first company may have missed.[91]

Exploration licences clearly detail onerous obligatory work programmes which can include a seismic survey and the drilling of one or more test wells. The details vary between exploration licences, and will generally form part of negotiating the bidding process for a licence. Licences generally provide for some form of sanction when the obligatory work programme is not fulfilled, often requiring the defaulting licensee to pay monetary compensation to the licensing authority for the value of the non-fulfilled programme.[92] Failure to complete the obligatory work programme is also grounds for the cancellation of an exploration licence, although this is often avoided through negotiations between the relevant parties.

Production licences often have a set initial period, often providing for one or more extensions. Often the total period comprises 30 or 40 years. Production licences often have less significant obligatory work requirements and can be granted subject to the development of a work plan and a corresponding work schedule, which must to be submitted to state authorities for approval before work is able to proceed. This can be done through a field development plan setting out in detail how the field will be developed, including the required structures, reservoir management, environmental and safety plans. In this way the state retains control over the development and production of its natural resources.

Depending on the regulatory framework governing the regime, the licence may confer exclusive rights, whereby the licensee is authorised to exercise the rights conferred by the licence against third parties. Generally, a non-exclusive licence is granted for geological and geophysical prospecting, whilst an exclusive licence is usually granted for exploration work that involves drilling and production operations.[93]

A licensing regime is often used in countries with relatively low reserves, and with offshore oil exploration and production which are associated with high

91 Hunter and Chandler, above n 48, 18–19.

92 Bernard Taverne, *Petroleum, Industry and Government: A Study of the Involvement of Industry and Governments in Exploring for and Producing Petroleum* (Kluwer Law International, 3rd ed, 2013) 126.

93 Hunter and Chandler, above n 48, 19.

costs. Countries that use the MLR include the United Kingdom, Norway, Australia and the Netherlands. In countries which are relatively unexplored, or where exploration is expensive and risky, as is typically the case offshore, usually a licence is given to an international oil company. When petroleum is known to exist, and exploration and production are less expensive and less risky, a production sharing arrangement can seem more attractive to a host country. In the MLR, the licensee is free to dispose of the production, since transfer of title and therefore ownership occurs when the oil is lifted (on the well-head), though there may be some restrictions requiring producers to sell a certain quantity of their production back to the domestic market.

The state 'fetters' its ownership rights when it grants a petroleum licence. The state is unable to transfer its ownership rights over the resource area for the period of the license.[94] However, once the licence has expired, the state is free to grant an authorisation, or transfer proprietary rights, in the acreage to others. The rights conferred by a petroleum licence are conditional rights, dependent on a condition being satisfied for the right to be either possessed or exercised. The conditions are usually outlined either within the legislation framework, or in administrative guidance notes that accompany a release of acreage for licensing.[95]

In an economic sense, the award of a petroleum licence by a state confers property rights on the licensee.[96] In Australia, the licence grants certain rights (exclusive or non-exclusive rights) over the licence area, depending on the type of licence awarded (the grant of an exploration licence confers the right to explore for petroleum in the Commonwealth's offshore zone under s 98 of OPGGSA).[97] These rights are proprietary in the sense that they are transferable and can be sold. A transfer of a title to a licence is authorised[98] and executed[99] using prescribed forms set out in Sch 4 of the Regulations. Similarly, it is possible to transfer a licence or participating interests to other countries, for instance, Norway.

In terms of why Australia chooses to implement the MLR, two main reasons emerge.

First, the states or territories frequently lack the risk capital to explore for petroleum – it is generally expensive and risky – and as a matter of domestic

94 J Davis, *Does one Size Fit All? Reflecting On Governance and North Sea Licensing Systems*, 2004, Background Paper: BC Offshore: Potential and Problems A MASC Workshop for Lawyers, Dunsmuir lodge, Sidney BC, 18–21 March 2004, 4.

95 Hunter and Chandler, above n 48, 74.

96 Property rights in in this context are those rights pertaining to the permissible (socially sanctioned) use of resources, goods and services. David W Pearce (ed), *The MIT Dictionary of Modern Economics* (MIT Press, 1986) 364.

97 While the Act does not expressly confer exclusive right over the permit area, the exclusivity of those rights are implied rights since the exploration for petroleum in the offshore area is prohibited under s 97(1) of OPGGSA, unless exploration activity is authorised by the grant of an exploration license under s 97(2) of OPGGSA. The grant of an exploration permit entitles the licensee to apply for a production permit to recover petroleum in the event of a commercial discovery.

98 OPGGSA ss 472–474.

99 OPGGSA ss 3–4.

law or philosophy they are not allowed to spend that capital on exploration or production operations.

Second, they lack the technical expertise for operation phrases. Therefore, the MRL is chosen by states or territories because they bear no liability as to the different risks inherent to every petroleum exploration project. Also, it allows them to access the latest technological equipment and technical expertise which is an inevitable feature of every valid oil company.

4.3.3 Australian modern licensing regime

The MLR is the licensing and concession system utilised by many developed petroleum-producing countries including the US, the UK, Norway, Canada and Australia.

In Australia, upstream petroleum operations can be divided into five stages or processes: exploration,[100] appraisal,[101] development,[102] production[103] and abandonment.[104] In turn, two separate types of licenses can be granted: an access (exploration) license and an operational license. The license that grants exclusive access to petroleum resources is known as a petroleum exploration permit. All other licences granted are operational licences; that is, licences granted as required during the further stage of petroleum activities. The regulation of petroleum activities including the granting of petroleum licences is undertaken through the Joint Authority (JA) and the Designated Authority (DA).

4.3.3.1 Access (exploration) license

The petroleum exploration and development permit is granted via the following process: nomination, acreage release, Minister calling for bids, assessed of bids by the JA and the granting of an exploration permit.[105]

The OPGGSA provides for the grant and authorises the permittee under a petroleum exploration permit to explore for petroleum in the permit area. There are three types of petroleum exploration permits provided for under the OPGGSA. All three types are granted through a competitive process following a notice in the Government Gazette calling for applications and the making of

100 Exploration is the process of identifying a prospective hydrocarbon (petroleum) region and structure.

101 Appraisal is the process of confirming the size, quality and therefor the commercial potential of a hydrocarbon discovery.

102 Development is the process of constructing facilities and infrastructure.

103 Production is the full-scale extraction of hydrocarbon reserves.

104 Abandonment is the final plugging of wells and permanent dismantling of production facilities and infrastructure, and is preceded by decommissioning.

105 Department of Resources, Energy and Tourism, 'Offshore Petroleum Acreage Release' (07 August 2012) Ningaloo Atlas <http://ningaloo-atlas.org.au/content/offshore-petroleum-exploration-acreage-releases>.

an offer. The notification provides details of the block(s) to be included in the permit and the data, manner and place of submission.[106]

A Work-bid petroleum exploration permit

Petroleum exploration permits are generally granted through work-bidding (which is also called work programme bidding). This is because the Australian government's approach has been one of increasing exploration in Australia, and of advancing knowledge of its petroleum potential.[107]

B Cash-bid exploration permit

Since 2014, cash-bidding has been utilised by the Australian government to allocate acreage in mature areas and in areas containing known petroleum accumulations. Consultation concerning the guidelines for the cash-bidding process commenced in 2013. The rules for cash-bidding are like those for work programme bidding, with the obvious difference being that instead of the bid containing proposals for work and expenditure, it must specify the amount that the applicant is prepared to pay for the granting of the permit. The process of inviting applications by way of cash-bidding and details which must accompany an application are set out by the OPGGSA.[108]

C Special petroleum exploration permit

Special petroleum exploration permits are granted over a block(s) where the subject of a petroleum title once was, but is no longer covered by it. This occurs when the former title is surrendered, cancelled, terminated or revoked in respect of those blocks. The situations applicable to the different titles are provided for in s 115(1) of the OPGGSA and include: when a petroleum retention lease is surrendered, cancelled or revoked; when a petroleum production license is surrendered, cancelled or terminated; or when a petroleum exploration permit is surrendered, cancelled or revoked.

The bidding rules are like those for work programme bidding. The only difference being that, in addition to containing proposals for work and expenditures, the bid must also specify the amount the applicant is prepared to pay for the granting of the permit. The details which must accompany an application are set out by the OPGGSA.[109]

4.3.3.2 Operational licenses

The OPGGSA provides for the types of licenses required during the various stages of upstream petroleum activities. As mentioned previously, the granting of a petroleum exploration permit is solely the start of petroleum activities and each type of activity requires operational authorisation. The type of license required depends on the result of the petroleum exploration activities. The options

106 *OPGGSA* s 7.
107 *OPGGSA* s 105(2).
108 *OPGGSA* s 110(6).
109 *OPGGSA* s 115(5).

are available once a discovery has been made, and the project is moving out of the exploration stage. The threshold question regards the commercial viability of the project. The petroleum production license is the license used for commercial production.[110]

A Licences during the appraisal stage

Once a discovery has been made in a petroleum exploration permit area by the exploration permit holder, several events will follow. First, the permittee must inform the titles administrator of the discovery before the end of the 30-day period beginning on the day of completion of the well that resulted in the discovery. Next, assuming the discovery is of a petroleum pool, the declaration process commences.[111]

If the permittee commences the process of recovering petroleum from the pool, it may nominate a block(s) of the extent of the pool for declaration as a location. The permittee would nominate block(s) for as much as of the pool is extended by him. If the permittee does not start the process, it can be started by the JA. If the JA believes a permittee is entitled to nominate blocks and has not done so, then s 130 of the OPGGSA can require the permittee to nominate within 90 days.

If the permittee does not comply, the JA can nominate the location blocks for declaration. Once a nomination has occurred (with the additional requirement in the case of a nomination by a permittee the JA regarding the permittee is entitled to nominate), under s 131 of the OPGGSA the JA must then declare the nominated blocks to be a location. Notice of the location declaration is published in the Government Gazette.

The permittee has two years from the declaration day[112] to apply for the granting of a petroleum production license[113] or a petroleum retention lease.[114] This can be extended to four years by the title administrator. Within this period, the permittee must decide whether to surrender the permit or to seek to obtain a petroleum retention lease or petroleum production license.

B Licences during the production stage

Achieving commercial production is the aim of the petroleum production license. In fact, the Australia regulator ensures that operations are carried out in accordance with appropriate oil master practices and are compatible with the optimum long-term recovery of petroleum.[115] Therefore, the OPGGSA provides for the granting of petroleum production licences. In addition, s 161 of the OPGGSA authorises the licensee to carry out petroleum recovery

110 Hunter and Chandler, above n 48, 99.
111 *OPGGSA* s 284(2).
112 The day of the declaration is called the 'declaration day'.
113 *OPGGSA* s 168.
114 *OPGGSA* s 141.
115 Available at <http://www.nopta.gov.au/> (accessed 29/08/2017).

operations in the licensed area and is therefore the title used for commercial production. Rules for the granting of a petroleum production license depend on the way in which it is granted. It is more desirable and logical that a petroleum production licensee to undertake recovery of petroleum is combined with an accepted petroleum development plan, and it is also acceptable to undertake an activity in the license area consistent with the plan.[116]

In conclusion, on the one hand, the MLR illustrates high capability at different stages to cover all parts of upstream and downstream petroleum and gas industry practices (from exploration to marketing) in Australia. On the other hand, the MRL is fundamental to attracting IOCs in Australia to invest millions, if not billions of dollar on petroleum activities. This is particularly in the exploration phase as they have security of title, in the sense that they will have the right to exploit a discovery once made.

4.4 United Kingdom

In the UK, the Department of Energy and Climate Change (DECC) is primarily responsible for the regulation of the oil industry and the granting of exploration and extraction licences. The license is in the form of a deed whereby the licensee is bound to observe the conditions of the license. Secondary legislation contains the conditions (known as model clauses) governing issues such as the granting of rights, implementation of development plans, working methods, measurements and work programmes and the relinquishment of a certain proportion of the license area.[117]

Licences are usually awarded in licensing rounds, although out-of-round licences may be granted in certain circumstance. In the UK, licences may be granted to one or more licensees. However, the license is legally held collectively by the licensees who are jointly and severally liable in respect to the obligations arising under, and operations conducted pursuant to, the license.[118]

4.4.1 Licensing system

The DECC currently issues two types of offshore licenses: exploration licenses, and production licenses. An exploration license allows the licensee to carry out seismic surveys in an area and to undertake shallow drilling. Exploration licences are usually granted for a period of three years, with the possibility of a further three-year extension.[119] In the production license, the licensee has the exclusive

116 Hunter and Chandler, above n 48, 109.

117 Mohammad Alramahi, *Oil and Gas Law in the UK* (Bloomsbury, 2012) 56.

118 Gunther Kuehne, 'Oil and Gas Licensing: Some Comparative United Kingdom German Aspects' (1986) 4(3) *Journal of Energy and Natural Resources Law* 29 (published online on 8 Jun 2015).

119 Taylor Tumnde, 'Petroleum License in United Kingdom' (30 July 2014) linked in <https://www.linkedin.com/pulse/20140630151031-137158292-petroleum-licensing-in-the-united-kingdom>.

right to explore for and subsequently exploit hydrocarbons in the geographical area covered by the license. It is also split into three phases: exploration (typically lasting for years); appraisal, during which time the field development plan must be submitted for approval (four years) and production (18 years, with the possibility of extension).[120] There is automatic expiry at the end of each phase unless the licensee has made sufficient progress to move to the next phase.

A petroleum exploration and development license is required for onshore exploration and production activities, similar in form to the offshore production license.

4.4.2 Features

Like other countries using a license framework, the UK license has common and individual provisions and characteristics including:

4.4.2.1 Ownership

Based on UK licensing, the holder of an exclusive production license has the right to acquire the ownership of any petroleum that enters any well drilled by the former in accordance with all terms and conditions of his license.[121]

4.4.2.2 Duration

Generally, there is an initial license period with the option for one or more extensions. The total license period may be up to 30 or 40 years if development and production forms part of the licensed operation. A license for exploration shall not extend beyond 10 years. Each license under application is treated as a special case.

The licensee must ensure that the authorisation duration does not exceed the period necessary to carry out the authorised operations. However, competent authorities may prolong the authorisation where the stipulated duration is insufficient to complete the operations in question and where the operations have been performed in accordance with the authorisation.[122]

4.4.2.3 Taxation

Currently, three types of taxes apply to hydrocarbons production activities in the UK:

i Ring-fence corporation tax – the normal UK corporation tax except for a ring-fence to prevent taxable profits from hydrocarbon extraction being

120 Alramahi, above n 117, 49–52.

121 *The Petroleum Regulations 1988* (production, seawards areas) schedule 4.

122 Kuehne, above n 118, 35.

reduced by losses from other activities or by excessive interest payments. Since April 1999, the rate of ring-fenced corporation tax has been 30 percent.

ii Supplementary charge – since April 2002, a supplementary charge has been applied to a company's ring-fenced profits without deducting debt financing costs. In 2011, the UK government raised the rate of supplementary charge from 20 percent to 32 percent in consideration of what it felt were unexpected profits made by oil and gas companies active in the UK.

iii Petroleum Revenue Tax (PRT) – a field-based tax applicable to profits arising from the exploitation of hydrocarbon fields for which development consent was given prior to 15 March 1993. Profits for PRT calculation purposes are based on the excess of proceeds from the disposal of hydrocarbons from the field over the field's expenditure. The current rate is 50 percent and is charged prior to the corporation tax. It is deductible for calculating ring-fence corporation tax and the supplementary charge.

The tax regime applied to a UK hydrocarbon field depends on the date on which development consent was received:

- Fields that received development consent before 16 March 1993 are subject to PRT, ring-fence corporation tax, and the supplementary charge.
- Fields that received development consent on or after 16 March 1993 are subject only to ring-fence corporation tax and the supplementary charge.[123]

4.4.2.4 Area relinquishment schedule

It is common practice that at certain intervals; for instance, at the end of the initial period, part or parts of the original area of the license must be relinquished. The part(s) to be relinquished must be of such a shape and size that they may again be offered once more for licensing.

4.4.2.5 Obligatory exploration work programme

According to licensing in the UK, during the initial period of the license an obligatory exploration work programme must be carried out. Extension of the license beyond the initial period shall depend on the satisfactory implementation of this condition. Details of the work programme belong to the conditions of a license and usually form an element of the competitive bidding for a license.[124]

123 Oil and Gas Authority, 'Taxation of Exploration For, and Production of, Oil and Gas in the UK and on the UK Continental Shelf' (9 October 2015) GOV.UK <https://www.gov.uk/guidance/oil-and-gas-taxation>.

124 Kuehne, above n 118, 22.

A license may provide for a sanction on the non-fulfilment of whole or part of the obligatory work programme. In case of non-fulfilment, the defaulting licensee may have to pay in cash the monetary value of the non-fulfilment programme to the competent authority. Non-fulfilment may also constitute grounds for cancelling the license, but the problem is usually resolved through further negotiation on compensatory work between the competent authority and the licensee.

4.4.2.6 Development plan

The licensee in the UK is obliged to prepare a development plan and corresponding production schedule with respect to any commercial discovery made. The plan and schedule must be submitted for approval to the competent authority and only approved plans may be carried out.

4.4.2.7 Participation

In the UK license, the government has the authority to demand as a condition for the granting of a license that the state itself or a wholly state-owned enterprise designated for that purpose becomes a participant in the venture. The applicant may meet this demand by accepting the state or the designated state enterprise as a co-licensee and by establishing a joint venture based on an agreement of cooperation, also known as a state participation agreement.[125]

If the state itself is participating in the license, a wholly state-owned enterprise may be designed to represent the state and to manage its interests.[126] State or designed state enterprises are hereafter referred to as the state participant. However, the state participant does not necessarily have to become a co-licensee.

The license may be awarded solely to the applicant with everything else (meaning the state participating agreement) remaining the same. If this option is chosen, the former applicant (now 100 percent license holder) is solely responsible for exercising the rights and for fulfilling the obligations attached to the license.

The modalities of state participation found in the state participation agreement concern:

- i The percentage share of state participation (whether fixed for the duration of the agreement or made dependent on factors such as production levels, etc.
- ii The timing as to when the state participant's financial participation (in accordance with its percentage participation) becomes effective; that is, either from the very beginning of the authorised operations or not before the first commercial discovery has been made.[127]

125 Alexander G Kemp, 'An Assessment of UK North Sea Oil and Gas Policies' (1990) 18(7) *Energy Policy Journal* 609–610.

126 Ibid. 610–611.

127 Kenneth W Dam, 'The Evolution of North Sea Licensing Policy in Britain and Norway' (1974) 17(2) *Journal of Law and Economics* 246–247.

If the latter option is chosen it must be settled irrespective of whether the state participant must reimburse its percentage share of the successful exploration expenditure that led to the commercial discovery. Text of the required agreement may be provided as part of the model license, if available. Otherwise, the agreement is subject to approval from the competent authority. Its contents are generally like those of the private or public sector.

The percentage share of state participation may be fixed in law or regulation as a standard condition of the license or state participation agreement. Alternatively, it may be negotiated in the context of a bidding round and so become a condition of the license concerned.

4.4.2.8 Settlement of disputes

A license creates a direct relationship between the licensee and the government granting the license in its capacity as representative of the state. Therefore, any dispute between the licensee and the government in countries with an advanced, well developed legal system shall as a rule is dealt with in accordance with the rules of public administrative law. In the event that no amicable resolution of the conflict appears possible, it is to be decided by a court of administrative law.[128] When the dispute relates to matters of a highly technical nature, the parties are more likely to choose arbitration than to allow the matter to go to court.

In conclusion, the UK licensing programme for its oil and gas industry comprises the exploration license and the production license. Although some features of the UK licensing system have not been mentioned (e.g. royalty payment, licensing area, relinquishment), detailed focus was given to the more important licensing terms appropriate to the oil fields in UK, some of which are compatible with other situations. The terms may even be offered to the oil and gas masters in other countries such as state participation and the accurate taxation system. The taxation system may be profitable if it is fulfilled correctly.

4.5 Norway

Norway is Europe's largest oil producer, the world's third-largest natural gas exporter, and an important supplier of both oil and natural gas to other European countries. Norway also has the largest oil reserves in Western Europe, with 5.83 billion barrels of proven crude oil reserves and 74 trillion cubic feet (TCF) of proven natural gas reserves.[129] All of Norway's oil reserves are located offshore on the Norwegian Continental Shelf (NCS) which is divided into three sections: The North Sea, the Norwegian Sea and the Barents Sea.

128 Ibid. 236–237.

129 Lars J Alveberg, 'Norwegian Petroleum History' (2013) FACTS 10 <http://www.npd.no/Global/Engelsk/3-Publications/Facts/Facts2013/FACTS_2013.pdf>.

4.5.1 Licensing regime

Petroleum legislation in Norway consists of Acts (formal law) and subsidiary legislation in the form of implementing and supplementary regulations. The *Petroleum Act* of 29 November 1996, provides the legal framework for the licensing system that regulates petroleum activities.[130] Licenses are granted in licensing rounds. In rounds one to three, licenses are granted under the 1965 Royal Decree. In rounds four to nine, licenses are granted under the 1972 Decree. From round 10, licenses are granted in accordance with the 1985 Act[131] and from 1 July 1997 (amended 27 June 2003; 7 July 2005; and 26 January 2007),[132] licenses have been granted according to this Act.[133]

The Ministry of Petroleum and Energy has the authority to award licenses. Following the submission of applications in each licensing round, the Ministry allocates each license to an individual licensee or group licensees. A consortium operator responsible for carrying out the day to day activities under the terms of the license is then appointed by the Ministry. Licensees are currently only awarded acreage for which they have submitted complete plans.

As in the UK, Norwegian regulations specify who may apply for licenses, the form of application and the conditions under which the licenses are granted. There are two kinds of licenses: the non-exclusive exploration (reconnaissance) license and the exclusive production license.

4.5.1.1 Exploration license

The reconnaissance license (which may be granted to foreign corporations)[134] has a three-year term and authorises all types of geophysical exploration. It may cover all or part of the Norwegian North Sea sector except an area covered by

130 The Act of 29 November 1996, No.72 as amended is currently in force. With effect from 1 July 1997, this act replaced its predecessor, the Act of 22 March 1985, No. 11 (1985 Act). Like its predecessor, the Act is a comprehensive petroleum law exclusively directed at the regulation of offshore petroleum operations. In turn, the 1985 Act was preceded by the Act of 21 June 1963, No. 12 and the regulations issued under this Act. In stark contrast to its successors, the 1963 Act was an enabling law, leaving the main provisions of the petroleum regime to be set out in regulations. The regulations concerned were the Royal Decrees of 9 April 1965 and 8 December 1972, respectively. Both related to exploration for and exploitation of petroleum on the Norwegian continental shelf.

131 *The Petroleum Act of 1985*.

132 Olav Hanssensvei, 'General Information on the Norwegian Regulatory Regime Pertaining to Fiscal Measurement of Oil and Gas from the Norwegian Continental Shelf' (2014) *The Norwegian Petroleum Directorate* 3 <http://www.npd.no/global/engelsk/5-rules-and-regulations/fiscal-measurement/fiskal-measurement.pdf>.

133 Mette Karine, 'Norway; Petroleum Regime' (2015) *Ministry of Petroleum and Energy* 8–11 <http://www.congreso.es/docu/docum/ddocum/dosieres/sleg/legislatura_10/spl_76/pdfs/19.pdf>.

134 Royal Decree of April 9, 1965, Note the dissimilarity with the UK regulations whereby an exploration license cannot be granted to a foreign corporation.

a production license. Through exploration licenses, the Ministry may grant to a body corporate a license to explore for petroleum within a limited area of the seabed or its subsoil. Exploration licenses may also be granted to a person domiciled in a European Economic Area (EEA) state. The exploration license provides the right to explore for petroleum. It does not, however, give exclusive rights to exploration in the areas mentioned in the license or any preferential right when production licenses are granted. An exploration license is granted for three years unless another period is stipulated.

The exploration license shall state the area covered by the license, but does not afford any rights to exploration in areas covered by production licenses unless determined by the Ministry.

4.5.1.2 Production license

The production license is the main license in Norway. It regulates the rights and obligations of companies vis-à-vis the Norwegian state. The document supplements the requirements in the *Petroleum Act* and stipulates detailed terms and conditions. A production license gives the licensee exclusive right to exploration, exploitation drilling and production of petroleum deposits in areas covered by the license.[135] The licensee is the owner of this proportionate share of the petroleum produced.

The Ministry shall, as a rule, announce the area for which applications for production licenses may be submitted. It shall be published through notification which stipulates a time limit for the filing of applications of not less than 90 days, as well as other information as determined by the Ministry. However, the Norwegian King may grant a production license without announcement.

The granting of a production license shall be based on factual and objective criteria, and the requirements and conditions must be stated in the notification. The King is not obliged to grant a production license based on the applications received. Also, the King may authorise as a condition for granting a production license that the licensees shall enter into agreements with specified contents with one another.[136]

Each license provides exclusive rights for the exploration and exploitation of hydrocarbons in the relevant geographical area and includes terms and conditions supplementing those of the *Petroleum Act*. The license is awarded for an initial exploration period of up to 10 years. Certain minimum exploratory activities, including seismic surveys and/or shallow drilling, must be carried out during this initial period. Following exploration, the licensee can only retain an area in which it plans to start production.[137]

135 Alveberg, above n 129.

136 *Directive 94/22/EC of 30 May 1994 of the European Parliament and of the Council on the Conditions for Granting and Using Authorisations for the Prospection, Exploration and Production of Hydrocarbons* article 3.

137 Alveberg, above n 129.

A licensee who has fulfilled the work commitment and the conditions otherwise applicable to the individual license may demand that the license be extended after the initial period has expired. The extension period is stipulated in the license and is generally up to 30 years (although in some cases it may be up to 50 years). If all licensees agree, the production license can be relinquished when the work commitment has been fulfilled. If the licensee wants to continue the work covered by the production license, the license will enter the extension period assigned for development and operations.[138]

4.5.2 Licensing system in Norway

The main licensing terms in Norway are like other commonwealth countries such as Australasia and the UK. The terms include license area, duration, license granting, bidding, licensee's obligation, fiscal regime, participation, relinquishment, settlement of dispute and ownership. All terms have individual importance and have been examined in their place. Therefore, to avoid repeating the terms, only the taxation regime and participation in Norway are discussed below.

4.5.2.1 Taxation regime

The overall objective of Norway's petroleum policy has always been to provide a framework for the profitable production of oil and gas in the long term. It has also been considered important to ensure that as large a share of the value creation as possible accrues to the state so that it can benefit the broader society. This is partly achieved by the tax regime. Currently, the taxation regime includes the Norwegian corporation tax rate of 28 percent plus a special tax of 50 percent. In respect to both taxes, consolidation between fields is permitted.

To shield the normal return from special tax, an extra deduction, the uplift, is allowed in the calculation base for the special tax. This amounts to 30 percent of the investment (7.5 percent per annum for four years from the year the investment is made).[139] Since 2005, Norway has also offered an annual refund of 78 percent of the taxable value of exploration costs. This is to incentivise new investment into Norway where new entrants are not able to offset exploration costs against taxable income from the other producing fields. Other important taxes linked to petroleum activities are the carbon dioxide tax and an area fee. The carbon dioxide tax rate in 2007 was Nkr 0.8 per litre of oil or standard cubic metre of gas. The area fees accrue on all licenses after expiry of the initial period.[140]

138 Karine, above n 133.

139 Ministry of Finance, Statistic Norway, *The Petroleum Tax System* (Updated 22 February 2017) <http://www.norskpetroleum.no/en/economy/petroleum-tax/>.

140 *Oil and Gas Taxation in Norway* (2014) Deloitte <https://www2.deloitte.com/content/dam/Deloitte/global/Documents/Energy-and-Resources/gx-er-oil-and-gas-taxguide-norway.pdf>.

4.5.2.2 Participation

The Norwegian government can participate directly in the proceeds arising from the exploration of oil and gas under the State Direct Financial Interest (SDFI), which is managed by Petoro. Petoro's participation is determined according to state preferences when the licenses are awarded and may vary from field to field. Once the relevant participation is decided, Petoro behaves like any other licensee, paying its share of costs and participating proportionately in production. This arrangement allows the state to adjust the amount of risk that it wishes to undertake while maintaining a licensing regime.

To conclude, the licensing contract chosen by the Norwegian government aims to achieve to its petroleum policy aims. Like other NCCs, licensing is dividing between the exploration and production sectors. The exploration licensing sector starts with the government announcing the licensing rounds before considering applications, and then negotiating and proposing the final award (based on certain conditions). The production licensing sector grants exclusive rights to explore for and produce oil and gas. The licensee becomes the owner of the petroleum produced.

It should be mentioned that all the countries profiled in this chapter utilise NCCs and a joint authority for the exploration, extraction and development of their common oil and gas reservoirs. The Thailand/Malaysia agreement of 1990,[141] the Australia and Indonesia agreement of 1989,[142] the Australia/East Timor agreement of 2001[143] and the Iceland/Norway agreement of 1981[144] are examples.

4.6 Conclusion

To achieve the objective of this chapter, the NCC (also labelled as MCC, MLR, License, lease or Permit) has been analysed in selected developed and developing countries for how they serve the national interests of the country. The countries currently use or have previously used the NCC in various ways in terms of level of development. The examples illustrate that these countries utilise the NCC irrespective of their level of development. Considering all the countries where the NCC is/was part of their oil and gas contract framework, they are/were

141 Gauult Ian Townsend, 'The Malaysia/Thailand Development Agreement' in Hazal Fox (ed), *Joint Development of Offshore Oil and Gas* (British Institute of International and Comparative Law, 1990) 102.

142 Burmester, 'The Zone of Co-Operation between Australia and Indonesia: A Preliminary Outline with Particular Reference to Applicable Law' in Hazal Fox (ed), *Joint Development of Offshore oil and Gas* (British Institute of International and Comparative Law, 1990) 128.

143 Ana Batista et al 'Cross Border Unitisation and Joint Development Agreement: An International Perspective' (2007) 29 *Houston Journal of International Law* 411.

144 Masahiro Miyoshi, 'The Basic Concept of Joint Development of Hydrocarbon Resources on the Continental Shelfs' (1988) 3(1) *International Journal of Estuarine and Coastal Law* 3.

seeking to maximise profitability from their oil and gas fields and to maximise attraction to IOCs.

Every country with inclusion content (such as bear risk and financial terms) appropriate to the significance their oil fields sought to maximise investment interest from IOCs in win-win proposition through the NCC. For instance, Brazil attempted to achieve this with its own individual bidding round, royalty and local content percentage, manifestation and IOC remuneration. Thailand applied the concessionaire obligation, financial regimes, SRB and EBG, and Australia utilised the high capacity of the MLR to attract capital from IOCs and development of the oil and gas industry simultaneously. The UK applied government participation and accurate taxation systems, and Norway applied important taxation regimes which could be practicable in Iran's oil and gas sectors.

Particularly, the NCC may be utilised as one of the most appropriate contract forms in common oil and gas reservoirs to maximise production. This is demonstrated by the oil contract pattern in the North Sea (under the name of license) and in the Thailand/Malaysia Agreement, Australia/Indonesia Agreement, Australia/East Timor Agreement and Iceland/Norway Agreement.

The NCC was analysed in regard to the extent to which it has facilitated achievement of national government objectives in developed and developing countries facing the risks and opportunities associated with the globalised oil and gas industry. It was argued that the NCC has distinct advantages over the CCC in this regard. The next chapter considers another aspect of main question 3. It includes an examination of the strengths and weaknesses of the NCC in relation to other contractual forms utilised in the oil and gas industry.

5 Current oil and gas contract framework in the world and comparisons between them

5.1 Production Sharing Agreement (PSA)

Under a PSA, also referred to as a Production Sharing Contract (PSC), the contractor is given the right to explore for and produce hydrocarbons within a given contract area, assuming all exploration risks and costs in exchange for a share of the oil and/or gas produced. The host country receives the remaining share. Under this type of Upstream Government Petroleum Contract (UGPC), like in a concession or license, if the contractor's exploration efforts do not materialise in a discovery, the contractor is not reimbursed by the host country. However, in the event of a successful venture, the resulting production is split between the parties according to participation formulas set forth in the contract.[1]

In addition, unlike a concession or license, the host government receives an amount of oil and/or gas which can be commercialised and monetised according to the government's development programmes and economic needs. The attendant benefits of the right to receive production are the host government's PSC's coverage of its domestic needs and a building up of foreign exchange reserves by way of exports to international markets. The PSA is now used in Indonesia, China, Peru, Malaysia, Malta, Guatemala, Libya, Jordan, Angola, Qatar, Bangladesh and the Philippines.

5.1.1 Definition

Agreements on production sharing are legal instruments that regulate the relationship between a government with commercial partners in the petroleum extraction industry.[2] A PSA is also defined in the Bill of Law in Brazil as a:

> Regime of exploration and production of oil, natural gas and other fluid hydrocarbons whereby oil companies will be granted rights to explore for,

1 Daniel Johnston, *International Petroleum Fiscal Systems and Production Sharing Contracts* (Pennwell, 1994) 38.

2 Anthony Jennings, *Oil and Gas Exploration Contracts* (London, Sweet & Maxwell Publish, 2002) 44.

develop, and produce petroleum reserves, at their cost. In the event of a commercial discovery, costs incurred will be reimbursed to oil companies through an entitlement to production referred to as cost oil. The remaining petroleum, after deduction of cost oil, is considered profit oil.[3]

5.1.2 Legal nature

The PSC is in fact a risky type of sharing contracts. In some sharing contracts, the risks are removed and the contract covers the explored oil or gas field.[4]

Within the production sharing scheme, the authorities retain ownership of the resources while hiring the IOC to provide technological and investment utilities for the various phases of the production process. The government is ordinarily actioned through the proxy of a national petroleum authority. Consequently, the IOC is granted a predefined percentage of the petroleum output as compensation for the risks endured and any facilities and services utilised. The remainder of the output is nonetheless owned fully by the government. Furthermore, the state party is afforded the ability to involve themselves in certain stages of the exploration and exploitation operations, ordinarily with a common governing body to supervise and direct the process.

PSAs are based on three main elements:

A Recovery of costs: by allocating a given percentage of production. This percentage varies from contract to contract, but is typically between 20 percent and 40 percent. The amount of oil production allocated to recover the investors' costs is called "cost recovery oil".

B Sharing the production: production will be split to recover the costs and the capital of the foreign investor. The remaining oil, called "profit oil" is split between investor(s) and the host country in the agreed proportion. This represents the profit to the parties from the project.

C Taxes: the host country can collect income tax from the foreign investor according to its national regulations. Income tax is only payable once production has begun.[5]

5.1.3 Structure

The contractual structure – while it has necessarily evolved to consider the circumstances of the venture concerned and to keep pace with the development of

3 Bill of Law (Projeto Lei) 5938-09 which followed the Law of Oil 9.478/97, would amend Brazil's law of hydrocarbons and establish a shared production model for exploration of pre-salt fields.

4 Marcia Ashong, 'Cost Recovery in Production Sharing Contract: Opportunity for Striking It Rich or Just Another Risk Not Worth Bearing?' *Centre of Energy Petroleum and Mineral Law Policy* 2.

5 Johnston, above n 1.

relationships between host countries and IOCs – has nevertheless retained its basic features. These features are[6]:

a The IOC is appointed by the host country as contractor for a certain area.
b The IOC operates at sole risk and expenses under the control of the host country.
c The oil field belongs to the host country and the production belongs to the operating company and will be split between the two according to the contract.
d The IOC is entitled to recovery of its costs out of the production from the contractual area. The State repays exploration and development costs only when production starts (cost recovery oil); that is, it forfeits an agreed percentage of its entitlement until the value of the cost oil has repaid the foreign investor.
e After cost recovery, the balance of production is shared on a pre-determined percentage split between the host country and the IOC.
f The IOC's income is liable to taxation. Income tax is only payable once production has begun.
g Some terms of the contract may oblige the operating company to provide technical and training requirements to the host state and to market the host state's produced oil portion.
h Equipment and installations are the property of the host country, either at the outset or progressively in accordance with their amortisation schedule.[7]

5.1.4 Main terms and features

Production sharing agreements are distinguished from other types of contracts in two ways. First, the IOC carries the entire exploration risk. If oil is not discovered the company receives no compensation. Second, the government owns both the resource and the installations. In its most basic form, a PSA has four main properties. The foreign partner pays a royalty on gross production to the government.[8]

After the royalty is deducted, the IOC is entitled to a pre-specified share (e.g. 40 percent) of production for cost recovery. The remainder of the production, namely, the profit oil, is then shared between the government and IOC at a stipulated share (e.g. 65 percent for the government and 35 percent for the IOC).[9]

6 Keith W. Blinn et al (eds), *International Petroleum Exploration & Exploitation Agreements: Legal, Economic, and Policy Aspects* (Barrows Company Inc, 2nd ed, 2009) 69.
7 Kristen Bindemann, *Production-Sharing Agreements an Economic Analysis* (Oxford Institute for Energy Studies, 1999) 12.
8 Ibid. 14.
9 Ingilab Ahmadov et al, 'How to Scrutinize a Production Sharing Agreement' (2012) *International Institute for Environment and Development (IIED)* 26.

The contractor then must pay income tax on its share of profit oil. Over time, PSAs have changed substantially and today they take many different forms.

To understand the PSA contract, it is crucial to understand the following terms and features.

5.1.4.1 Ownership

Ownership of petroleum is one of the most noticeable characteristics of the PSCs and can be interpreted as a change in the legal nature of oil and gas arrangements. It is regarded as the necessary corollary of its claim to sovereignty over its natural resources.

Ownership may be divided into three parts:

a Ownership over oil reservoir
b Ownership over produced oil
c Ownership over installation

Due to agreement types, it is based on the consent of the parties. Therefore, it is common for the parties to have different ideas about the aspects of the contractual framework. Hence, there are different conceptualisations of ownership in relation to the PSA. On the one hand, there is a belief that in the PSC the producing countries transfer only the exclusive right to conduct exploration and production activities of subsoil minerals. However, the hydrocarbons produced remain the property of the host country (or the national oil company) that hires the IOC to exploit the hydrocarbons.[10]

Another common characteristic of the PSC is that at the end of the contract, all infrastructures shall be transferred to the host country without extra charge. In this context, a case study from Angola can be useful to illustrate the common arrangements in a PSC. That is, at the end of the contract all equipment, instruments, materials and any other property acquired for the operations during the PSC, as well as all information of an economic and technical nature, should be passed on to the nation (Sonangol), without any payment or reimbursement.[11]

There is obviously a belief that the explored reserves belong to the host country and the operating company only has exclusive rights to produce the oil in each period. However, the produced oil and all constructions and installations belong to the operating company.[12] Therefore, it should be noted that in PSCs the ownership of any petroleum discovered belongs to the state or its national oil company and the contractor acquires title to its share of petroleum when oil

10 Irina Paliashvili, 'The Concept of Production Sharing' (Paper Presented at the Seminar on the Legislation on Production Sharing Agreements, The Russian-Ukrainian Legal Group, 14 September 1998).

11 República de Angola, 'Lei das Actividades Petrolíferas' [No. 10/2004, de 12 de novembro de 2004].

12 Ashong, above n 4, 6.

reaches the export point or mutually agreed delivery point. Title to production in the agreed share that will pass to the oil company at a defined point. However, the government may seek to retain or obtain title to other assets and equipment.

5.1.4.2 Rights and obligations of contractor

The status of the contractor under a PSA is characterised by a set of rights and obligations which are included in all PSAs.

A Contractor's rights

The contractor shall conduct petroleum operations within the contract area in accordance with the Petroleum Law, and the contractor shall have the following rights:

- a Subject to requisite approvals, to construct pipelines, bridges, roads, storage facilities, houses, landing fields, radio towers and communication facilities.
- b To use in petroleum operations any petroleum produced within the contract area.
- c To store and transport petroleum from the contract area to the point or points of sales and exports.
- d To use or sell the contractor's share of production sharing oil.
- e To repatriate or retain abroad and freely dispose of all proceeds, from such sales or other dispositions.
- f To sell, assign, transfer, convey or otherwise dispose of all or part of its rights and interests under this contract to any third party with the prior written consent of the government representative.
- g Some PSCs contain a general grant of rights to the contractor and specifically reserve certain rights for the host government with respect to the area of the contractor's operations. An example of such a grant is contained in one of Qatar's PSAs executed in 1997.[13]

B Contractor's obligations

The contractor's main obligations under a typical PSC entail two core activities: the exploration and production of the reserves within the contract area, both of which must be done at the contractor's own risk and

13 2.1.1 Subject to the terms and conditions set forth in this Agreement, the *GOVERNMENT* hereby grants to the *CONTRACTOR* the following: The above rights include all functions necessary for the proper and reasonable exercise of all Petroleum Operations.

- i The exclusive right, excepting those rights reserved by the GOVERNMENT in Article 2.2, to explore for, appraise, develop and produce crude oil and non-associated gas from the contract formation in the contract area
- ii The right to store, transport and export for sale or otherwise deal with or dispose of, all crude oil and non-associated gas, subject to Article 17

2.1.2 The above rights include all functions necessary for the proper and reasonable exercise of all petroleum operations.

expense. In terms of exploration, the contractor is usually subject to a contractually agreed work programme whereby the contractor must perform certain exploration activities such as shooting seismic and drilling of exploratory wells. In terms of production, oil discovery the contractor must appraise its commercial potential and prepare a development plan, usually subject to approval by the host government. Likewise, the contractor is obliged to conduct production operations according to the terms of the PSC.

After commercial production commences, the contractor shall fulfil its obligations towards supply of the domestic market in the host country.[14] A contractor is also required to give preference to such goods and services which are produced in the host country or rendered by host country nationals, provided such goods and services are offered at equally advantageous conditions regarding quality, price, and availability at the time and in the quantities required.[15]

5.1.4.3 Government participation

Most PSAs give the national oil company an option to participate in the venture.[16] This, however, does not imply that the national oil company shares in the costs and risks involved in the exploration period. They generally have a carried interest which means the IOC bears the costs and the risk during exploration and carries the national oil company through. If the field is declared commercial the national oil company can (but does not have to) take up its option of working interest.

Participation rates vary from 5 percent (some Indonesian PSAs) to up to and over 50 percent (Algeria 1991, China, some Indonesian PSAs). However, 15 percent (Malaysia, Vietnam) and 25 percent (Angola, some Malaysian PSAs) appear to be rather common clauses. Apart from the extent of their involvement, some issues to arise once the national oil company decides to participate in the project are the point of entry, the kind of participation, the sharing of costs and the way in which the stake is financed. The national oil company's financial contribution will usually come out of production.[17]

From the IOCs perspective, any participation by the host country tends to be unattractive as the partner can interfere with the day-to-day management of the operation. Conflicting views may lead to a less efficient running of the project.

14 Bindemann, above n 7, 16.
15 Blinn et al, above n 6, 71.
16 PSAs without participation can be found (e.g. in Egypt, Oman, Qatar, Yemen, the Philippines, Nigeria and Turkmenistan).
17 Bindemann, above n 7, 24.

5.1.4.4 Government revenue

Perhaps the most noteworthy aspect of the PSA is the division of production between the foreign company and the host government (or its state company).

A Profit oil

Three related issues inevitably arise when working out this division: (1) whether any provisions exist for recovery of the foreign company's costs, (2) whether any provisions are made for accelerated recovery of costs or interest on the costs and (3) how such costs will be reimbursed. All three bear upon the extent to which the host country will share in the costs of exploring and developing the area subject to the contract. The early Guatemalan contract stood at one extreme of the spectrum. It contained no express cost recovery provision whatsoever. Instead, the oil company simply received a stated share of production which was graduated from 45 percent for production under 15,000 barrels a day to 25 percent for production of more than 100,000 barrels a day.[18]

More commonly, the PSA provides that the operator will receive a specified fraction of production (generally ranging from 30 percent to 50 percent) from which it reimburses itself for its capital expenditures and operating costs. There may be an amortisation period for capital costs such as drilling. For example, less than one variant of the Indonesian agreement, a maximum of 20 percent of capital costs may be taken from cost oil in a year. Depending upon the country, financing costs may or may not be included in the concept of reimbursable expenses. From the operator's standpoint, express provisions to determine overhead costs are also necessary. These can be stated as a flat percentage of actual operating costs, as is done in the PSA between the Nigerian National Petroleum Company and Ashland Petroleum Company which calculates overhead as 2 percent of actual operating costs.[19]

Once all authorised expenses have been deducted up to the maximum percent of cost oil set out in the agreement, the remaining profit oil or 'production split' is divided between the host country and the operator in accordance to a specified formula. There are several systems for production splitting: (1) either a sole profit oil split as in Indonesia (85 percent to the host country and 15 percent to the IOC, considering the income tax) or (2) a progressive split based on the following:

i Daily production according to a given scale 60 percent/40 percent up to 20,000 b/d, 65 percent/35 percent from 20,000 to 40,000 b/d, 70 percent/30 percent from 40,000 to 60,000b/d etc.
ii Accumulative production.

18 Paliashvili, above n 10, 63.
19 Yinka Omorogbe, 'The Legal Framework for the Production for the Petroleum in Nigeria' (1987) 5(4) *Journal for Energy & Natural Resource Law* 273–279.

iii The profitability of operations. It is also to be noted that distinctions are sometimes made between onshore and offshore productions, or production of oil as opposed to production of natural gas.

B Sliding scale

Alternatively, the split may be based on a sliding scale analogous to the royalty discussed earlier (Chapter 3). One can find many variations of sliding scale rates, but the two most common methods for calculating payments using sliding scales are based on either average daily production or R-factors.[20]

An example of a volume-based sliding scale is one of the Indonesian contracts. This stipulates for profit oil that Pertamina receives at least 61.5385 percent of production and the IOC share will not drop below 19.2308 percent (Table 5.1).

The R-factor is the ratio of revenue to expenses. This means that the cumulative contract revenues earned by the IOC from cost recovery and profit oil are divided by the cumulative expenses incurred during a specified period. An example of this is one of the Azeri PSAs (Table 5.2).

The design of the scale is usually based on the expected size of the discovery.

Table 5.1 Profit oil in Indonesia

Average daily production (bbl)	*Pertamina (%)*	*IOC (%)*
0–50,000	61.5385	38.4615
50,001–150,000	71.1538	28.8462
^150,001	80.7692	19.2308[a]

a Kristen Bindemann, *Production-Sharing Agreements an Economic Analysis* (Oxford Institute for Energy Studies, 1999) 18.

Table 5.2 Profit oil in Azerbaijan

R-Factor	*SOCAR (%)*	*IOC (%)*
R ^ 1.50	50	50
1.50 – R ^ 2.00	60	40
2.00 – R ^ 2.25	62.5	37.5
2.25 – R ^ 2.50	65	35
2.50 – R ^ 2.75	70	30
2.75 – R ^ 3.00	75	25
3.00 – R ^ 3.25	80	20
3.25 – R ^ 3.50	85	15
R ^ 3.50	90	10[a]

a Kristen Bindemann, *Production-Sharing Agreements an Economic Analysis* (Oxford Institute for Energy Studies, 1999) 18.

20 Bindemann, above n 7, 18.

Regardless of whether the contract is volume or R-factor based, caution needs to be applied when setting the rates. If they are too high, the scale loses most of its flexibility.[21]

Depending on the expected size of the deposit and its special characteristics, a threshold of say 50,000 b/d can be unprofitable. By the same token, if we have a 100 mb field which produces 20 percent of reserves in the peak year of production (20 mb), the average daily production is 55,000 b/d.

Thus, a sliding-scale tranche of say 100,000 b/d would be rather useless. Generally speaking, sliding scales add flexibility to a contract. The government return increases as the project profitability increases. In this system, the former is a function of the latter; whereas, under a fixed system (e.g. the government always receives 60 percent of available profit oil) profitability is a function of government take.

C Payment of taxes

Under a PSA, IOCs are usually subject to the payment of taxes on the income from operations (i.e. on the profits related to their share of production). However, the PSAs originally negotiated did not provide for the payment of income tax and the host countries' share of production was regarded as its total take. Over the years, that situation has changed and IOCs are liable to pay 45 percent tax on their income arising from operations and a withholding tax of 20 percent on the dividends paid to them.[22]

For all practical purposes, whether the tax is included in the host countries' share of profit oil or paid by the IOC – in other words, whether or not the production split is made on a pre-tax basis – is not of significant importance. The adopted mechanism really depends on its political and administrative convenience for the host country, as well as on the host country's need for a payment in kind (i.e. oil) instead of a cash payment.

Under some PSAs, the host country is to pay taxes on behalf of the IOC. To that end, an extra share of production is allocated to the IOC for that specific purpose. It is then physically taken by the host country. Such was the case under the first Peruvian PSAs in the 1970s, as well as in Gabon, Egypt, Oman and Trinidad-Tobago. The wording in the agreement for the latter country is as follows:

> The contractor shall receive, in consideration for the obligation assumed under this contract, the following shares of petroleum production from the contract area:
>
> a A share of production at the focalisation point;
>
> b A share of production equivalent to (the taxes) related to petroleum operations hereunder which the contractor must pay to the government … this share will be delivered by contractor to the Minister.[23]

21 Hooman Farnejad, 'How Competitive is the Iranian Buy-Back Contracts in Comparison to Contractual Production Sharing Fiscal Systems?' (2009) 7(1) *Oil, Gas and law Intelligence* 7.

22 Ibid. 9.

23 Blinn et al, above n 6, 77.

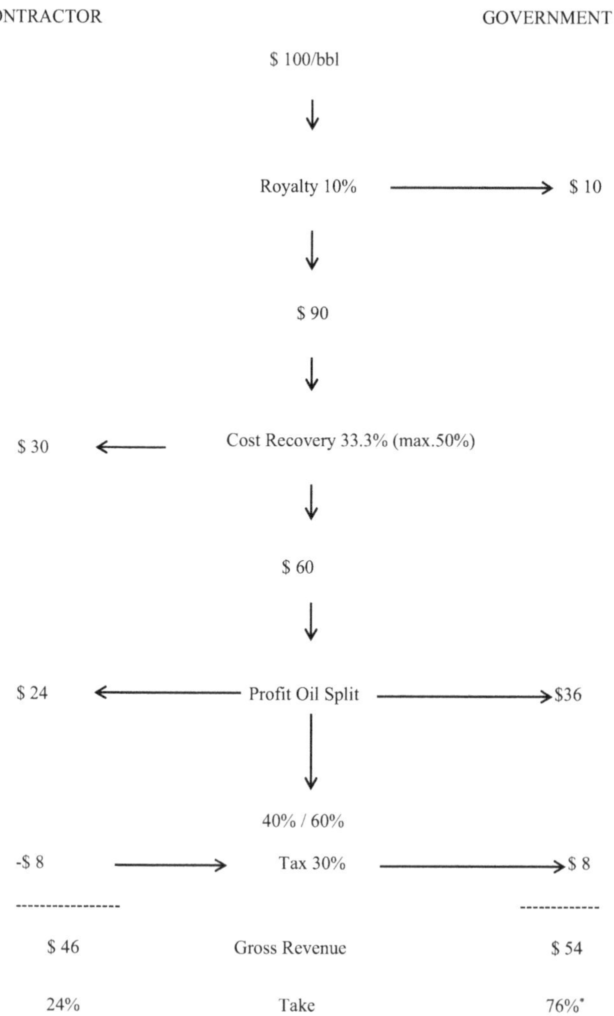

Figure 5.1 PSA flow chart.

* Kristen Bindemann, '*Production-Sharing Agreements an Economic Analysis*' (Oxford Institute for Energy Studies 1999) 15.

To further clarify the PSA contractual framework, Figure 5.1 illustrates the average cash flow and the return each party receives over the lifetime.

5.2 Joint venture (JV)

Any association of two or more entities, private or public companies, or a combination of private and public may be identified as a JV. For illustration purposes, a JV can be considered to comprise a contractor and a national oil company. The JV was built on the same concept as the PSA and was a reaction to extensive domination of oil companies in the industry. However, in addition to share in production, states gained access to management of petroleum operations.

The JV is a way of balancing state and company interests by jointly bearing the rights and obligations in the petroleum operations. The basic benefit to the state is that it receives ownership in production.[24] This can be obtained either with equity (equity JV with 50/50 share) or proportionally to its interest agreed between the parties to the agreement or in a concession.

The concept of JV is not a legally defined term and attempts to clarify the definition have been made by courts and scholars. It is typically described as a form of partnership with mutual objectives: expectation of profit and limitation of risks.[25]

5.2.1 Legal nature

In the petroleum JV, the state is both an authority regulating petroleum operations and a participant through the joint committee, an entity created as a forum for cooperation between the state and foreign contractor. In the JV, both the state and the company take control, monitor and participate in operations through the Joint Management Committee. This committee usually includes representatives of all parties involved and oversees key decision-making on operations through voting. In practice, management rests in the hand of international companies as they have the technical and technological capabilities.[26]

Both parties are represented in the committee, which has a board of directors and chief executive appointed by the foreign company. It is also possible in non-incorporated agreements to establish a separate non profit making company in charge of managing operations or to entrust management to the national oil company.[27] The non-profit-making organisational structure however has no financial flexibility.[28]

24 *World Petroleum Arrangements* (The Barrow Company, INC, New York, 1985) 574.

25 Talal Al-Emadi, 'Joint Venture Contracts (JVCs) Among Current Negotiated Petroleum Contracts: A Literature Overview of JVCs Development, Concept and Elements' (2012) *Georgetown Journal of International Law Online* (8 November 2012) <http://www.gjil.org/2012/10/articles-joint-venture-contracts-jvcs.html>.

26 Kamal Hossain, *Law and Policy in Petroleum Development. Changing Relations between Transnationals and Governments* (Nichols Publishing Company, New York, 1979) 122.

27 *World Petroleum Arrangements*, above n 24, 577.

28 Kamal Hossain, above n 26, 128.

5.2.2 *Main terms*

According to law, in a JV the host country participates as a commercial partner with the IOC, or as part of a consortium. In this form of oil and gas contract, the host country contributes a percentage share of capital investment, and receives a portion of oil produced equal to its investment. The remarkable terms of the use of the JV structure is that it enables the sharing of risk. Not being as a partnership is the main effective reason why JV structure enables for the sharing of risk. In JV the joint venturers will agree to contribute a specified percentage of the costs and liabilities of the venture and take the same percentage of any petroleum produced, rather than a share of net profits.[29] They will agree to own the property of the JV in this same percentage. This structure will enable a company to invest in a number of JV in conjunction with other companies, which will allow it to spread its capital over different projects, thereby increasing its chances of a successful discovery, but keeping its liabilities within controlled parameters.

General partnerships are rarely used in upstream sector of petroleum because of joint liability of partners. It meant that the participants are severally liable for the obligations of the venture in their participating interest shares. A JV is different from a partnership, where each partner will be liable for all the debts of the partnership. It is very important consideration in drafting the JV contract to ensure that a partnership is not created.

For more understanding about this type of contract, the following main terms of JV are explained.

5.2.2.1 *Ownership*

The ownership rules differ according to the type of JV. Two typical forms are the incorporated and non-incorporated model, from which the non-incorporated model is considered as more beneficial for the state.[30] The non-incorporated model is not based on the undivided direct interest principle. This means neither that state nor the oil company jointly participate in production and management. The produced petroleum is not jointly owned either. Each party directly participates in production and is entitled to its share in production, and the petroleum produced remains at their disposal pursuant to provisions in the contract or concession.

The incorporated model is considered as less beneficial to the state due to lack of flexibility. In this model, a separate management company – an independent legal entity – is created on a non-profit-making basis. The oil produced is sold by a joint company and the revenues are then split according to shares. Subsequently, the participants obtain their benefits in dividends set beforehand in the contract or concession.

29 *United Dominions Corporation Ltd v Brian Pty Ltd* (1985) 157 CLR 1 at 14.
30 Irina Paliashvili, above n 10.

In other words, a non-incorporated joint venture is also different from an incorporated joint venture, although most, if not all, of the participants in an non-incorporated JV will be companies (it is common for the ownership of an interest in a joint venture to be structured using project specific subsidiary; often a petroleum company will have one wholly-owned subsidiary that holds the JV interest and above it an intermediate holding company. If the subsidiary holding the JV interest has no other assets, this can assist in isolating the risk of the JV).

In holding the project assets and its attendant liabilities, an incorporated JV will usually utilise a company. A company is a separate legal entity and the participants will hold shares in that entity instead of a direct interest in the assets. The company will be a separate entity also from a tax and accounting perspective. Profits which are earned from the project will be allocated to the participant shareholders as dividends by the company.

5.2.2.2 Government participation

Joint Ventures entitle the state to share in production and to participate in operations. It is possible to include a provision allowing for an increase in the state's share in case of change in production up to the limit of maximum participation in exchange for compensation either in cash or in kind. Usually, participation in production varies according to level of production, but is however limited to a certain percentage agreed by the contractors.

5.2.2.3 Costs and risk bearing

The case of cost-sharing and cost reimbursement is a one of the key issues in a JV. Of importance is the exploration phase where the risk is high – at this stage, little information on the commerciality of the discovery is known. Moreover, at this stage a state may participate in costs of exploration on an equal basis, proportionally, or as non-reimbursable. More often, the so-called carried-interest system is applied which is more beneficial to a host state as it transfers the exploration risks to the oil company.

In the JV, the state's financial input is dependent on whether production commences; that is, whether the discovery is considered commercial. A state 'is carried through exploration',[31] but only through the exploration phase. As soon as a discovery is made, its commerciality is evaluated and a decision on production is made. At this point the state begins to participate in costs. It is important to establish clear criteria for defining the commerciality of the discovery to avoid a deadlock. Duration of the carried interest phase is relevant to the state's future share in the JV or production. The longer a company bears the costs of operations, the lower the state's share becomes. In this context, it is practical for a state to consider bearing costs in the development phase where the risk is lower.

31 *World Petroleum Arrangements*, above n 24, 546.

It may also be advantageous to share the costs to obtain better participation in the production phase.[32]

Before the production phase begins, a decision on commerciality must be taken. It is in the state's interest to clearly determine the criteria for evaluation to avoid a situation when a deposit remains passive. Clear criteria are necessary for the state, not only to ensure development of deposits, but also to highlight the point from which it will participate in costs. Participation in costs requires substantial resources which may not be available, especially in developing states. Hence, the outside financing system is usually applied. If no commercial discovery is made, it is generally the company's loss and the state is not required to compensate. However, a company is reimbursed from the profits if the discovery is considered commercial.

The question of commerciality may be a source of dispute between participants. As was previously mentioned, the criteria for evaluating a discovery should be clearly set down and agreed to by the parties. A state may also introduce provisions that allow it to develop the field, even if the company is unwilling to do so, and to maintain efficiency of petroleum development. The sole risk clause provides the possibility for the state to produce oil at its own cost and risk.[33]

During the production phase, a state participates jointly with the foreign company in operating costs and, if the contract or concession so decides, the oil company is reimbursed the costs borne in the exploration phase. Obtaining benefits from produced oil is resolved differently in different forms of JVs. A state may secure its interests by adding provisions that enable or require a company to buy or sell its share of production.

Regimes for liability differ, depending on the type of JV. In the non-incorporated type, both the state and the company are jointly and severally liable for obligations, with their liability unlimited. The advantage of unlimited liability is larger influence and control over operations, as opposed to limited partnerships.[34]

It should be mentioned that the parties to the JV will usually be defined as the participants.

The Joint Operation Agreement (JOA) has usually a provision which provides the interests of the participants. The interest of the participants is usually described as 'participating interests' with a definition which says that a participating interest is the participant's share, expressed as a percentage in the rights, interests, liabilities and obligations of the participants. It includes an undivided share of joint venture property. This will be supported by an operative provision stating that the joint venture property is owned by the participant in proportion to their participating interests. A participating interest composed of both

32 United Nations Centre on Transnational Corporations, *Alternative Arrangements for Petroleum Development. A Guide for Government Policy-Makers and Negotiators* (New York, 1982) 51.

33 Kamal Hossain, above n 26, 126.

34 Al-Emadi, above n 25.

proprietary and contractual rights.[35] The contractual rights are the rights of the participant under the JOA itself, which can be characterised as a chose in action, and any contracts which constitute joint venture property, such as construction and maintenance contracts.[36] The proprietary rights are the interest of the participant as tenant in common in the JV property which is real, personal or other property. This is totally different from the interest of a partner in partnership assets.[37]

5.3 Service contract

As the title illustrates, in a service contract the mining-right holder (government or host country) buys the services of an IOC which functions in the legal status of a contractor. The service contract in international petroleum oil contracts came into use for the first time in the 1960s. The move towards service contracts is reminiscent of the transition from concessionary systems to the PSA commencing in the 1960s.

The new interest in service contracts may be explained partially by heightened sovereignty concerns on one hand (opposition against IOCs' control over the world oil price and issues over natural resources the main driving factors behind the adoption of PSA in the 1960s); and, on the other hand, the need for IOC capital[38] and know-how in developing oil and natural gas fields[39] in the host countries.

The service contract is a regime under which the host state at all points retains full ownership of all hydrocarbons produced on its soil. In turn, the IOC performs the exploration and production work as a service to the state. The adoption of service contracts in countries reflects elements of nationalism, including those in which the constitution prohibits foreign control or ownership of natural resources. These countries usually have substantial capital at their disposal, but

35 W Manning, 'Assignment Clauses in Mining and Petroleum Joint Venture' (1986) *AMPLA Yearbook* 119 at 120.

36 Tina Hunter and John Chandler, *Petroleum Law in Australia* (Lexis Nexis, 2013) 265.

37 QC Merralls, 'Mining and Petroleum joint venture in Australia: Some Basic Legal Concepts' (1988) 62 *ALJ* 907.

38 The degree of need for IOC capital varies in each country and for different projects inside a country. In some cases, a country's bad credit rating may leave it with no other option than to fund the projects through the IOCs' capital and to reimburse them later. This may be the case in production sharing as well. In addition, the IOCs might have access to cheaper capital compared to what is available for the host governments. In other words, it might be cheaper for countries to borrow from IOCs than to finance their development projects through other sources. In the case of Iraq, due to the fast cost recovery mechanism embedded in the technical service contracts, it may look as though the country did not need the IOCs' capital. However, the total cost of development of all awarded fields in the first two rounds may suggest that financing through government annual budget was difficult or even impossible.

39 This is particularly the case for mature fields that require enhanced oil recoveries or fields in more challenging locations.

seek the technical expertise of IOCs to carry out the exploration and production activities.

In the late 1980s and early 1990s, service type contractual frameworks started to appear in the political economy of several major oil or natural gas producing countries. Venezuela, Kuwait, and Iran signed their first service contracts in 1991, 1992 and 1995, respectively. More recently, Iraq, Mexico, Bolivia, Ecuador and Turkmenistan signed new service contracts, or have shown increasing interest in adopting variations of service type contracts rather than PSCs to explore and develop their oil and natural gas field.

Essentially, in proceeding from concession to production sharing to participation, the discussion has shifted from arrangements permitting the most foreign involvement to the least; or alternatively, from the least host country participation in developing its resources to the most.

The final form of arrangement in this analysis involves a service agreement between the country and a company. In fact, under a service arrangement, the company agrees to a fee or a share of production to provide the country and its state oil company with services and information to help the country develop its own resources.

Three contract arrangements have been developed to take advantage of the multinationals technological and managerial expertise and capital resources while allowing the host country to maintain the appearance that its state oil company has control and ownership:

1 The pure service contract
2 The technical assistance agreement
3 The risk service contract[40]

The 'pure' service contract, as its title indicates, is to distinguish it from the other service contracts which implies the notion of risk-taking by the IOC. In the pure service contract, all exploration and production risks and rewards are retained by the state. The IOC is contracted to perform certain services (e.g. consulting, engineering, construction, operational, managerial, service and so on) as defined by the service contract in return for a flat fee. The IOC is a mere contractor, working under the supervision of the state, and has no legal or beneficial interest in the enterprise itself. Service contracts within this category include management contracts (e.g. contracts for management service, start-up and operational assistance and so on) and turnkey contracts (under which the contractor will be responsible for the construction and commissioning of a whole facility). Occasionally, the IOC may be given the right to buy back a proportion of hydrocarbon production from the government under a separate sales arrangement.

40 Willem J H van Groenendaal and Mohammad Mazraati, 'A Critical Review of Iran's Buyback Contracts' (2006) 34 *Energy Policy Journal*.

The service agreement, or 'technical assistance' agreement, is in some ways a more sophisticated version of the service contract. In these agreements, the contractor agrees to provide technical assistance in the exploration, development, production and, in some cases, refinement of oil. The contractor services may include the provision of equipment and training employees to operate the petroleum facilities. In return, the country agrees to reimburse the company for the expenses incurred plus a fee based on production. For example, Venezuela entered into technical assistance agreements as part of its plan for nationalising its oil industry. Under these agreements, several of the multinational oil companies agreed to help operate the facilities they had constructed in return for a per-barrel-produced fee.[41]

The 'risk' service contract is the same as the pure service contract, but rather than pay a flat fee, payment is based on the level of initial investment. Under the risk service agreement, the oil company agrees to explore a specific area and evaluate its potential for discoveries. If the existence of petroleum reserves is suspected, the company is obligated to develop the reservoir. Throughout this period, the company invests only its own money with no expectation of payment unless it results in commercial production.

Thus, the company bears the entire financial risk without receiving any rights in the explored territory. When commercial production commences, the company has the right to be paid for its services with cash, or the right to take oil at a discounted price. Although the risk service agreement contains features like a production-sharing arrangement, it gives the oil company fewer rights in the acreage that is explored.

5.3.1 Legal nature

The above agreements are service contracts whereby a host country (or its judicial delegate as national oil company) hires the services of an IOC which assumes the legal status of a 'contractor'. In case of commercial production out of the contractual area, the IOC is reimbursed for its costs and investments and paid for its services. Although this is a service contract, the financial risk is borne by the contractor. This explains why the emphasis is placed on that risk feature in its classification. The legal consequences attached to this type of agreement are that the IOC is granted no mining or mineral rights and that the production belongs in its entirety to the host country or its national oil company. Also, all assets and equipment are the property of the host country.[42]

41 Peter Fischer and Thomas Waelde, *A Collection of International Concessions and Related Instruments* (London Oceana, 3rd ed, 1982) 288–290.

42 M Me, 'The Iranian Buyback Model and Its Efficiency in the International Petroleum Market – A Legal View' (2009) 7(1) *Oil, Gas and Law Intelligence* 2.

5.4 Iranian Buy-Back Contract

Since 1979 in Iran, granting ownership and control over oil and gas reservoirs and total hydrocarbon extraction to foreign companies has been prohibited by the Constitution. As such, all exploration and extraction of hydrocarbons is implemented by the NIOC on behalf of the Ministry of Petroleum. However, indirect foreign participation is allowed.

According to Iranian Buy-Back Contract (IBBC), the IOC as investor accepts all costs for exploration, development and production operations on behalf of the NIOC, coinciding with an agreed scope of work. The IOC, in return, will receive remuneration for advances on these invested funds, capital cost, operation costs, related bank charges with interest and the negotiated Rate of Return (ROR) through the NIOC's allocation of production. The remuneration is paid from the sale of petroleum up to a maximum of 60 percent of production under a Long-Term Export Oil Sale Agreement (LTEOSA). The sale agreement continues until the IOC has fully offset its petroleum costs and has earned the agreed remuneration.[43]

5.4.1 Definition

The buy back as a type of counter-trade transaction was defined in 1990 by the Council of Ministers.[44] However, this definition may not be precisely applied in the Iranian upstream oil and gas industry. In the Iranian buy-back contract, the contractor funds all investments and receives remuneration from the NIOC in the form of an allocated production share. The contractor then transfers operation of the field to the NIOC after the contract has been completed.[45]

The IBBC is a short-term service contract, between the NIOC and an IOC, under which the latter undertakes to provide funding and to carry out development operations in respect of a gas/oil field. In return, the NIOC agrees to reimburse the IOC, either through direct sale of the resulting oil/gas to the

43 A Brexendorf et al, 'The Iranian Buy-Back Approach' (2009) 7(1) *Oil, Gas & Energy Intelligence* 22.

44 Articles 1 and 3 state: the counter trade is a contract concluded between two legal or natural persons under which one party (supplier) is committed to supply material, equipment, machinery, parts and service enabling other the party (exporter). An exporter is an Iranian natural or legal person who assumes obligation under the contract to export or make available for the supplier to export agreed goods produced from the same facilities or the productions of the same industrial group in certain quantity and within a defined period personally or by an intermediator in exchange of receiving equipment, tools, machinery or service from the other party to the contract. To accomplish its undertakings in exchange of other party's (exporter) commitment to produce and deliver certain goods for export outside the country during an agreed period.

45 Seyed Nasrollah Ebrahimi and Abdolhossein Shiroui, 'The Contractual Form of Iran's Buy-back Contracts in Comparison with Production Sharing and Service Contract' (2003) 2 *SPE International Society of Petroleum Engineers* 2.

IOC, or by payment of proceeds generated by selling the IOC's portion of oil/gas to third parties.[46]

5.4.2 Why and how Iran acceded to buy-back

The answers to the questions of why and how Iran acceded to buy-back contracts have significant importance because they reveal Iran's oil and gas upstream industry aims, achievements and limitations.

The buy-back contract could be result of Iran's economic needs, the need to optimise the petroleum industry, or the result of the legal frameworks. Therefore, the buy-back could be the best oil and gas contractual form according to Iran's requirements and legal circumstances. The following section examines the Iranian buy-back contract based on Iran's domestic requirements and legal frameworks.

5.4.2.1 Iran's requirements

After the Islamic revolution in Iran in 1979, the ruinous eight-year Iraq-Iran war and the frequent political and economic crises at that time resulted in disruption to the oil supplies and crippled production and transportation of oil. As matter of fact, lack of oil extraction in Iran during the 1990s meant the nation was unable to reach the levels achieved in the 1970s. This is because the country's oil wells were getting old and new wells were required if it was to achieve production capacity. To increase oil production, Iran had to seek out new oil fields and wells, but to do this new capital and technology was required. In addition, there was a lack of adequate domestic investment in the upstream oil and gas fields.[47]

5.4.2.2 Iran's regulations

Although the buy-back contract (service contract) had been used in Iran since the 1979 revolution, it first emerged a few years before this. The Petroleum Law enacted in 1974 imposed considerable limitations on any foreign oil company's participation in upstream oil and gas operations. Article 3 of the Petroleum Act states that "all oil and gas resources, as well as the oil industry itself should be nationalised; and that any activities related to exploration, development, production and distribution of oil and gas were to be carried out solely by NIOC, either directly or through its appointed contractors and agents".[48]

According to the provisions of this law, the engagement of IOCs in exploration, development and production was restricted to cases where the foreign

46 Ibid. 3.

47 Hedayati Kakhki, Mohammed Mehdi, *A Critical Analysis of Iranian Buy-Back Transactions in the Context of International Petroleum Contractual Systems* (PhD Thesis, The University of Durham, 2008).

48 Brexendorf et al, above n 43, 2–3.

companies acted on behalf of the NIOC as its contractors. The conclusion of any agreement, such as concessions, production sharing or JV contracts in which the IOCs were not engaged as contractors under NIOC was prohibited. Instead, a kind of risk service contract was developed within the mandate of the legislation, and several such contracts were concluded.[49]

The nationalisation of many sections of the economy after the Islamic revolution in Iran in 1979 saw the new Constitution impose significant restrictions on participation in economic activities by the private sector in general, and particularly by foreign investors. It forbid foreign investors the right to establish a company (Article 81), foreign experts were restricted from employment (Article 82), and foreign persons were prohibited from acquiring control over natural resources (Article 153).

To avoid domestic damage by foreign person during the Iraq-Iran war (1980–1988), the Petroleum Act 1987 was enacted by parliament. Article 6 of this Act states; any investment will be carried out using the operational segments' budget and based on proposals by the Ministry of Oil. These investments will be included in the county's budget bill after the general assembly's approval. Foreign investment in these operations is not allowed under any circumstances. In turn, Article 6 is of utmost importance to fully understand the prohibition of direct investment in upstream oil and gas industry; whereas Article(5) of the Act permits the Ministry of Petroleum and affiliated companies (e.g. the NIOC) to enter into contracts with local and foreign individuals or companies to carry out oil and gas projects.[50]

A further step was taken by the Iranian parliament in 1987 when it authorised the NIOC to take out short- and medium-term loans to finance limited oil and gas projects. Limit amounts of oil were allocated for a period of three years to service a loan. Through this law a sort of buy-back process emerged in Iran. The parliament authorised the NIOC to enter into agreements up to US$3.2 billion with competent foreign companies for the development of the gas fields.[51] This was on the condition that all costs would be recovered by output from these fields. In addition, IOC as NIOC contractors were required to provide funding for, and to carry out, oil projects. When a project came on stream, the IOC's entitlement was paid from the output of the project and the risk of any shortfall in the production was taken by NIOC. The Iranian Central Bank guaranteed repayment of costs.[52]

In 1993, the Budget Act authorised the NIOC to enter into oil contracts with IOCs up to the value of US$2.6 billion. The following conditions were applied: instalments shall be paid exclusively from exports of resultant outputs of the project, and therefore no guarantee shall be provided in terms of any shortfall in production; utilisation of Iran's existing potential in design, engineering,

49 Abdolhossein Shiravi and Seyed Nasrollah Ebrahimi, Exploration and Development of Iran's Oilfields through Buyback (2006) 30(3) Natural Sources Forum, 199.

50 Ibid. 199–201.

51 Ibid. 199–201.

52 Ibid. 201–202.

construction and installation shall be maximised; transfer of technology shall be accomplished through JV agreements between local and foreign companies and a minimum of 30 percent of Iranian content shall be achieved.[53]

Gradually, the Iranian buy back scheme took shape and the Budget Act in 1994 played a major role. Not only was the term 'buy back' first mentioned in this Budget Act, but by virtue this Act the IOCs were permitted to invest in certain oil and gas projects under buy-back schemes. Therefore, Article(6) of the Petroleum Act of 1987, which prohibits any foreign investment in oil and gas projects, was amended by implication. The authorisation to conclude buy-backs was restated in the second, third, fourth and fifth 'five-year economic, social and cultural development plans' of 1995–1999, 2000–2004, 2005–2009 and 2010–2015, respectively.[54] A significant upheaval in the Iranian buy-back scheme took place with the Budget Act of 2002–2003, which expanded the buy-back contract from development only to exploration and development of Iran's oil and gas field.

5.4.3 Buy-back generations

There have been four generations of buy-back contracts that together showcase the government's attempts to make foreign investment more attractive. An evaluation of the Iranian buy-back contracts by generation sequence is presented below:

5.4.3.1 First generation

The first-generation IBBC was a simple buy-back agreement between the NIOC and a foreign company. In this generation, the exploration phase and development phase were separate. That is, if during the exploration phase a contractor found a commercial oil field, it would not necessarily become the developer of the field since this contract would be rewarded separately. It emerged gradually because of low-level interest among international companies as they could not be certain to recover operational costs and capital investments during the exploration. Also, according this type of contract, the IOC was entitled to a fix price for services provided. Each party's responsibilities and shares from the produced oil during the production phase were also ambiguous during this first-generation contract.

5.4.3.2 Second generation

The second-generation contract, like the first-generation contract, also covered all phases from exploration to production in different contracts that were not necessarily given to the same contractor. Moreover, if the contractor could

53 Ibid. 201–202.

54 The economic, social and cultural development plans were approved by the Iranian parliament, *inter alia* to advance the market orientation of the economy and to improve the living standards of the population.

successfully finish the exploration phase, they could directly, and without a new contract, go to the development phase, but at a fixed and predetermined price. This may have also resulted in problems because the cost of operations is volatile and could therefore negatively impact the contractor's investments.

5.4.3.3 Third generation

The third-generation of IBBC was significantly different to its previous generations. In this generation of contract, a single contract comprised both exploration and development phases. Furthermore, open public tender determined the manner and cap on the price of the contract. Transferring the technology according to a predetermined plan was also included in this generation of contract. This generation, like its predecessors, also had major ambiguities, however. It lacked clarity in defining each party's responsibilities and shares in the production phase. It also generated tension between the contractor and the NIOC or its affiliate as to the way the tender was executed and the way the costs were calculated.

5.4.3.4 Fourth generation (Iranian Petroleum Contract IPC)

The new and fourth-generation buy-back contract in Iran is the Iran Petroleum Contract (IPC). The IPC may appear to be similar in many aspects to its previous three generations, but it combines with IBBC with the PSC. In fact, the IPC is similar to the buy-back in that the contractor's entitlements are paid only from the defined master's revenue. The IPC is similar to the PSC in that the contractor receives the benefits of the production. Therefore, the IPC has been categorised as a service contract, though some terms are shared with the PSC. The strategic objective of the IPC is to encourage IOCs to deploy the latest technological advancement in reservoir management, optimisation and production. Therefore, transfer of the latest technology and building local capacity are the aims of the IPC.[55]

5.4.4 Main terms of IPC

Regarding the importance of the IPC to the future of Iran's oil and gas industry, the key terms to consider are as follows:

A Remuneration fee

The IOC is entitled to fees defined and formulated proportionate to the magnitude of the risk taken while participating in the exploration, development and operation. The remuneration fee is anticipated to be a fee per barrel of oil or per standard cube feet of gas produced. This will vary depending on the applicable 'R factor' (based on the ratio of cash receipts to petroleum costs) and production rates.

55 Tavana Energy, 'Iran Petroleum Contract' (21 July 2016) Tehran University <http://tavana-energy.com/iran-petroleum-contract/>.

According to IPC, the remuneration fee will be implemented as a true volumetric fee structure extended over the life of the agreement. Based on the IPC, the life of the agreement is from 20 to 25 years in the case of successful discoveries leading to production. There is also the possibility of tail extensions of up to five years where enhanced oil recovery techniques can be implemented.

B Cost recovery

There are some limitations on the recovery of certain costs incurred during the development and production phases. The cost recovery year commences from the first year of production. In the IPC, any Direct Capital Cost (DCC) and Indirect Cost (IDC) incurred prior to first year of production are to be amortised within five to seven years of the commencement of first production. After first production, the DCC incurred is amortised within five to seven years from the date of expenditure. The DCC does not cover Cost of Money (COM) in the development phase and after the first production date. The COM is calculated and applied in the event of delay of the payment of petroleum cost to the unpaid amount.[56]

After achieving first production, other costs including the IDC and Opex is recovered by the contractor at cost without the COM based on submission of the quarterly invoices confirmed by the NIOC. In the other words, the IDC incurred after first production and operating expenses is recovered on the current basis. If the IOC is unable to recover its costs within the contract terms, the terms are extended to allow for additional cost recovery subject to NIOC approval.

C Joint venture

Regarding Iran's objective to facilitate the transfer of technology and know-how, particularly which required for modern EOR techniques, the IOC is mandated to join with either the NIOC or a pre-selected company(s) by Iranian government in form of a JV.[57] In the IPC, the IOC must make a commitment to an Iranian local designated entity – selected by the government – which has a specified stake-hold in the JV formed to develop the field. In addition, the contractor in an IPC is operator during the exploration phase. However, a 'joint operating company' is established to operate defined fields during the development and production phases. Nevertheless, the management terms of the JV Company are complex and vary by phase of exploration and development as follows:

56 Hamed Sahebonar, Ali Taheri Fard and Fazel M Farimani, 'Economic Analysis of New Iranian Petroleum Contract (IPC): The Case Study of the Caspian Sea Fields' <http://www.iaee.org/baku2016/submissions/ExtendedAbs/Sahebhonar.pdf>.

57 Joanna Addison, 'The New Iranian Petroleum Contract (IPC)' (February 2016) Herbert Smith Freehills <file://ad.uws.edu.au/dfshare/HomesPTA$/90923458/Downloads/%D0%AD%D0%B4%D0%B4%D0%B8%D1%81%D0%BE%D0%BD_%D0%B0%D0%BD%D0%B3%D0%BB%20(1).pdf>.

1 Exploration phase

The Joint Exploration Committee (JEC) comprising an equal number of members from both the IOC and NIOC has control over several operational issues. All decisions about this phase should be taken unanimously, though the important decisions will ultimately be taken by the NIOC such as composition of final reports and statements, any sort of changes in project targets, and the determination of commerciality.[58]

2 Development and production phases

During the development and production phases, a 'contractor' JV company implements operation and all major decisions are assigned to a Joint Steering Committee (JSC). The JSC comprises equal representation of the IOC and NIOC, with annual chairmanship alternating between the two parties. The NIOC and the JSC have combined approval/oversight over the Annual Work Plan and Budget (AWPB).

3 Operation

The operation phase is implemented by the JOC which is owned by the IOC and NIOC. The important issue in this stage is Iran as a third party. In fact, Iran as a third party does not exact shareholding in principle, but is decided on a case by case basis.

D Periods of time

According to the IPC, the 'phase' times are anticipated as follows:

1 Exploration

Based on the IPC, the period of exploration is four years. It may be extended for two years more.

2 Appraisal

After exploration, which is four years (with two-year potential extension), the appraisal phase is a further two years.

3 Development and production

The development and production phase in the IPC is 20 years plus a potential five-year extension for IOR/EOR operations.[59] The main purpose of the longer periods of time is to be an incentive to foreign investors to make long-term investments and to implement measures to maximise the life of the reservoir.

E Settlement of dispute

The IPC includes an escalation dispute resolution clause which provides for arbitration as the final resolution method. This is used to settle within a limited period any contention arising out of, or in connection to, the

58 Mahdi Haddadi, 'The Nature of Iranian Petroleum Contracts in Upstream Section' (2015) 44 *International Letters of Social and Humanistic Sciences* 53.

59 Shervin Darvish, 'Legal Aspects of Iran's New Oil Contracts' (18 July 2016) *Natural Gas Europe* <http://www.naturalgasworld.com/legal-aspects-of-irans-new-oil-contracts-30651>.

contract; or related to a breach, revocation or termination of the contract. Thus, any dispute, claim or controversy related to the contract or arising out of it shall be finally settled by arbitration set out in the annex of the IPC. In an IPC, all risk and expenses incurred when a master or a commercial reservoir is not discovered, when the contractual aims are not met, or when there is insufficient reserve for setting financial debts, should be borne by the contractor.[60]

5.4.5 Critical analysis of IPC

It should be noted that there has been a long series of controversies about the IPC structure. Although the IPC was approved by the parliament and its key terms were released,[61] up to present, some terms and structures of the IPC remain unclear and uncertain. For instance, in terms of ownership, it is not clear in what circumstances foreign investor can book reserves; in relation to remuneration fee, the extent to which the mechanism based on the average annual export oil price from Iran works in practice, or whether to link it to a local reference like Iran's Asian standard pricing formula or an international reference such as plats; in regards to the JV, as it is uncertain as the point during development that a local party can elect to participate, and also the nature of its contribution; in terms of management, as the disaggregation of the IOC funding obligations from the ownership and voting mechanism particularly given the IOC's obligations to fund all exploration and production, together with NIOC's/local designated party's percentage share of carry through such phases; and more detail is also required regarding the criteria used to determine commerciality.

Nonetheless, the IPC is still confidential[62] such as the signed contract between Iran and a consortium including France's Total (50.1 percent interest), China's CNPC (30 percent interest) and Iran's Petro Pars (19.9 percent interest) in granting the phase 11 of the gas field in South Pars.[63] Although the IPC released the contract almost two years ago, there has been much conflict and struggle between the IPC designer and parliament, and its details have not yet been cleared.[64]

60 Ibid.

61 The IPC key terms were released at the Tehran Summit, a two-day conference held in Tehran on 28 and 29 November 2015.

62 On July 2016, Iran's supreme leader said: "These contracts (IPC) will not be signed unless the necessary reforms are implemented in the framework of national interest. Bozorgmehr Sharafodin, 'Iran's Supreme Leader Says Reform in New Oil Contracts Are Necessary' (3 July 2016) Reuters <http://www.reuters.com/article/us-iran-oil-contract-idUSKCN0ZJ067>."

63 The NIOC and Total signed a contract for the development and production of phase 11 of South Pars (SP11), the world's largest gas field, on 3 July 2017.

64 Behrooz Akhlaghi, 'Iran Petroleum Contract (IPC)' (Bi-Weekly News & Analysis of the International Law Office No. 1, Behrooz Akhlaghi & Associate, 2015).

5.4.6 Features of buy-back

The IBBC is type of service contract allowing the IOC to explore and develop oil and gas resources as a contractor, with financial reimbursement from sales revenue.

Once production has commenced, the investment is handed over to the NIOC or its affiliate who manages the operations. Annual capital expenditures are stipulated by the contract and the IOC is entitled to full reimbursement including cost recovery, remuneration and ROR, if the NIOC approves all cost and expenditures according to the contract.

For better understanding, Ebrahimi[65] asserts the key features of the IBBC can be categorised as follows:

5.4.6.1 Objective

A Preserve government sovereignty

The objective underpinning the government's use of IBBC is to preserve its sovereignty right over oil and gas resources and to maintain government control over oil and gas operation. This is affirmed in the Constitution, and in the 1974 Act and 1987 Act. Thereafter, the IOC was authorised to carry out petroleum activities on behalf of the NIOC. This means the IOC acts as a contractor of the NIOC, rather than owner or partner in the project.

B Attract foreign investment

One of the Iranian government's ongoing concerns is how to attract foreign investment in the oil and gas industry. Utilising IBBC supports access to foreign funds, particularly for costly projects.

C Access to advanced technology

Lack of modern technology and the Iraq-Iran war reinforced the need for an efficient means of transferring modern and advanced technology to Iran's exploration, development and production industries, as well as to help increase domestic capabilities.

5.4.6.2 Executive procedure

Any contract valued above US$1 million must be passed through a tender according to the 2002–2003 Budget Act. Approval from the High Economic Council is required to use foreign funds.[66] The NIOC as a state company should require the contractor to grant product operations, works and services to Iranians. Iranian content should be up of 50 percent of the value of the contract, technically.

65 Ebrahimi and Shiroui, above n 45, 2.

66 *Law of the Five-Year Economic, Social and Cultural Development Plan* (Iran) art 85 (year 2000–2005).

5.4.6.3 Contents

- Fiscal regime

  Financing in IBBC can be divided to five categories:

  1. Capital Cost (capex): the capital needed to fund all the direct expenses incurred during the development phase, payable by the investor. This term encompasses the following expenses: engineering; purchase and installation of major equipment; service-provider fees; instrumentation and secondary facilities, buildings and structures. The buyer in a buy-back contract is not responsible for any of the above expenses.
  2. Non-Capital Costs (non-capex): includes indirect costs accrued while operating the development which are not covered by the capital costs category. For instance, training and education to employees, paying taxes, and customs duties.[67]
  3. Cost Recovery: according to an Iranian buy-back contract, the foreign party is charged with developmental operations as well as costs for exploration. In exchange, the party will be reimbursed for expenditures (both funding and undertaken during operations) from the output of production. The party in charge of operations is ordinarily compensated in the form of petroleum output and bears the risk of both exploration failure and market fluctuations.
  4. Operating Costs (opex): the equipment required to conduct oil operations, including pipes, drilling machinery, storage equipment, drilling platforms and any other standard expenses related to the process of producing oil. This also includes the cost of maintaining the labour force, conducting repairs and supporting the related infrastructure.
  5. Bank charges: refer to financing and investment costs calculated according to the London Interbank Offered Rate (LIBOR), plus a premium of 0.5 percent–1 percent. Still, this percentage is rather low given the risk involved in oil and gas projects.

- Reimbursement

  If the NIOC approves all costs and expenditures according to the contract, the IOC is then entitled to full reimbursement. This typically covers the following areas.

  1. According to IBBC, during the amortisation period (usually five to eight years), the contractor receives his costs plus interest at LIBOR, plus an agreed uplift. In addition, the contractor receives a monthly remuneration fee.[68]

67 Faranak Rabiei, *Contracts Law* (translated by author, Behnami, 2002) 71 [trans of: *Hoghoogh-e-Gharardadha* (1381)].

68 Michael A G Bunter, 'The Iranian Buy Back Agreement' (2009) 3(1) *Oil, Gas & Energy Law Intelligence (OGEL)* 5.

2 All financial expenditures such as opex, capex, non-capex and bank charges will be paid by the contractor after commencement of production and during the amortisation period.
3 In exploration contracts, the IOC is entitled to develop the field according to an agreed plan by the NIOC if a commercial field has been discovered. Otherwise, if agreement is not achieved the contractor may withdraw and his costs are repayable by the NIOC plus uplift.
4 In addition to costs, a fixed amount in the buy-back contract is agreed to be paid to the IOC as reward for its investment and risks taken. This reward, commonly referred to as the remuneration fee, is paid if the objectives of the contract as defined in the MDP[69] are duly achieved by the IOC and the project is successfully handed over to NIOC.
5 All costs should be reimbursed through a LTEOSA according to the market price. This clause guarantees IOC access to the crude oil during the contract period.
6 The IOC is entitled to purchase a percentage of oil produced from the field at a discount (i.e. 5 percent less than the market price) as reward for risks taken. If no commercial field is found, the contract is terminated and expenses are borne solely by the IOC.
7 The risk of change of crude oil price to cover instalments has borne by NIOC.

- Dispute settlement

The buy-back contract in Iran provides an opportunity for the use of international arbitration to settle satisfactorily within a limited period any contention arising out of or in connection to the contract. Thus, any dispute, claim or controversy related to the contract or arising out of it shall be finally settled by arbitration set out in the annex of the contract.[70]

5.4.7 Result and analysis criticism

Regardless of the political and diplomatic ramifications, Iran's oil and gas industry has always been complicated, particularly regarding oil and gas contractual terms. In this section, Iranian buy-back contracts are analysed in relation to their legal structures, performance in practice, and IOC feedback. The critical analysis considers here the deficiencies of the contract from the contractor's point of view and from the perspective of the Iranian government.

69 Master Develop Plan (MDP) defines in detail the scope of work and activities to be carried out and a comprehensive plan for development of the field. Capital expenditures are calculated as well. The MDP is an essential part of Iranian buy-back contract, which is a mandate for development operations.

70 Ebrahimi and Shiroui, above n 45.

5.4.7.1 Deficiencies from the contractor's perspective

The Iranian buy-back model has many shortcomings from the perspective of the contractor. It is considered as risky by the contractor in terms of the performance guarantees associated with production rates, development costs, and project schedule. These risks are not compensated for in the same manner as other contract regimes. The most significant and important shortcomings of the Iranian buy-back contracts are as follows:

A Short contract life

The most important deficiency of IBBC is its short life; generally 5 to 10 years, with an additional five years as a designated 'investment recovery period'. The host-country's desire to ensure limited obligation has two adverse effects. First, in short duration contracts there are no incentives for the contractor to introduce measures to maximise the life of the field, even when the contractor damages the reservoirs to achieve cost recovery by abnormal maximisation of the rate of production. Second, the contractor often feels discouraged from using the latest technology and to transfer technology to the host country.[71]

B Financial structure

The assets acquired by the contractor remain the property of the NIOC, subject to per- determined purchases of oil and remuneration until the contractor's control is repealed.

C Higher level of risk

The contractor bears risks such as higher capital expenditure requirements than originally estimated and agreed upon, or its distribution over the construction period. In this case, the contractor is forced to pay the difference. Even factors beyond the contractor's control such as an unforeseeable drop in oil price[72] can result in serious financial pressures as the contractor is obliged to make up for the costs and agreed return by using a limited amount of oil.

D Inaccurate prediction of expenses

Another issue which negatively affects IBBC is related to insufficient data or costs. Due to the nature of contract, which requires all expenditures and potential returns from the field to be accurately documented in the MDP and then in contract, with that estimate eventually used for compensation.

Regardless of what goes into calculating the compensation, the extent of the oil reserves, the time required for production and production expenses particularly are much more difficult to accurately predict before the start of operations. As such, the deficiencies in seismic or wells offset data may lead to inaccurate calculations which in some case prove to be significantly different to the correct numbers.

71 Bunter, above n 68, 7.

72 Such as the most recent nadir, reached in January 1999, after increased oil production from Iraq coincident with the Asian financial crisis, thereafter curtailing demand.

E Bank interests repay

The NIOC offered an uplift of costs at the LIBOR rate,[73] plus a negotiated percentage. According to Iran's legal system, however, the domestic courts have jurisdiction over disputes and certain vital commercial transactions such as interest charges through LIBOR are banned. As previously mentioned, the issue is that LIBOR is a specifically interest-based yardstick, but according to Islamic law an Iran's legal system on which it is based, charging interest (usury) is forbidden.

F Inflexible terms and sensitive to negotiation

Flexibility in the contract terms had always been a component of a good contract, provided the contract's form and structure is maintained. Also, parties can guarantee the durability of the contract via a negotiation clause or even via renegotiation. Of course, the degree of flexibility in terms of responding to changes in circumstance is up to the parties to anticipate and how they wish to negotiate protection against such changes. But in IBBC, the terms are inflexible and do not provide a mechanism for renegotiation.[74]

G Quantity bureaucracy

Technically, most companies working with the NIOC express concerns about the excessive bureaucracy in the administration of the projects. Some decisions must be made in a speedy manner and this is inherently inconsistent with the bureaucratic and slow NIOC executive process. No doubt this matter will be resolved in a matter of time when the NIOC becomes convinced that a co-operative relationship with the contractor is in everyone's interest.[75]

H Oil price risk

One of the issues the contractor commonly complains about is that the repayment of capital expenditures, bank charges, and remuneration will be postponed if the international price of oil or gas is below the agreed upon level. Under IBBC, the contractor should bear this substantial risk.

I Fixed rate of return (ROR)

Perhaps one of the most notable deficiencies of IBBC is the fixed ROR. If the oil price returns to its previously low level, it will encourage inefficiencies and may even cause problems because the amount of oil available from the project might be insufficient to meet the costs of the project and the agreed return. In addition, oil price risks are borne to a large extent by the government, as opposed to other contract regimes in which the contractor has relatively more risks. As a result, any incentives for the contractor to improve total return from the project – which is also the government's desire – such as discovery of additional reserves, employing enhanced oil

73 London Interbank Offered Rate, a daily interest reference rate.

74 Maximillian Kuhn and Mohammadjavad Jannatifar, 'Foreign Direct Investment Mechanisms and Review of Iran's Buy-Back Contracts: How Far Has Iran Gone and How Far May It Go?' (2012) 5(3) *Journal of World Energy Law & Business* 15.

75 Ibid. 16.

recovery techniques, and introducing cost saving measures are not provided in a fixed ROR.[76]

J Transfer of capital and technology skills

The fact that IBBC target is proposed over the short duration is another major deficiency. The contractor will ask if it is worth using state of art technology only to see it taken over by the Iranian party when the development phase ends. Of course, it is not worth it, and it is simply not enough time for the NIOC to gain as much new technology from the foreign partner as it should. Moreover, during the decline phase of the project, when the application of new technology could have its greatest impact, the foreign partner is no longer around to help.[77]

K Transfer of management skills

The IBBC can also hinder long-term field development. This is because the NIOC's or its representative's knowledge is insufficient for optimal long-term reservoir development, or that the oil and gas reservoirs require new investments during production due to changing reservoir behaviour.

So, although there is no doubt that there is immense expertise in the Iranian oil and gas sector, the contractor's expertise and funding is required. However, without detailed knowledge of the reservoir behaviour over time, a contractor is unable to optimise the extraction over the lifetime of the reservoir. Because of this, most IOCs favour of other contract types such as the PSA or NCC.

L Long process of accountancy and calculation

Every international and national contract regime needs to accountant for and calculate the oil and gas contracts regime specifically if it is to share the revenue and divide the gain. However, the accounting and audit of some oil and gas contract is easy; whereas, for others it is a long and complicated process. The Iranian buy-back contract expansion of the audit and scrutiny levels in areas such as sub-contracting is designed to decrease costs, but has not worked to the advantage of the contract. In addition, the auditing and accountancy processes are often controversial and result in disputes.

5.4.7.2 Deficiencies from the Iranian perspective

From Iranian perspective, buy-back contract has deficiencies too.[78] In fact, an evolved version of oil and gas contract will emerge in future Iranian oil and gas industry contracts which address IBBC shortcomings.

76 The profit or ROR on the IOC's investment varies from project to project, normally between 15 percent and 20 percent.

77 Mohammad Reza Moghaddam, 'Analysis of Buy-Back Contracts and Adduction Optimization Model of Contract for Iran' (Farsi) (2008) 76 *Economy Research Journal* 161.

78 Iranian perspective refers to persons known as domestic critics.

The deficiencies from the Iranian perspective include:

A No financial incentive for improvement reservoir performance

An insufficiency of the current buy-back contract lack of incentives for the contractor to improve efficiencies. A point on which both domestic and contractor critics agree is the short duration of the contract to maximise effective exploitation of Iran's natural reserves. The contractor (e.g. IOC) is compelled to recover costs through the sale of oil at the peak stretch of the field's performance, rather than to ensure a longer period of high performance and product sales during this 'plateau' period. Vitally, there are no incentives to ensure high performance prior to turning production over to the NIOC after the contract.

B Problems with comparing competing project bids and inaccurate project demands

The process of determining the optimal arrangement for oil exploitation and exploration is vital for maximising profits for the NIOC. However, the bidding process is itself mired with problems; namely, that bids not conforming to the stated requirements and therefore not easily comparable. For instance, the recent bidding for the three Bangestan fields by BP, Shell, Total, FinaElf and Eni resulted in varied multi-phased bids with 15 to 20 years work duration rather than the requested five-year buy-back contract format.[79]

This example is indicative of a secondary problem of bidding; namely, the unrealistic requirements of the NIOC which the companies believe are not economically worthwhile or practically possible. Due to the lack of bid standardisation, extensive negotiations between Petroleum Engineering and Development Company (PEDC), a NIOC subsidiary charged with oil buy-back contract negotiation, and each participant is instead required. Therefore, economic efficiency and speed in the bidding approach is lost.

C Possibility of mortgage for the future

This is rather a serious objection to the whole Iranian buy-back principle because the foreign contractor is rewarded in cash rather than crude oil. The cash is raised by the NIOC from the sale of the crude oil produced by contractor. If the crude oil price falls, the NIOC is presented with a substantial liability.[80]

D Inflexible concept

As from the contractor's perspective, the inflexibility of IBBC terms is a criticism help by Iran. Although there is nothing to be gained by making the contract terms rigid, there is nonetheless no way to amend the contract in the event of changing circumstances.[81]

79 Moghaddam, above n 77, 161.
80 Moghaddam, above n 77, 162.
81 Brexendorf et al, above n 43, 28.

E Unforeseen proceedings

Another IBBC shortcoming is the unpredictability of core elements such as costs, reservoir performance, regional events, sudden changes in capital markets, etc. This causes contractors to be always under extreme pressure.

F Lack of appropriate time for Capex

The IBBC is also problematic in that it is signed with oil firms looking to invest in Iran. This means that a contractor pays the exploration and development project operation costs up-front; to be recovered from the sale of the commercial's petroleum output over a minimum five to ten-year period. Hence, the contractor is in a position whereby he never gains any equity rights in under the contract.[82]

G Lack of appropriate profit with inherent output

Under IBBC, the contractor does not profit from uplift in production. It is logical that an incentive for investors to optimise production would be to receive extra profit or award for boosting output beyond a certain target. In Iranian buy-back contracts the contractor receives no extra profit even if production is beyond the agreed level.[83]

In addition, another shortcoming such included:

- Fixed ROR;
- Only limited transfer of capital and technology;
- Risk of non-compliance with maximum efficient rate and doing damage to reservoirs; and
- Little to no motivation to cut down on expenses.

Thus, the main question is, after consideration of all these factors, is the buy-back contract efficient enough to attract foreign investment and protect Iran's national interests at the same time? In other words, Iran as a member of OPEC would like to keep its quota within OPEC to remain a key and effective player on the international oil market. This is a significant issue on the agenda of Ministry of Petroleum and Iran's energy horizon. The aspiration is to have production capacity of seven million barrel per day by the year 2020. Iran also urgently needs investment funding, up to $170 -200 billion in its oil and gas industry, particularly in the upstream sector, for the next 10 to 15 years. Hence, Iran will need all the finance and help it can get because without sufficient capital input it will not be able to invest in the improvement of its domestic energy sector.[84]

82 Moghaddam, above n 77, 162.
83 Brexendorf et al., above n 43, 31.
84 Me, above n 42, 22.

5.5 Criteria for evaluating and comparison between oil and gas contractual framework

To compare the regimes, it is important take into consideration not only the fiscal aspects of a system, but also how effective it addresses the different phases of the operation. Other aspects such as how important the oil is to the economy of the country should also be taken into consideration. Basically, the following criteria can be applied to the five main contracts (CCC, NCC, PSA, JV and service contract) along with IBBC based on current standards: objective, ownership, management, cost and risk bearing and government revenue.

5.5.1 Objective

In terms of objective structure, in a CCC the government is interested in discovery, exploration and developing their petroleum deposits. In an NCC, the host country is initially interested in discovery, exploration and developing their petroleum deposits. As such, it enters into a contractual relationship with an IOC with enough capabilities and experience to perform oil and gas operations, as well as the transfer of their technology to host country.

Underlying the PSA is that the state acquires its share in production and the objective of the JV system is that petroleum is jointly shared by state or its national company and the IOC. Lastly, the service contract provides services, 'know how', technology and funds, and IBBC is same as a service contract.

5.5.2 Ownership

In matters of ownership structure, the operating company has full ownership over production resources in the CCC. In the NCC, oil resources are owned by the government, but the petroleum is owned by the concessionaire at well-head subject to government approval.

It is only the ownership over certain parts of production that is transferred to the company according to terms in a PSA. In a JV contract, the operating company has ownership over production reserves to the level it has invested.[85] In the service contract and Iranian buy-back contract, ownership belongs to the host country, although in some cases remuneration to the company is to be paid by share in production.

5.5.3 Management

In matters of operation and management structure, in the CCC the concession holding company has control over exploration, exploitation, development, refining and marketing operations; whereas, in the NCC, the national oil company

85 Paliashvili, above n 10.

or some authorised company on behalf of the government is a partner via participation in the petroleum operation.

In JV and production sharing contracts, a common committee represented by both parties has control over the operation and determines the extent of investment and production.[86] However, in a PSC, the host state has the upper hand in the committee in comparison with the JV contract. In a service contract, as well as the Iranian buy-back contract, operations, at least theoretically, are under absolute control of the host state.

5.5.4 Cost and risk

In matters of risk-taking rate, the CCC structure means host countries grant rights to foreign companies for the exploration, exploitation, production and development of the fields for a fixed or flexible time (depending on the concession). The IOC bears all risk and costs associated with the operations. That is, the operational risks during the exploration and exploitation phases are fully upon the concession holding company, as is the case in an NCC.

In a PSA, the contractor undertakes to provide the funding for, and to carry out exploration, exploitation and production activities bearing commercial risks involved either because of not finding a commercial discovery or not achieving a commercial production after performing development operations. In a JV agreement, every phase has different conditions, and during the exploration phase, for instance, the risk is high because little is known about the commerciality of the discovery. At this stage a state may also incur equal costs for exploration, proportionally or non-reimbursable. More often, the so-called carried-interest system is applied which is more beneficial to the host state as it transfers the exploration risks to the oil company.

In the JV agreement, financial input is dependent on whether production commences; that is, whether the discovery is considered as commercial. A state "is carried through exploration",[87] but only through this phase. As soon as a discovery is made, its commerciality is evaluated and a decision is made on production, the state begins to contribute to costs.

The service contract is divided into two forms: pure service contract, and risk service contract. This distinction entails legal consequences for the company regarding risk bearing and compensation of costs. Under the pure service contract, all risks are borne by the state and all the costs are reimbursed to the company, regardless of commerciality of discovery. In terms of risks, the service contract is like the standard PSA – the company takes all the exploration risks and may be compensated only if production starts (discovery is economically profitable). However, in contrast with the PSA, under the service contract the foreign company is not entitled to share in production.

86 *World Petroleum Arrangements*, above n 24, 575.
87 *World Petroleum Arrangements*, above n 24, 570.

In a PSA and JV, the risks are shared between the IOC and the host state at the exploitation phase, but the risk is borne by the investor at exploration phase. Practically, the issue of exploration risk in service contracts is never addressed. Also, in the exploitation and development phases the risk is borne by the operating company.

In IBBC, a fixed fee is payed to the contractor to cover its risks. It is calculated proportionate to the capital costs, and only costs incurred and paid by IOC are recoverable.

5.5.5 *Government revenue*

In matters of government take, in a CCC the government only takes a fixed royalty from the oil produced. In an NCC, revenue to state is included as a signature bonus, annual bonus, annual benefit, royalty by cash or kind (calculated on the value of production based on a sliding scale), and income taxes.

In a PSA, the resultant output of the project is shared by the parties when extracted, and at the point specified in the agreement (agreed formula). In other words, the state extracts revenues as a profit share according to an agreed formula, and income taxes in the PSA.

In a JV, the state receives a return from its share in production. In other words, the state can obtain equity in a JV with 50/50 share or proportionally as agreed. In a service contract, the contractor is paid its fee in kind (oil and/or gas) or is given a preferential right to purchase the production from the host country. The contractor may thus be remunerated from the petroleum produced; with the payment either in cash or in kind.

Lastly, in IBBC, reimbursement or ROR and cost of recovery, exploration, appraisal and development will be recovered within the ceilings agreed to, from the proceeds of sales of oil and gas allocated to the IOC.

5.6 The NCC positive and negative points compared with other oil and gas contract form

This section examines the positive and negative aspects of the NCC in regard to other oil and gas contract forms. Therefore, the elements of the NCC are studied relative to other regimes based upon the criteria described in the previous section (i.e. objective, ownership, management, cost and risk taking and government revenue).

5.6.1 *Objective*

In terms of objective structure, the NCC seems to provide more benefits compared to other contract forms. One could consider the NCC as a wide umbrella that covers all oil and gas contract objectives from the CCC to the service contract. Also, this is an advantage of the NCC over other oil and gas contract forms like PSC, JV and service contract.

5.6.2 Ownership

In matters of ownership, although ownership over reservoirs is always a controversial issue in the CCC; in the NCC, the oil is owned by the concessionaire at well-head contingent on state approval.

5.6.3 Management

In matters of control and management, due to the awareness of host countries about the benefits of their natural resources, they maintain the right to control and manage the oil operations. This is expressed not only in the NCC, but also within service contracts and IBBC. Technically, however, because of the paucity of requisite skills and technology for oil and gas operations, they have not been able to achieve such a purpose.

5.6.4 Cost and risk take

In terms of cost and risk, the NCC is an acceptable and desirable form of oil and gas contract for host countries because the costs and risks are carried by the IOC. The oil-producing states, although eager to participate in investment, do not agree to take investment risks and loss of project implications.

Host countries are generally willing to remain out of such matters and allow the investing company or contractor to discharge their obligation as to investment costs. This is particularly in oil and gas fields where there is lack of exploration records and impassable places that have high cost associated with oil production. Therefore, the most positive points of the NCC is that the government's financial involvement is largely free of risk. Only the NCC has this advantage over other oil and gas contract forms (PSC, JV and service contract).

5.6.5 Government revenue

In matters of government revenue, of most importance in the structure of financial relations between the host country and IOC is the agreed rates and percentage payable to parties in the division of oil revenue. Revenue accruing to the host country under the NCC can compare favourably with other oil and gas contract forms when the oil and gas rent and revenue collecting system is diversified. One such system is the royalty payment which increases progressively or on a sliding scale as the value of production rises. The royalty system is also advantageous for the parties in that relying on the extracted product for the purpose of calculating host state royalty, there is no need for complicated accountancy and calculations of net income of the company. The added advantage for the investing company is that governmental bodies of the host state will have no reason to supervise the operation and audit the IOC's financial statements to determine the real income of the company.

5.7 Conclusion

This chapter reviewed the major forms of oil and gas contract in the world. This completes the review of all relevant current oil and gas contract regimes; including the PSA, JV agreement, service contract and Iranian buy-back contract (in this chapter), and the CCC and NCC (in the previous chapters) in terms of their structure, provisions and appropriateness to serve the national interests of oil-rich countries.

The comparisons made between current oil and gas contractual forms in the world indicate that, in practice, the dividing lines between different types of contracts are not as clearly defined as they seemed initially to be. In fact, no concluded agreement can be found to lie exactly within the framework of one of the above-mentioned contracts and reflect fully its characteristics. The stereotypes and formal definitions for oil contracts are not much evidenced. Therefore, in practice we see a mixture of ideal types in the contracts being concluded.

Despite this, consideration of the positive and negative points of the NCC in regard to other oil and gas contract forms shows that it has some advantages for developing the upstream oil and gas industry of some host countries like Iran. However, it remains necessary to consider which type of contract will most appropriately serve the national interests of the government of Iran within the Iranian legal system to support the flourishing of Iran's oil-based economy and to attract more foreign investment. These issues are considered in the next chapter.

6 Discussion of the challenges in proposal a new concession contract for Iran's oil and gas industry

6.1 Islamic (Sharia) law

This section is concern with a brief discussion of Islamic law as it may be relevant to the legal status of oil and gas contracts in Iran. It includes a brief description of Islamic Law, as well as explanation of the sources of rules in Islamic (Sharia) Law as a background to the arguments and opinions of Muslim scholars about assisted conception. It also outlines the conception of Islamic jurisprudence as a means to derive and apply rules of Islamic law. It followed by the Islamic denomination and *Shi'a* prospective on natural resources.

Undoubtedly, Islam is a worldwide system which comprises a complex social organisation; a doctrine of politics; economic order; manner of governing; cultural behaviours; military activities; modes of commerce and international, criminal, environmental law.

The term Sharia is defined generally as the path or way to follow to the watering-place,[1] the clear path to be followed by the believer in order to obtain guidance in this world and deliverance in the next.[2] Islamic Sharia (Islamic law) broadly refers to the whole legal system consisting of Islamic principles and jurisprudence, and including the primary and secondary sources as well as providing a methodology for applying the law.[3] Sharia specifically refers to the rules,[4] which are included in the *Quran* and prophetic Sunna.[5] The rules regulate and cover different aspects of life. Sharia law consists of injunctions and guiding principles established for humankind associated with this life and thereafter.[6] Rules of Islamic law can exist in specific or general texts; the general text could be interpreted and understood differently by Muslim scholars.

1 H Patrick Glenn, *Legal Traditions of the World* (Oxford University Press, 5th ed, 2014) 183.
2 Mohammad Kamali, *Shari'ah Law: An Introduction* (Oneworld, 2008) 14.
3 Irshad Abdal-Haqq, 'Islamic Law: An Overview of Its Origin and Element' in Hisham Ramadan (ed), *Understanding Islamic Law* (Altamira Press, 2006) 3.
4 There are two major categories of rules in Islamic Sharia; devotional matters *(Ibadat)* and civil transactions *(Mu'amalat)*. Kamali, above n 2, 17.
5 Mashood Baderin, *International Human Rights and Islamic Law* (Oxford University Press, 2003) 33.
6 Kamali, above n 2, 14. Also, Abdal-Haqq, above n 3, 4.

Regarding to objectives of Islamic Sharia, recognising and obtaining legitimate advantages are the principal purpose of Islamic Sharia. This objective reflects two main elements: promoting human welfare and preventing harm.[7] The advantages could be classified into three types: essentials, complementary and embellishments.[8] The priority of Sharia is to safeguard the first type, the essential interests, as this kind of interest touches the lives of all human beings and neglecting it might cause chaos in the community.[9] The purpose of the principles of Sharia is to protect the interests of humankind.[10]The essential interests which have priority in Islamic Sharia are represented in preserving human life, faith, intellect, property and legal parentage.[11]

Islamic Sharia includes religious matters, moral values and regulatory principles for humankind.[12] In terms of regulatory provisions of Islam, Islamic Sharia contains two categories of rules; the first category is those provisions which regulate specific matters, and second general principles that are able to be applied universally. Islamic law is considered one part of Islamic religion; it is linked to, and inseparable from, other unities of Islam such as doctrine, value and beliefs.[13]

According to the common view amongst Muslim scholars, principles of Sharia are meant to have the flexibility to adapt to changing circumstances[14] and to apply in different times and places.[15] Adaptability could be accomplished through re-interpretation of general principles of Sharia and new understanding of Islamic provisions according to time and place to enable it to deal with new issues and resolve them in accordance with contemporary changes and needs.

A variety of opinions about an issue is acceptable as long as they are not conflicting with the spirit and purpose of principles which are established in the primary sources of Sharia. Justice in Islamic Sharia is the principle that should be applied on all individuals without regard to religion, race or colour.[16]

Applying those provisions of Sharia which regulate some legal issues should be consistent with purpose of principles of Islam, specifically those aiming to obtain advantages and avoiding disadvantages, as well as achieving social justice. This may mean that provisions of Islam should not be considered or applied whenever they may conflict with this main purpose of Sharia. Changing circumstances and situation might require enacting modern provisions in order to regulate legal issues provided it is compatible with purpose and core of Islamic principles.

7 Baderin, above n 5, 40.
8 Kamali, above n 2, 33.
9 Ibid. 33.
10 Baderin, above n 5, 40.
11 Kamali, above n 2, 33.
12 Ibid. 18.
13 Ibid. 14.
14 Dariusch Atighetchi, *Islamic Bioethics: Problems and Perspectives* (Springer, 2007) 1.
15 Hashmat S Moinifar and Amir Ashraf Vaghefi, 'Gamete Donation and the Role of Religious Leaders in Iran' (2010) 8 *Journal of Women of the Middle East and the Islamic World* 247, 251.
16 Kamali, above n 2, 15.

Islamic Sharia is considered a powerful influence on all aspects of life, policies, practices and behaviours in the Muslim community.[17]

Islam's influence over Iranian society, particularly its legal frameworks and law is undeniable. Therefore, Islamic law governs the interactions between people, governance and many other things.

6.1.1 Sources of Islamic law

There are four main sources of Islamic law: the *Quran*, *Sunnah*, *Ijma'* (consensus) and *'agl* (reasoning). These four sources can be further subdivided into two categories: primary sources (the *Quran* and *Sunnah*) and secondary sources (*Ijma'* and *'agl*).

The primary sources have priority. In the absence of an applicable rule in the primary sources, secondary sources which are based on general principles of Sharia are relevant. The principal source of rules of the Islamic Sharia are considered sacred for Muslims and to be obeyed and followed.[18] The primary sources are recognised and admitted by all Islam schools and Muslim scholars and jurists. It includes the *Quran and Sunnah.*

The *Quran* was revealed to the prophet Muhammad and is considered to have the most influence over all Muslim affairs and the laws in Muslim countries. The *Quran* is the revelation of Allah to the Prophet Muhammad and its legal rules are to be followed in absolute terms. It comprises over 6,000 verses that broadly describe a variety of issues. It covers both the temporal and spiritual aspects of life and thereafter,[19] such as religious and devotional matters, moral guidelines, legal rules as well as matters of universe and historical stories.[20] With regard to the regulatory principles of the *Quran*, there could be detailed provisions on some issues such as marriage, inheritance commerce, and crimes. General principles represent to the then contemporary events and problem.[21]Roughly, 600 of the 6,000 verses in the *Quran* deal with specific legal matters and rules of law.[22] In addition, fundamental principles such as those related to freedom, equality, public interest and justice could be understood and interpreted by specialised scholars in order to adapt to new situation.[23] The *Quran* rules of law reign supreme in the establishment and construction of laws and nothing can contradict them.

The *Sunnah* is the second main source of Islamic law. The *Sunnah* refers to traditions of Prophet Mohammad encompasses his deeds and sayings, as well as his implicit approval on some issues, and the *Imamas*. They have been codified

17 Moinifar and Vaghefi, above n 15, 248.
18 Baderin, above n 5, 34.
19 Ibid. 35.
20 Kamali, above n 2, 19.
21 Ibid. 19.
22 Muhammad S. Karim, *Oil, Islamic and International Petroleum Industry Legal, Economic, Politic and Cultural Issues* (L.L.M. Dissertation, The University of Dundee, 2001).
23 Jamila Hussain, *Islam, Its Law and Society* (Federation Press, 2011) 36.

by people who were so close to them and are viewed by the *Ulema* (learned scholars) as a reliability source. It should be noted the *Sunnah* and *Hadith*[24] are sometimes referred interchangeably because they reflect the same content in a different context. Some *Sunna* is a divine source of Islamic Sharia and could have a significant role interpreting the *Quran*.[25] Not all narrations of Sunna are considered as part of Sharia but only those which have a legal nature.[26] Some *Sunna* explains and clarifies rules and principles which are mentioned in the *Quran*[27]; other *Sunna* contains rules and regulations pertaining to specific conditions which are not stated in the *Quran*.[28]

There are also secondary sources derived through examining rules and principles of the primary sources of Sharia and recognising the purpose and spirit of rules of Islamic law, by following human reasoning as well as considering the consequences of the examined matter. Secondary sources of Sharia basically can be utilised to cover new circumstances and solve issues which are not addressed in Quranic or prophetic Sunnah. (Whereby, the primary sources were revealed during the life of Prophet Mohammad, so rules of Sharia about new cases and events could be revealed through the secondary sources of Sharia.).[29] There is considerable disagreement between scholars and different schools of Islamic jurisprudence about the authority of the sources and extent and range of reliance on different secondary sources of Sharia.[30]

The *Ijma'* could be translated to 'consensus' or 'unanimity' and is the compilation of rules and laws agreed on by the *Ulema*. In addition, the Consensus *(Ijma')* might be considered a source in this context; the consensus refers to unanimous opinion by Muslim scholars on a particular issue.[31] The consensus of Muslim scholars about a specific issue usually is difficult to be established, where debate and discussion relying on individual reasoning might lead to various opinions.[32] Relying on individual reasoning is a secondary source. They are based on interpretations of the *Quran*, *Sunnah*, *Hadiths* and rulings of past scholars.[33]

24 The prophet's actions are recorded in the *Sunnah* and the teachings based on his saying and Imams saying are recorded in the *Hadiths*. Karim, above 22, 11.

25 Mawil Dien, *Islamic Law: From Historical Foundations to Contemporary Practice* (Edinburgh University Press, 2004) 39.

26 Hussain, above n 23, 36.

27 Ibid. 37.

28 In this context, Imam Al-Shafai (the founder of one of major schools of Islamic jurisprudence, will explain in Section 6.1.2) says 'the Sunna of the prophet is of three types: first is the Sunna which prescribes the like of what God has revealed in His Book; next in the Sunna which explains the general principles of the Quran and clarifies the will of God; and last is the Sunna where the messenger of God has ruled on matters on which nothing can be found in the Book of God.' Baderin, above n 5, 35.

29 Baderin, above n 5, 37.

30 Kamali, above n 2, 19.

31 Arif Khan, *Concept of Islamic Law* (Pentagon Press, 2007) 86.

32 Glenn, above n 379, 185.

33 Mike Bunter, 'Sovereignty over Minerals and Petroleum in the Islamic Law and the Question of Ownership' (2006) 4(1) *Oil, Gas & Energy Law Intelligence (OGEL)* 8.

The *'agl*, or reasoning by *'agl*, is defined as the "categorical judgments drawn from both pure and practical reason".[34] *agl'* is the process by which learned jurists draw analogies from the *Quran* and the *Sunnah.*[35] The principle dates back to a precedent set by the Prophet Muhammad's support for a judge in Yemen.[36] The judge announced that in case he could not find any evidence from the *Quran*, *Sunnah* and *Hadiths*, he would use his own judgement to draw principles.[37]

It is accepted that such principles and legal provisions of Sharia could be expanded and applied to other circumstances allowing scope for a new understanding in order to regulate specific and modern issues.

It could be deduced that, if the primary sources of Islamic law do not include any text about new life, the examination of secondary sources would allow the development of provisions of Islamic Sharia with new and modern understanding of it which is consistent with changes in the situation and needs of people.

It is important to note, however, that both *Ijma'* and *'agl* are considered as secondary sources of Islamic law. The *Quran* and *Sunnah* remain the indisputable sources of Islamic law and indeed have become the pillars of the post-revolution Iranian legal system.[38]

6.1.2 Islamic denominations

There are several sects in Islam, but the two major divisions are the *Shi'a* and the *Sunni* schools. They concur on the principle that either a member of the Prophet's family or a member of his tribe can exercise the divine sovereign will for the Muslim community. The *Shi'a* (which has one widespread school of *Ja'fari*)[39] contends that the divine sovereign will can be exercised in a just way only by an *Imam*at.[40] The *Sunnis* believe that membership in the larger circle of the Prophet's tribe was quite adequate for the requirements of political justice.[41] The doctrinal difference between *Sunnis* and *Shi'as* has led to the latter's acceptance of the legitimacy of the principle of the *Imamat* as the sole manner for establishing a just socio-political system.

34 Hossein ModarressiTabataba'i, *An Introduction to Shi'i Law* (Ithaca Press, 1984) 2–6. See also Noel J Coulson, *History of Islamic Law* (Edinburgh University Press, 1979).

35 Brian Rusell and others (eds), *An Introduction to Business Law in the Middle East* (London, Oyez Publishing) 3.

36 Sayed Hassan Amin, *Commercial, Arbitration in Islamic and Iranian Law* (Vahid Publication, 1988) 61.

37 Ibid. 61.

38 Nader Entessar, 'Criminal Law and the Legal System in Revolutionary Iran' (1988) 8 (1) *Third World Law Journal* 94–95.

39 The Ja'fari School is the school of jurisprudence of most *Shi'a* Muslims, derived from the name of Ja'far al-Sadiq, the 6th Shi'a Imam. This school of jurisprudence draws upon traditions from all legitimate successors of Prophet Muhammad, a total of twelve Imams. The Ja'fari School will be more explained in Islamic Jurisprudence and Its Major Schools (Section 6.1.3).

40 *Imamat* refers to persons who are member of the Prophet's family.

41 Majid Khadduri, *The Islamic Conceptions of Justice* (Johns Hopkins, 1984) 14–20.

That is, acceptance the Prophet's son in-law (Ali), as the first rightful successor to Prophet Muhammad as Shi'a Scholars believes, followed by Ali's male descendants in direct line, is for the *Shi'as* an indispensable part for establishing a just political order. However, according to the Twelver *Shi'ism*[42] (the dominate sect in Iran), the Twelfth imam went into occultation and will return as named *Mahdi* to once again establish justice on earth.[43]

In the absence of the Twelfth Imam, the *Ulema*, or religious scholars (*velayat-e fagih* in Iran), guide the *Shi'a* community on the righteous path. The *Ulema* are obligated to take authority and put an end to corruption and injustice. Ayatollah Khomeini established an Islamic government under the guardianship of *velayat-e fagih* (government of the just jurist) and institutes the Sharia as the only source of law in the Iran.

6.1.3 Islamic jurisprudence and its major schools

In this subsection, the Islamic jurisprudence and its major Schools of thought will be discussed.

It also provides brief information about the major schools of Islamic jurisprudence and methodology of each school used to derive rules of Sharia about matters which are not stated in Islamic Sharia.

The process which is utilised to derive rules and apply principles of Sharia in real or hypothetical situations is known as the jurisprudence.[44] Islamic jurisprudence (*figha*) was developed by the early great Muslim jurists, in order to reach the real understanding of Islamic Sharia rules,[45] and sources of Sharia; in the other word, in this context, the principal theme of Islamic jurisprudence is based on saying that God has revealed his revelation and has given us a brain to understand it, so understanding and applying Sharia should be through using our brains and thought.[46] Where matters are not regulated or stated in the original sources, a process called *Ijtihad* (personal reasoning) can be used in interpreting Sharia materials or reaching an opinion about particular issues.[47] The process of

42 Twelver shi'a is the largest branch of Shi'a Islam and the term Shi'a Muslim often refers to the Twelvers by default. The term Twelvers Shi'a are derived from the doctrine of believing in twelve divinely ordained leaders, known as Twelve Imams. The Twelve Imams are the spiritual and political successors to Muhammad for the Twelvers. Based on theology of Twelvers, the successors of Muhammad is an infallible human individual who not only rules over the community with justice but also is able to keep and interpret the diving law and its esoteric meaning. The words and deeds of Muhammad and the Imams are a guide and model for community to follow; as a result, they must be free from error and sin. Modarressi Tabataba'i, above n 412, 10.

43 M Khadduri, *The Islamic Conceptions of Justice* (Johns Hopkins, 1984) 16. Also, Hossein Nasr, *Expectation of the Millennium: Shi'ism in History* (State University of New York Press, 1989). Also See Entessar, above n 38, 95–98.

44 Abdal-Haqq, above n 3, 5.

45 Kamali, above n 2, 16.

46 Baderin, above n 5, 37.

47 Kamali, above n 2, 25.

personal reasoning can assist in developing a modern understanding of Sharia in the light of contemporary changes and developments of society, specifically about legal matters.[48] Therefore, the personal reasoning can be used to reveal the Sharia perspective through examining and realising the reason and spirit of rules of Islamic Sharia in light of general principles of Sharia.[49]

The jurisprudence covers legal and juridical aspects of Islamic law exclusively. The Islamic jurisprudence not only covers civil or criminal matters but also it includes different legal subjects of law as well.[50] Also the Islamic jurisprudence determines a method to understand and apply rules of Sharia which can be compatible in accordance with time, circumstances and situations.[51]

Although all schools of Islamic jurisprudence accept the primary sources of Sharia, the interpretative method and application of the original sources of Sharia (especially general principles) may vary depending upon the particular school.[52] Therefore, it could lead to different interpretations of the primary source texts.[53]

Basically, the principal sources of Sharia in in the scope of understanding are restricted by the *Sunni* decision making.[54] Some scholars of the *Sunni* reject personal reasoning in religious and legal matters of Islam.[55] Sunni scholars are restricted to consideration and decisions based on the major schools. This may limit the capacity to respond to contemporary changes in society. While, In the *Shi'a*, a qualified Scholar can decide about new matters which are not stated in the original sources of Sharia according to their personal interpretation. Therefore, the *Shi'a* could be more flexible as there is more scope for variable opinion of scholars about new issues.[56]

In relation to the major Schools of Islamic jurisprudence, there are five principal who represent Islamic jurisprudence within the two major sects of Muslim (*Shi'a and Sunni*).[57] The four Schools of jurisprudence for the *Sunni* are *Hanafi*, *Maliki*, *Shafia* and *Hanbali*; and School of jurisprudence for the *Shi'a* is the *Ja'fari* School.[58] These Schools were stablished in the early centuries of Islam (during the 8th century AD) and continue to present.[59]

Undoubtedly, the main sources of Islamic Sharia are considered by all different schools of Islamic jurisprudence in decision-making. However, the

48 Hussain, above n 23, 42.
49 Khaled Hamad Fayadh, *The Legal Regulation of Assisted Reproductive Technology in Iraq-Lessons From the Australian Approach* (PhD Thesis, Western Sydney University, 2015).
50 Abdal-Haqq, above n 3, 5.
51 Baderin, above n 5, 34.
52 Abdal-Haqq, above n 3, 6.
53 Baderin, above n 5, 37.
54 Atighetchi, above n 14, 6.
55 Hussain, above n 23, 46.
56 Hamad Fayadh, above n 49, 101.
57 Abdal-Haqq, above n 3, 6.
58 Atighetchi, above n 14, 6. Also, Abdal-Haqq, above n 3, 7.
59 Kamali, above n 2, 16. Also, Atighetchi, above n 14, 6.

methodology of interpretation and the understanding of sources of Sharia used for decision-making are different from one school to another.[60]

Before turning to *Shi'a* perspective on natural resources, it is useful to briefly review the methodology of each of the schools of Islamic jurisprudence.

There is not any priority to begin among the Islamic Schools in terms of rank, particularly in research studies. It starts with the *Hanafi* School.[61] The *Hanafi* School is the most widely followed in Muslim world.[62] It is dominant among Sunnis in countries such as Iraq, Pakistan, Syria and Turkey.[63] The method of decision making in this school could be described as a rational method based on reasoning and analysis of provisions of Sharia. In fact, the research methodology of this school which make it distinguished from others School that is based on consultation, discussion and analysis before reaching a decision.[64] This school adopts individual freedom in order to reach a decision with reliance on personal opinions and analogy, as well as discussion and research on actual as well as theoretical problems and hypothetical issues.[65]

Second, The *Maliki* School[66] is considered as school which is located largely in North and West Africa.[67] This school, unlike other schools, considers that customary practices of the people of Medina (the city where Prophet Mohammad lived and died) as a source of evidence after the main sources of Islamic Sharia as a basis for applying and revealing rules of Islamic Sharia.[68] This is based on assumption or belief that people who lived in city of Prophet Mohammad realise and understand rules of Sharia rules better than other societies do. Thus, the using analysis and rational reasoning are limited for this school.[69]

The third school is the *Shafia* School.[70] This School is dominant among *Sunni* in southern Egypt, southern Arabia, east Africa and in countries such as Syria, Jordan, Malaysia and Indonesia.[71] The founder of this school was considered the first to have classified the main principles of jurisprudence, and established principles and criteria for applying analogy.[72] These were later revised in the light of a new environment and circumstances when the author moved from Baghdad to Egypt.[73] Consequently, this school of Islamic jurisprudence takes the approach that rules could be changed in accordance with the different circumstances.

60 Abdal-Haqq, above n 3, 38.
61 The Hanafi School was founded by Abu Hanifa; he was born in Iraq (702–767 CE). Ibid. 26.
62 Atighetchi, above n 14, 6.
63 Baderin, above n 5, 37.
64 Abdal-Haqq, above n 3, 26.
65 Kamali, above n 2, 70.
66 The Maliki School was founded by Malik ibn Anas (died 795 CE), who lived in Madinah (Saudi). Ibid. 73.
67 Baderin, above n 5, 37
68 Abdal-Haqq, above n 3, 27.
69 Hamad Fayadh, above n 49, 103.
70 The founder of this School is Muhammad al-Shafie (d. 820 CE). Atighetchi, above n 14, 6.
71 Kamali, above n 2, 83.
72 Abdal-Haqq, above n 3, 27.
73 Kamali, above n 2, 81.

Unlike the *Maliki* School, the *Shafia* School considers traditions, and it examines them critically.[74] And, it provides the middle ground between the *Hanafi* School, which depends on analysis and examining in understanding and revealing rules of Sharia, and the *Maliki School* which largely follows custom and traditions.[75]

The *Hanbali* School[76] is considered as fourth School which is prevalent in Saudi Arabia.[77] This School has many followers in countries such as Bahrain, Oman, Kuwait and Qatar.[78] The research methodology of this school is based on personal reasoning. It also rejects any opinion which might conflict with the primary source of Sharia, specifically the *Sunnah*.[79] Unlike the *Hanafi* School which is based on to reach a decision with emphasis on personal opinions and analogy, the *Hanbali* School has limitation for using of analogy. It should be considered that the analogy is using as last option in very limited cases in this school.[80]

The principal school in the *Shi'a* sect is the *Ja'fari* School.[81] This school predominantly prevalent in Iran southern Iraq and has followers in some West African countries, Syria and Lebanon.[82] The methodology of this school is based on the primary sources and *Ijtihad*[83] of the *Imams*.[84] This provides flexibility in dealing with new issues which are not stated in the main source of Islamic law.[85] Therefore, this School not only considers the main sources of Sharia but also it has more compatibility with new situations in accordance with circumstances and time with reliance to *Ijtihad*.

6.1.4 Shi'a *perspective on natural resources*

The *Quran* does not impose the ownership of natural resources and allows the different schools of Islam to interpret their standing. The schools' interpretations will be acceptable if they do not contradict the *Quran* and *Sunnah*.[86] However, *Ijtihad* is a distinctive element between Sunni and Shi'a as the latter are open to use it to accommodate the teachings to ever-changing society. Basically, as

74 Hussain, above n 23, 40.
75 Hamad Fayadh, above n 49, 104.
76 Ahmad ibn Hanbal is founder of this school; (died 855 CE). Kamali, above n 2, 83.
77 Atighetchi, above n 14, 6.
78 Kamali, above n 2, 84.
79 Ibid. 84.
80 Abdal-Haqq, above n 3, 28.
81 Name of this school has taken from name of *Shi'a* imams, Ja'far al-Sadiq. Abdal-Haqq, above n 3, 29.
82 Baderin, above n 5, 37. Also Kamali, above n 2, 92.
83 *Ijtihad* is the process where rules are derived from interpretations made of *Quran* and *Sunnah* and rulings of past scholars.
84 Abdal-Haqq, above n 3, 29.
85 Hamad Fayadh, above n 49, 105.
86 Arash Nazhad, 'The Link between Islamic Law and Hydrocarbon Agreements' (2008) 10 2 *Journal of Islamic Law and Culture*.

Shi'a school believes, *Ijtihad* allows for greater flexibility in the development of laws and has been essential in adopting Muslim teachings to meet the changing requirements of Iranian society. *Vali-e Faghih*[87](supreme leader)[88] is the person responsible for issuing *Ijtihad* while Imam is on occultation. Of course, this flexibility is not as yet reflected widely in the construction and implementation of Iran's mineral laws.

What relates to hydrocarbon subject is that *Shi'a* school of thought does not recognise the privatisation of companies for minerals. Furthermore, only government has the right to extract oil due to believe that it is the government that is entitled to be observant of the entire community's needs.[89]

Therefore, the privatisation of industry can only be justified provided that there are firm regulations and the interests of community are assured.

6.2 Oil and gas legal framework in Iran

Natural sources in general, and particularly oil and gas contracts, are an important and sensitive issue in Iran's legal framework. After the Islamic revolution in Iran, the legal framework for the oil and gas sector has undergone change. In fact, the changes to Iran's oil and gas legal framework were affected by either objective legal fact or the circumstances of that time, or both.

Iran's oil and gas legal frameworks are based on: the Constitution (which was affected by the 1979 revolution and its influences), the Petroleum Act 1987, the Five-Year Economic, Social and Cultural Development Plans (implemented to improve and develop Iran's economy and cultural affairs, especially in the oil and gas industry), the Foreign Investment Promotion and Protection Act (FIPPA) 2002 (which were/are under objective legal fact and to attract foreign investment), the Petroleum Act 2011 and the Act of Duties and Authorities of the Oil Ministry 2012 (which imposed financial terms, economic sanctions, and objective legal fact). In consideration of the importance of oil and gas in Iran, experts in the field and scholars are codifying and modifying petroleum law, Acts and legislations. For further understanding of Iran's oil and gas legal frameworks and their structure, the following details are provided.

6.2.1 Constitution

Iran's laws derive from the Constitution of the Islamic Republic of Iran which is based on interpretations of Islam. The Constitution primarily declares that only God is sovereign and has the right to legislate. It is also the main source of the Convention of Iran. Since 1979, the legal regime of natural resources has

87 He is the highest ranking religious figure in Iran since the country has been wholly governed by Islam. This makes him the highest ranking political leader.

88 David Smock, 'Applying Islamic Principles in the 21st Century' (Special Report No. 150, United States Institute of Peace, September 2005) 3.

89 Bunter, above n 33, 6.

changed fundamentally and the Islamic Republic of Iran, made specific reference to natural resources. The key articles of the Constitution which are relevant to natural resource are now examined.

ARTICLE 4

As previously mentioned, Iranian law is based on the Islamic (*Sharia*) law and under Article 4 of Constitution it is explicitly expressed; "All civil, penal, financial, economic, administrative, cultural, military, political and other laws and regulations must be based on Islamic criteria ..." Due to the Islamic legislative base of Iranian law, all of the above aspects should stem from the principles of Islam and all legal provisions must be in accordance with Islam criteria.[90]

ARTICLE 43

Article 43 is designed to avert foreign economic domination over the Iran's commercial sector. The article emerged from Iran's previous difficulties related to excessive foreign political power related to foreigners' control over the natural minerals and economy of the country. The following is an extract from the Constitution relevant to issues of foreign investment:

> "The economy of the Islamic Republic of Iran, with its objectives of achieving the economic independence of the society ... is based on the following criteria:
>
> 5 The prohibition of infliction of harm and loss upon others, monopoly, hoarding, usury, and other illegitimate and evil practices;
> 8 Prevention of foreign economic domination over the country's economy ..."[91]

ARTICLE 44

Iran's post-revolution economic policy as defined in Chapter 4 of the Constitution of Iran covers three sectors:

> State, co-operative and private, and is to be based on systematic planning. The state sector is to include all large-scale and mother industries, foreign trade, major minerals, banking, insurance, power generation, dams and large-scale irrigation networks, radio and television, post, telegram services, aviation, shipping, roads, railroads, and the like; all those will be publicly owned and administrated by the state. The co-operative sector includes

90 *Iranian Constitution 1979* (Iran) (to view the Constitution in English, go to: <http://www.iranonline.com/iran/iran-info/government/constitution.html> (accessed 18/02/2017).
91 Ibid. art 4.

> co-operative companies and enterprises concerned with production and distribution, in urban and rural areas, in accordance with Islamic criteria. The private sector consists of those activities concerned with agriculture, animal husbandry, industry, trade, and services that supplement the economic activities of the state and co-operative sectors.[92]

Ownership in each of these sectors is protected by the laws of the Islamic republic, except to the extent permitted by other articles in Chapter 4 of the Constitution) and should not go beyond the bounds of Islamic law. They contribute to the economic growth and social progress of the country.

In fact, Article 44 not only forbids any form of private ownership, it also prohibits private participation (i.e. investment), be it foreign or domestic as evidenced in the words; "publicly owned and administrated by the state". However, privatisation of most mother industries later became legally feasible through legislation.[93]

ARTICLE 45

This article grants the Islamic government the authority to manage non-privately-owned entities and resources such as natural deposits as they see fit.

"*Anfal*[94] (i.e. public wealth such as uncultivated or abandoned land, mineral deposits, seas, lakes, … and public property recovered from usurpers, shall be at the disposal of the Islamic government for it to utilise in accordance with the public interest".[95]

As previously mentioned, Iranian law and acts of legislation are driven by and should accord with *Shi'a* Islamic scholars. Public wealth such as mineral deposits are components of public property and therefore any ownership of oil and gas deposits or granting of its exclusive right is in contravention of Iran's Constitution.

ARTICLE 81

Article 81 denies foreign individuals the right to establish a company in Iran. It also states that foreigners may not receive any concessions. It prescribes that "The granting of concessions to foreigners for the formation of companies or institutions dealing with commerce, industry, agriculture, services or mineral extraction, is absolutely forbidden".[96] There are various interpretations of this

92 Ibid. art 44.

93 Exigency Council, 'General Policies of Article 44 of the Constitution of the Islamic Republic of Iran' (1 July 2006) Iran Data Portal <http://irandataportal.syr.edu/the-general-policies-pertaining-to-principle-44-of-the-constitution-of-the-islamic-republic-of-iran>.

94 The public domain in its Islamic sense.

95 *Iranian Constitution 1979*, above n 90, art 45.

96 Ibid. art 81.

article. On the one hand, some supporters of Iran's current oil and gas contracts believe that this prohibition is absolute, and that the government is therefore not granted the power of consent to foreign ownership. On the other hand, some opponents suggest that Article 81 prohibits the government from giving foreigners the right to form companies or institutions dealing with mineral extraction. Nonetheless, it should be noted that this article simply states that foreigners who want to form a company or entity dealing in commerce, industry ... may not receive any concession.

Therefore, Article 81 does not refer to ownership or granting of ownership. In addition, the objective of the article is the prohibition of foreigners dealing in commerce and industry, not ownership or ownership granting. Further, this article does not restrict corporation of the branches of foreign companies in Iran. The Guardian Council[97] (as the sole qualified source to interpret the Constitution in Iran)[98] has clarified this issue in response to the government's request for interpretation on 28 March 1981. Although there was a limit placed on foreign shares in Iranian companies – according to the Company Registration Act, but based on a dominate interpretation of the FIPPA – this restriction has since been abolished. Finally, formation of the branches for foreign company's incorporation of companies with 100 percent foreign investment is now allowed and is currently implemented in practice.

ARTICLE 153

Under Article 153, control over natural resources by foreign persons is prohibited. It reads:

"Any form of agreement resulting in foreign control over the natural resources, economy, army, or culture of the country, as well as other aspects of the national life, is forbidden".[99]

This article expresses Iran's political, economic, social and cultural independence. In the other words, the purpose of this article is to prohibit of any sort of agreement which may lead to foreign domination.

6.2.2 Petroleum Act 1987

On 1 October 1987, the first Petroleum Law after Islamic revolution of Iran was ratified. It was approved by parliament during the eight-year war (1980–1988) which undoubtedly affected the mentality of the law makers; namely, the development of a pessimistic view regarding the domination of foreign investors in Iran's economic activities. The *Petroleum Act* authorised the government to

97 According to Article 91 of the Constitution of Islamic Republic of Iran, "in order to examine the compatibility of the legislation passed by the Islamic consultative assembly with Islam, a council to be known as a Guardian Council is to be consisted ..."

98 *Iranian Constitution 1979*, above n 90, art 98.

99 Ibid. art 153.

control all activities related to all of oil and gas operations. Hence, the government assumed strict control over the oil and gas industry. Regarding to this Act the obstacle on the foreign control of reserves is meaning of the obstacle on foreign ownership of minerals in Iran. In turn, this Act permits the establishment of contracts between the Ministry of Petroleum, state companies, and local and foreign national persons and legal entities.

ARTICLE 2

Under Article 2, all petroleum reserves count as public wealth. Moreover, Article 45 of the Constitution states the reserves are at the disposal and exclusive control of the Iranian government, administrated by the Ministry of Petroleum with Iran's best interests in mind:

> "The petroleum resources of the country are part of the public domain (properties and assets) and wealth and according to Article 45 of the Constitution (of the Islamic Republic of Iran) are at the disposal and control of the Government of the Islamic Republic of Iran and all installations, equipment, assets, property and capital investments which have been made or shall be made in future within the country and abroad by the Ministry of Oil and its affiliated companies will belong to the people of Iran and remain at the disposal and control of the government of the Islamic Republic of Iran.
>
> The authority for exercising sovereignty and ownership rights over the petroleum resources and installations is vested in the government of the Islamic Republic of Iran which based on the regulations, rights and powers prescribed in this Act shall be undertaken and executed by the Ministry of Petroleum in accordance with the general principles and policies of the country".[100]

ARTICLE 5

Article 5 permits the Ministry of Petroleum and affiliated companies to enter into contracts with local and foreign individuals or companies to carry out oil and gas operations.

> Conclusion of important contracts between the Ministry of Oil or petroleum companies and the local and foreign natural persons and legal entities and determination of the important cases shall have governed by the By-Laws to be approved by the council of ministers upon the proposal of the oil ministry. The contract ...[101]

100 *The Petroleum Act of 1987* (Iran) (to view *The Petroleum Act of 1987* in English, go to: <http://www.alaviandassociates.com/documents/petroleum.pdf> (accessed 18/02/2017) art 2.

101 Ibid. art 5.

ARTICLE 6

According to Article 6, all capital investments are based on the budget of operational units proposed through the Ministry of Petroleum and approved through the country's general budget. Also, this article emphasises the prohibition of foreign investment in the petroleum sector. As such, this article provides utmost clarity as to the prohibition of direct investment in oil and gas industry:

> All capital investment shall be proposed through the Ministry of Oil on the basis of the budget of the operational units and be included upon approval of the general assembly, in the General State Budget. Foreign investment in these operations in any manner will not be allowed whatsoever.[102]

ARTICLE 12

Article 12 is a continuation of previous policy and nullified any previous conflicting law and regulation:

> Any law and regulation contrary to this Act shall be abrogated and stand null and void by approval of this Act.[103]

6.2.3 Foreign Investment Promotion and Protection Act (FIPPA)

To encourage foreign investment, the Foreign Investment Promotion and Protection Act (FIPPA) was approved on 4 May 2002. The enactment of FIPPA not only succeeded in changing previously held strict attitudes, it's also opened a new opportunity towards foreign investment. This Act consists of grant assurances to foreign investors, facilitates the approval procedure and introduces new contractual mechanisms for foreign investment. In further consideration of the oil and gas issue, two Articles (2 and 3) of FIPPA are discussed below.

ARTICLE 2

Article 2 includes the protections applied to investments undertaken for the promotion and development of production activities in mining, agriculture, service and industrial sectors.[104] Article 2(d) states that the value of services and commodities resulting from the foreign investment must compare to the service and commodity supplies to domestic markets in every economic sector and in every field and should proportionally exceed 25 percent and 35 percent, respectively.

102 *The 1987 Petroleum Law*, above n 100, art 6.
103 Ibid. art 12.
104 Ardeshir Atai, 'A New Paradigm for Attracting Foreign Investments: Restructuring Investor-State Arbitration for Resolution of Petroleum Disputes: Dynamics of the New Iranian Oil Investment Contract' (2015) 12(2) *Transnational Dispute Management (TDM)* 7–8.

The fields and the amount of foreign capital should also be approved by the Council of Ministers. The end of Article 2(d) mentions that exemptions from the proportions are provided for foreign investments related to the production of services and commodities for export purposes, but explicitly not for crude oil investment.[105] It states:

> Admission of foreign investment shall be made, in accordance with the provisions of this Law and with due observance of other prevailing laws and regulations of the country, subject to the following criteria:
>
> (d) The ratio of the value of the goods and services produced by the foreign investments, subject matter of this Law, to the value of the goods and services supplied to the local market at the time of issuance of the investment license, shall not exceed 25 percent in each economic sector and 35 percent in each field (sub-sector). The fields and investment ceilings in each field shall be determined in the by-law to be approved by the Council of Ministers. Foreign investment to produce goods and services specifically for export purposes other than crude oil shall be exempted from the ratios.[106]

ARTICLE 3

Under Article 3, the major investment modes are: Foreign Direct Investment (FDI) in the field where private sector activity is authorised; and foreign investments in all sectors within the 'civil partnership', 'buy-back' and 'Build, Operate and Transfer' (BOT) frameworks. Return of principle and profit arises solely through the economic activity of the same investment project and does not rely on any guarantee by the government or bank or government companies. It states:

> Foreign investments admitted in accordance with provisions of this Law shall enjoy the incentives and protections available under this Law. Such investments may be admitted under the following two categories:
>
> a FDI in areas where the activity of private sector is permissible;
> b Foreign investments in all sectors within the framework of "civil participation", "buy-back" and "build-operate-transfer" arrangements where the return of capital and profits accrued is solely emanated from

105 Hedayati Kakhki, Mohammed Mehdi, *A Critical Analysis of Iranian Buy-Back Transactions in the Context of International Petroleum Contractual Systems* (PhD Thesis, The University of Durham, 2008).

106 *The Foreign Investment Promotion and Protection Act (FIPPA) 2002* (Iran) Article 2 (to view the FIPPA in English, this is accessible at: <http://centinsur.ir/ShowPage.aspx?page_=form&order=show&lang=2&sub=0&PageId=2252&codeV=1&tempname=EnglishTemp> (accessed 27/08/2017)).

> the economic performance of the project in which the investment is made, and such return of capital and profit shall not be dependent upon a guarantee by the Government, state-owned companies or banks.[107]

Some experts believe that FIPPA primarily funds very capital-intensive economic projects particularly in the upstream petroleum industry. It should be noted however that oil and gas downstream industry projects appear to come under FIPPA's protection for their share of capital.[108] Nevertheless, it seems that the upstream oil and gas industry cannot benefit from the provisions of direct foreign investment.

6.2.4 Five-year economic, social and cultural development plans

The successive five-year economic, social and cultural development plans (hereafter development plan) may similarly provide for basic instruction, predominantly in generalities, aimed at revamping the country's infrastructure for foreign investment. Since 1989, the development plans have been renewed and update every five years. The first development plan (1989–1994) aimed to remove the legacy of the economic burdens brought about by the Iraq invasion of Iran. Article 29 in the plan permitted the state party to utilise profits from petroleum contractual schemes. The second development plan (1995–2000) was drawn up specifically with the achievements and failures of first plan in mind. Therefore, Article 22 of the second development plan states that the government was permitted to participate in such arrangements. The third development plan (2000–2005) then set the groundwork for the subsequent Iranian development policies.

The commencement of the new set of policies within the framework of this plan generated new hope for a more successful liberalisation of the Iranian economy. In the fourth development plan (2005–2010) provisions are included regarding the use of current oil and gas contractual schemes to appeal to outside investors. Finally, the fifth development plan (2010–2015) was passed in 2010 and sets out detailed provisions (articles 125-126-129) on the development of upstream petroleum (these details are examined below).

Finally, in the sixth development plan (2016–2020) oil-related objectives are increasing crude oil production capacity and export, and also observing priorities regarding development and operation of shared oil fields (paragraph 13, 14, 15).

107 Ibid. art 3.

108 Maximilian Kuhn, Mohammadjavad Jannatifar, 'Foreign Direct investment Mechanisms and Review of Iran's Buy Back Contracts: How Far Has Iran Gone and How Far May It Go?' (2012) 5(3) *Journal of World Energy Law and Business.*

ARTICLE 125

This article applies to the granting of licenses on a joint field. It aims to protect Iran's interests and to avoid delays in exploration arising from disagreements between Iran and the licensed country:

> The Ministry of Oil should create a competitive climate through issuing license (permits) for the exploration, development and production of the oil and gas fields to increase the oil output by one million barrels per day and natural gas by two hundred and fifty million cubic meters. The Ministry of Oil should prioritise joints fields and South Pars Gas Field, following the approval of the technical and economic plans by the Economic Council and pursuant to provisions of the national budget law and exchange of agreements with the Deputy, shall take the following actions:
>
> 1 Utilisation of the methods for the exploration, development and production for a defined period in oil and gas field.
> 2 Placement for the issuance of foreign and domestic currency bonds in Iran and abroad pursuant to the applicable laws and regulations without any government guarantees.
> 3 Utilisation of buyback arrangement in accordance with principles and conditions lay down in Article 14(b) of the Fourth Development Plan.[109]

It is important here to provide further explanation of Article 14(b) in the Fourth Develop Plan.

In order to increase oil production, Article 14(b) of the Fourth Development Plan permits that the NIOC to enter into contracts with foreign investors or qualified domestic companies for the exploration and development of upstream oil and gas fields.[110]

The provisions of Article 14(b) set forth the conditions for the exploration and development contracts as follows:

1 The government retains sovereignty and proprietorship rights over oil and gas resources.
2 There should not be any guarantee by government, state banks and Central Bank of Iran (CBI) regarding obligations on returns of investment.

109 *Law of the Fifth Five-Year Economic, Social and Cultural Development Plan* 2010–2015 (Iran) Article 125(a) (to view the development Plan in English, this is accessible at: <http://www.wipo.int/wipolex/en/details.jsp?id=14565> (accessed 27/08/2017)).

110 *Law of the Fourth Five-Year Economic, Social and Cultural Development* 2005–2010 (Iran) Article 14(b) (to view the development Plan in English, this is accessible at: <http://www.paris21.org/sites/default/files/2924.pdf> (accessed 27/08/2017)).

3 The return of original investment, remunerations or profits, risk and costs accrued for securing financial resources and other costs incurred for implementation of the project must be allocated from a portion of products recovered from the field or revenues which must be based on the market price of sold products.
4 The contracting party must bear the risk associated with not achieving the targets set by the contract, when the fields are non-economic, or when the quantity of products recovered from the field is inadequate.
5 The rates of return of investment for the contracting party must be commensurate to the circumstances of each project and observe the incentives for employing optimised methods for excavation, development and utilisation of fields.
6 To guarantee sustainable production of oil and gas during the contract period.
7 Observation of the domestic content rules.
8 Observation of laws and regulations concerning environment protection.[111]

ARTICLE 126

This article states:

> The Ministry of Oil is authorised to act for discovery and exploration of more oil and gas fields across the entire country, as well as to the transfer and use of new technologies for exploration operations of onshore and offshore joint fields shared with neighbouring countries in which the relating exploration operations concerns risk-taking by the contracting party and leads to discovery of fields capable of commercial production.[112]

The Ministry of Oil is permitted to conclude buy-back agreements to achieve the goals covering exploration and development of new fields by holding tenders and selecting the contracting party in accordance with legal requirements. The framework of agreements determines the repayment of exploration costs (both direct and indirect costs) as well as the development costs from the source of sale of produced goods from the same field. The Ministry of Oil is responsible for issuing the permission which is in place for a definite period. In addition, the permission is on a case-by-case and renewable only once. By the completion of the exploration stage, if no commercial field is discovered in any of the areas in the block, the agreement will be terminated and there would be no right to claim any amount for the contracting party.[113]

111 Ibid. art 14(b).
112 *The Development Plan 2010–2015*, above n 109, art 126.
113 Atai, above n 104, 3–5.

ARTICLE 129

Under Article 129, the Ministry of Petroleum is authorised to issue licenses for exploration, development, extraction and production of oil and gas. The Ministry of Oil should:

- a take action for exercising sovereignty and ownership rights over the oil and gas resources and to execute legal duties by designing a management plan for the exploration, development and production. The Ministry of Oil shall equip the organisational posts by employing skilled work force and deployment of available human resources for undertaking duties stipulated in this law and other relevant laws.
- b the Ministry of Oil should adopt a framework concerning exploration activities, development, extraction and production of oil and gas by companies affiliated to the Ministry of Oil and qualified companies concerning sustainable production and to issue permits for exploration without conferring ownership rights over the produced oil and gas. The Ministry of Oil must take action on the basis of an approved plan, concerning the supervision of exploration, development and production operations of abovementioned companies from the point of view of production, quantity, preservation of the deposits, health and safety, and environmental standards.[114]

6.2.5 The Act to Modify Petroleum Act (1987) of 2011

Upon legislative approval to modify the Petroleum Law (1987) in 2011, the *Petroleum Act 1987* was amended and the *Petroleum Act 1974* (before the Islamic revolution in Iran) was clearly abrogated.[115]

As previously mentioned, the *Petroleum Act 1987* banned any form of foreign investment in the oil and gas sectors. Moreover, according to the *Petroleum Act 1987*, any FDI activity that entails ownership of resources, equipment and installations is prohibited.[116]

Subsequently, the *Petroleum Act 1987* was amended on 29 June 2011 to the Petroleum Act of 2011. The *Petroleum Act 2011* defines oil contracts as bilateral or multilateral agreements concluded between the Ministry of Oil and any of its subsidiaries or between any operational units and one or more operation units or natural or legal persons inside or outside the country. Also, its definition covers downstream and upstream activities and extends to trading oil, petroleum and petrochemical products.[117]

114 *The Development Plan 2010–2015*, above n 109, art 129(a).

115 *The Petroleum Act 2011* (Iran) art 16 (to view *The Petroleum Act 2011* in English, this is accessible at: https://www.ilbconsultancy.com/insights/2011-Amendment-on-Iran-Petroleum-Act (accessed 27/08/2017)).

116 Atai, above n 104, 8–9.

117 Ibid. 8–9.

ARTICLE 1(16)

In Article 1(16), competent authorities to conclude petroleum contracts are both Ministry of Petroleum and NIOC:

> Oil contracts as bilateral or multilateral agreements concluded between the Ministry of Oil or any of its subsidiaries or between any operational units and one or more operation units or natural or legal persons inside or outside the country in accordance with the applicable laws, concerning the implementation of all or part of downstream and upstream petroleum or trading oil, petroleum products and petrochemical products under taken.[118]

ARTICLE 2

In Article 2, the right to exercise of sovereignty over petroleum resources was granted to the Ministry of Petroleum on behalf of Islamic governance.

> The petroleum resources of the country are part of the public domain (properties and assets) and wealth. The exercise the right of governance and public ownership on petroleum resources is on responsibility of Ministry of Petroleum, on behalf of Islamic Republic of Iran.[119]

Accordingly, competent authorities to conclude petroleum contracts in upstream section are the Ministry of Petroleum and the NIOC.

6.2.6 The Duty and Authorities of Oil Ministry Act (2012)

The *Duty and Authorities of Oil Ministry Act 2012* replaced the Bill for the establishment of the Ministry of Oil in 1979. The aim of the Act is to clarify and determined the duties of the Ministry of Oil and to oversee its organisational structure. As with the fifth five-year development plan, this Act looked to include the operation phase in Iran's petroleum contracts. The most notable aspects of this Act are the licensing and nominating participation contracts.

ARTICLE 3

In Paragraph C of Article 3, the executive affaires of the Ministry of Petroleum are defined. Clause (5) of paragraph C of this article states; licensing and license activity for qualified juridical persons for exploration, development, extraction and production for all oil and gas fields. Paragraph D of this article aims to attract foreign investment via the granting of special conditions or rights such as

118 *The Petroleum Act 2011*, above n 115, art 1(16).
119 *The Petroleum Act 2011*, above n 115, art 2.

changing the framework of the contract (participation contract), and transferring the ownership. Paragraph D (3) of Article 3 of the Act states:

> ... attracting and leading internal as well as foreign investment to develop hydrocarbon field with the priority of common field, through designing and introducing new contractual schemes such as participations contracts with internal as well as foreign contractors, without transferring the ownership of oil and gas in place ...

Arguably, this Act was a turning point in the contracts to exploit Iran's oil and gas fields. In this Act, Ministry of Petroleum can participate alongside foreign contractors in the operation phase and share the output according to an agreed amount. In this case, it is a win-win game because it allows the contractor to stay in the production phase of the project for the life of the field resulting in more profits through a long-term contract. From the NIOC's point of view, it allows for the use of contractors know-how and experience in production or other operational phases. Therefore, the NIOC develops an understanding of contractors who are efficient based on the profits from production.

6.3 Challenges of adopting new concession contract in Iran

Iran has almost a century of valuable experience in oil and gas sectors, is an OPEC member and is located in the Persian Gulf at the centre of 70 percent of the oil and gas resources. It has reserves close to sea ways for easy access to world markets, huge high-pressure petroleum reservoirs with the possibility of natural production, low oil and gas production expenses, a relatively cheap work force and gas reserves in comparison with other countries. It is also a competent country that presents notable opportunities for investors to upgrade their level of contribution to attract greater profits from the oil and gas sectors.[120]

Therefore, considering Iran's potential to attract foreign investment to upgrade its oil and gas industries, it is necessary to examine the opportunities for, and barriers to, accessing foreign investment. Generally, foreign investment is conducted directly or indirectly and may be via new oil and gas framework contracts such as the NCC.

6.3.1 Opportunities

Recent evolutions and transitions in the structure of Iran' oil and gas legal framework have provided new condition in which to increase the level of production in the oil and gas industries to achieve upmost efficiency. These evolutions include enacting and amending crucial petroleum legislation and Acts (the *Petroleum*

120 Leila Zabbah, 'Investment Challenges in Iranian Oil & Gas Sectors – A Legal Approach' (2011) 10 *Institute for International Energy Studies* 12.

Act 2011 – the *Duty and Authorities of Oil Ministry Act 2012*),[121] ratifying infrastructures to attract foreign investment like the FIPPA,[122] and providing the five-year development plans.[123] Conversely, the NCC has specific characteristics which differentiate it from other oil and gas contractual frameworks such as ownership over reservoir, control and supervision over oil deposit, bidding and tax. Thus, it is important to identify the Iranian legal framework opportunities for accepting NCCs.

6.3.1.1 Acceptance of another framework beside/instead of buy-back

Despite Article 6 of the *Petroleum Act 1987* prohibiting foreign investment in the petroleum sector, and statements in the annual *Budget Act* that the buy-back scheme is the only accepted form in the oil and gas industry, Article 3 of FIPPA states explicitly that the major means of investment are: FDI in fields where private sector activity is authorised and foreign investments in all sectors within the frameworks of 'civil partnership', 'buy-back' and Build, Operate and Transfer (BOT). Therefore, although Article 3 does not offer an alternative framework to the buy-back approach, it at least accepts other frameworks beside the buy-back scheme such as civil partnership and BOT.

In addition, according clause A, Article 125(a) of the fifth development plan,[124] the Ministry of Petroleum has the authority to issue licenses for the exploration, development and production of the oil and gas fields by limited manners such as utilisation of the methods for exploration, development … It is clear that it permits the utilisation of other methods for the exploration, development and production in the oil and gas fields.

In addition, in the *Duty and Authorities of Oil Ministry Act 2012* another contractual framework is offered. Paragraph D (3) of Article 3 of the Act is a real turning point in the history of oil and gas contract frameworks after the Islamic revolution in Iran. To attract foreign investment, this part nominated other framework (participation contract). It states, "investment to develop hydrocarbon fields with the priority of common fields, through designing and introducing new contractual schemes such as participations contracts with internal as well as foreign contractors …".

The significance of this change is evidenced by recalling the history of oil and gas contract framework after revolution in Iran. All Acts and legislation regarding oil and gas contracts were restrictive. Even Article 6 of the *Petroleum Act 1987* prohibited foreign investment in the petroleum sector.[125] In contrast, this Act not only accepted foreign investment but also encourages the Ministry of Petroleum to design new contractual schemes likes participation contracts. This position started to emerge in other oil and gas contractual framework in Iran.

121 *The Petroleum Act 2011*, above n 115.
122 *The FIPPA*, above n 106.
123 *The Development Plan 2010–2015*, above n 109.
124 *The Development Plan 2010–2015*, above n 109, art 125(a) clause A.
125 *The Petroleum Act 1987*, above n 100, art 6.

6.3.1.2 Ownership

The issue of ownership is perhaps the most challenging aspect of Iranian's oil and gas history. Ownership conflict has been an interminable issue since oil was discovered in Iran. In turn, a review the Petroleum Acts and relevant legislation in Iran reveals that legislators had a specific perspective on this issue and always ratified strict ownership conditions. Granting ownership rights was prohibited either explicitly or implicitly in the *Petroleum Act 1987* and other relevant legislation. However, this problem was almost resolved by the *Duty and Authorities of Oil Ministry Act 2012*. Article 3(D)(3) of this Act states explicitly:

> Attracting and leading internal as well as foreign investment to develop hydrocarbon fields with the priority to common fields, through designing and introducing new contractual schemes such as participations contracts with internal as well as foreign contractors, without transferring the ownership of oil and gas in place.

Up to the enactment of this Act, some scholars believed that – according to Acts and legislation which emphasise ownership – the prohibition of transfer of ownership does not distinguish between oil in place and produced oil. Therefore, no type of ownership should be offered to a contractor. These scholars cite some articles of the five development plans and other previous relevant legislation to support their position. Alternatively, some oil and gas scholars believe that Iran should draw a distinction between ownership of petroleum 'oil in place' and 'oil in output'. These scholars support their position with reference to Article 3(D)(3) of the *Duties and Authorities of Oil Ministry Act 2012*, particularly the last phrase which states; "without transferring the ownership of oil and gas in place".

As a result, it should be mentioned that according to the above phrase, utilisation of domestic and foreign investment for developing hydrocarbon fields is allowed without transferring the ownership of oil and gas in place. This means that ownership can be transferred in oil output or in oil of well-head. Thus, it is possible to use other oil and gas contractual frameworks for ownership of oil in place to belong to the government and ownership of oil in output to transfer to the contractor.

6.3.1.3 Licensing

Licensing or permit activity is an inevitable element of the NCC. If any country intends to use the NCC, it should provide the legal and operational infrastructures for licensing. Opportunities in Iran's legal frameworks surrounding licensing are discussed below.

Article 125 of the fifth development plans which states the Ministry of Petroleum is authorised to create a competitive climate through issuing the exploration, development and production licenses required to develop of oil and gas fields.[126]

126 *The Development Plan 2010–2015*, above n 109, art 125.

In addition, paragraph B of Article 129 of the fifth development plan states that the Ministry of Oil should adopt a framework concerning exploration activities, development, extraction and production of oil and gas by companies affiliated to the Ministry of Oil and qualified companies concerning sustainable production and to issue licensing for exploration.[127]

Lastly, Article 3(C)(5) of the *Duties and Authorities of Oil Ministry Act 2012* explicitly gives authority to the Ministry of Petroleum to issue permits and licenses to qualified juridical persons for exploration, development, extraction and production from Iran's oil and gas fields. Therefore, having these opportunities makes the NCC distinguishable from the PSC and JV.

6.3.1.4 Duration

One of the main differences between oil concessions contract and the NCC is the duration of the concession. As discussed in Chapter 3, the duration of an oil concession contract may be six, seven or even nine decades; whereas, the duration of the NCC is limited.[128] Therefore, Article 125(a)(1) of fifth development plan states utilisation of the methods for the exploration, development and production of oil and gas fields for a defined (limited) period.[129]

6.3.1.5 Training and employment

Training and employment is a bilateral desire. In other words, host countries are willing to have domestic personnel receive training to improve their employment skills, and some IOCs are willing to train and employ domestic personnel as part of the contract. Iran's legal system provides this opportunity, with Article 43 of Constitution stating; to achieving the economic independence of the society, uprooting poverty and deprivation, and fulfilling human needs in the process of development while preserving human liberty, the economy of the Islamic Republic of Iran is based on the utilisation of science and technology and the training of skilled personnel in accordance with the developmental needs of the country's economy.[130]

6.3.1.6 Admission of foreign investment

The conditions for admitting foreign investment is significant to attracting foreign investment. Countries pay special attention to better investment opportunities, particularly in foreign countries. To support Iran's economic growth, opportunities to admit foreign investment in the construction and manufacturing sectors are provided. Article 2(A) of FIPPA states that for construction and manufacturing activities in the industrial, mineral, agricultural and service sectors,

127 *The Development Plan 2010–2015*, above n 109, art 129.
128 See Chapter 3, subsection 3.2.
129 *The Development Plan 2010–2015*, above n 109, art 125(a) (1).
130 *Iranian Constitution 1979*, above n 90, art 43.

admission of foreign investment shall be made in accordance with the provisions of this law and with due observance of other prevailing laws and regulations of the country to support economic growth, upgrade technology, promote quality products and to increase employment opportunities and exports.[131]

Article 3(B) of FIPPA undertakes to support foreign investment. The major foreign investment forms are as follows: FDI in fields where private sector activity is authorised, and foreign investment in all sectors.[132]

6.3.1.7 Protect and guarantee of foreign capital

Chapter 4 of FIPPA expresses how to protect and guarantee foreign capital. To protect foreign investments, Article 8 of FIPPA states; foreign investments under this law shall equally enjoy all rights, protections and facilities provided for domestic investments.[133] Article 9 of FIPPA states, foreign investments shall not be subjected to expropriation or nationalisation, unless for public purposes, in accordance with due of law, in a non-discriminatory manner, and upon payment of appropriate compensation based on the real value of the investment immediately before the expropriation.[134]

6.3.1.8 Settlement of dispute

Settlement of disputes is always an important element of a contract. Although, the terms of the contract are usually agreed to by parties, countries have their own judicial systems. Settlement of a dispute can be a controversial and complicated issue. Therefore, having the appropriate legal system in place is important for all parties. Article 19 of FIPPA is relevant to the settlement of disputes between foreign investors and the government. It states disputes arising between the government and the foreign investors in respect of the mutual obligations within the framework of investments under this law, if not settled through negotiations, shall be referred to domestic courts, unless another methods for settlement of disputes have been agreed under the Law for Bilateral Investment Agreement with the respective government of the foreign investor.[135]

6.3.2 Barriers

6.3.2.1 Pessimistic mental background

The first barrier to presenting the NCC to Iran's oil and gas legal framework is the history of oil exploration in Iran. The concession contract originally posed

131 *The FIPPA 2002*, above n 106, art 2(A).
132 Ibid. art 3(B).
133 *The FIPPA 2002*, above n 106, art 8.
134 Ibid. art 9.
135 Ibid. art 19.

a threat to the territorial integrity and political and economic independence of Iran. This generated mistrust from Iran towards other countries and, more than anything else, against the concession form. This impacted Iranian politics, society, culture, economy and law, culminating in the 1953 coup in Iran. Hence, this pessimistic view of the contract remains in Iran.[136]

6.3.2.2 Legal system

Use of any contract form should be clarified by a legal structure, and it needs to be valid in any countries' legal system. In Iran, using other types of oil and gas contracts – except the current buy-back contract framework – has not been clearly clarified in Iran's legal system.[137]

Although, the use of other types of contract is implied in Iran's oil and gas legal framework such as Article 3 of FIPPA,[138] Article 125(a)[139] of the fifth development plan and paragraph D (3) of Article 3 of the *Duties and Authorities of Oil Ministry Act 2012*,[140] according Article 125(3) of fifth five development plan, the buy-back contract is still the sole permitted contractual scheme in Iran.[141] Iran's legal structure has not codified other forms of oil and gas contracts. Therefore, acceptance of other oil and gas contract frameworks in Iran's legal system is not enforceable unless other types of oil and gas contract such as the PSA, JV and NCC are ratified by Acts of parliament.

6.3.2.3 Granting concession

Concession granting in Iran is not only usual, it is prohibited in some cases. For example, Article 2(c) of FIPPA states:

> It does not entail the grant of *concessions* by the government to foreign investors. 'Concession' refers to the special rights which place the foreign investor in a monopolistic position.[142]

The fear of foreigners influencing the politics in Iran is perhaps the main reason for avoiding concessions in Iran. Their political influence might undermine Iran's national security and the public interest by foreign investments or the IOC. The article makes explicit that foreign investment shall not involve concessions granted by the government to foreign investors.

136 Mark Gasiorowski, *Mohammad Mosaddeq and the 1953 Coup in Iran* (Syracuse University Press, 2004) 145.
137 *Budget Act of 1994* (Iran), Islamic Parliament of the Islamic Republic of Iran, Iranian Official Gazette 1994 [No. 14313 dated 7/2/1373 (April 27, 1994)].
138 *The FIPPA 2002*, above n 106.
139 *The Development Plan 2010–2015*, above n 109.
140 As stated in Section 6.3.1
141 *The Development Plan 2010–2015*, above n 109, 125(3).
142 *The FIPPA 2002*, above n 106, 2(c).

6.4 Efficiency of new concession contract in Iran's oil and gas industry

Control exerted by the State over all oil production stages – especially upstream stages – is popular from a historical point of view and has always been viewed as a target. However, it should be born in mind that the high costs of investment and risks associated with oil projects, along with the costs to government; means the government is generally not interested in investing public funds in fields where the profitability and return on capital is doubtful. This general principle is better understood when added to the fact that oil-rich countries like Iran generally lack the required financial resources for infrastructure investments. In fact, one of the biggest issues which make conditional the type of interference and participation of states in oil contracts is the lack of preparation and required diplomacy for investment, and the preparedness to assume the risks associated with a non-functioning project.[143]

This has led to various contracts concluded by states, irrespective of their framework, to include a clause stating the operating company incurs exploration phase costs up to the time when production becomes commercial. The state is then obligated to pay off the investment costs only in cases where the operation leads to the desired result. For this reason, the oil-producing states do not agree to take investment risks and loss of project implications, even though they are eager to participate in investment. They want to have immunity against such matters and for the investing company or the contractor to discharge their obligation as to investment costs. Therefore, oil-producing countries aim to achieve a formula which may assist them to avoid the heavy costs of investment, and at the same time ensure the government share of revenues from the project is protected. In this case, the NCC might be the suitable and appropriate formula for Iran to adopt rather than other oil and gas contract forms such as PSC, JV and service contract.

Furthermore, it should be borne in mind that in these circumstances a country just like Iran with high investment costs and no record of exploration or exploitation, capacities, the concession system can provide the platform for the achievement of national development goals. History has shown that the government will be forced to resort to complicated or indirect mechanisms such as buy-back schemes under which the rights and duties of parties are subject to misinterpretation because of the complex structure of such mechanisms. Alternatively, because of the long-time functioning of the concession system, the rights of parties are more transparent. Moreover, in cases of dispute over the interpretation of the contract provisions, a wide range of legal and judicial precedents and customs exist within the parties' reach to help them to reach an agreement.[144]

143 Mahmoud Mansouri Naraghi, *Legal Bases and General Terms of Middle East Oil Contracts* (Bita Publication, 1972) Osool –e- Hoghooghi va Sharayete 'omoomi Ghharardadhaye Nafti Dar Khavar-e- Mianeh1350, 153.

144 Mohsen Mohebbi, *Some Issues Related to Oil and Gas Law within the Purview of International Arbitration Precedent* – Expropriation and Compensation in Oil Contracts (Shahre Danesh Legal Studies and Researches Association, 2008) 78.

The biggest advantage of the concession system for a country like Iran is that the state bears no liability for the different risks inherent to every oil project. Costs which may put pressure on the public budget are avoided. Considering the economic problems the Iranian government must deal with to regulate its public finances, this is a matter which is undoubtedly important to the Iranian government. However, in the buy-back system the government has also tried to discharge its financial obligations by incorporating clauses into the contracts that discharge the state's financial liabilities.[145]

The most important comparative advantage of the NCC over other oil and gas contract forms like PSC, JV and service contract regarding to efficiency in Iran's oil and gas industry is the extraction and production costs. The extraction and production cost is known to be one of the most effective factors in choosing financial arrangements and legal regime governing oil and gas contracts in upstream sector. On this ground, the basis of categorising oil and gas contracts are their proportion to extraction and exploitation costs and oil and gas discovery with a commercial level. Therefore, in regions where oil fields lie in deep water, impassable place and the oil production costs is more than intermediate the common and agreed contract is the NCC because the governments have special problems to deal with for extracting oil and gas in this regions and high costs are incurred by the treasury and the requirement of applying sophisticated technology all makes governments unwilling to take part in initial investment and incur eventual losses.

In this respect, a study of the geological conditions of oil fields shows that in recent decades, only a rather small portion of the country's resources has been extracted and exploited. Indeed, large oil fields have practically remained unexplored or unused for various reasons, the most important of which is undoubtedly the lack of sufficient capital and preparation of domestic companies to take investment risks in these fields. These fields form a considerable part of Iran plateau. Taking into consideration the lack of exploration record, the impassibility of many of these regions, lack of necessary infrastructures, remoteness from ports and consumption markets, and the high-risk factor of the project, use of new concession framework can be efficient.[146]

6.5 Modernising Iran's oil and gas contract framework and regulation

Iran is a major supplier of petroleum products to global market. Currently, the country is estimated to possess over 157.8 billion barrels of proven oil reserves, which is almost 10 percent of the world's oil reserves and over 12 percent of OPEC's collective stockpile. Iran also has over 18.2 percent of the world natural

145 Farhad Iranpour, 'Different Types of Oil Contract; the Evolution of Oil Contracts from Barter to Joint Ventures' (2008) 38(2) *Fasl nameye Hoquq* 153.

146 Zabbah, above n 120, 13.

gas reserves.[147] As such, Iran ranks among the world's top three holders of both proven oil and natural gas reserves. However, despite its many advantages (see Section 6.3), the rate of production in Iran compared to global production is not adequate. Therefore, modernising Iran's oil and gas contract frameworks and regulations is imperative.

6.5.1 Modernising Iran's oil and gas contract framework

For Iran, development of the oil and gas industry requires almost $200 billion[148] for the exploration, development and production of the oil and gas fields to increase the oil output by one million barrels per day and natural gas by two hundred and 50 million cubic meters.[149] Iran also needs up to $100 billion of investment in the medium term to raise production capacity to an ideal level of seven million barrels per day in 2020.[150] Undoubtedly, this level investment cannot be provided by Iran itself and thus requires contributions from foreign investors. Such investment would lead to economic growth, promote technology and consequently improve the quality of productions, increase employment opportunities, raise exports and help Iran enter into international markets.

It is, however, questionable as to whether Iran's oil sector can absorb this amount of investment under the current legal framework. Does the current buy-back agreement provide enough incentives for IOCs to cooperate? The buy-back contract system is believed to be sub-optimal. Based on the current level of foreign investment in Iran's oil and gas industry, the buy-back contract is not investor-friendly enough and does not provide investors with the certainty they seek compared to the alternatives; namely, the PSA and NCC. Iran should therefore look to create modern oil and gas frameworks if its intentions are to achieve a sustainable oil and gas industry.

The oil and gas contract framework in Iran needs to be elaborated to encourage foreign investment, but this is an extremely difficult task. In practical terms, Iran's oil and gas contracts should be preserved the following three principles:

- Safeguard the national sovereignty
- Maintain control and management
- Grant long operational phases to IOCs by extending the contract period

147 *BP statistical Review of World Energy* (June 2017) <www.bp.com>.

148 Director of Strategic Planning of the Ministry of Oil, 'Chesh-andaz Jazb Sarmaye Khareji dar Naft' (Speech delivered at the Fars News Agency, Tehran, November of 2015) <http://www.farsnews.com/newstext.php?nn=13940603001049> (in Farsi).

149 *Law of the Fifth Five-Year Economic, Social and Cultural Development Plan* 2010–2015 (Iran) art 125(a).

150 Mirmoezi, 'Role of Middle Eastern NOCs in World Oil Industry and Necessity of Structural Reforms and Productivity' (Paper presented at the Ninth International IIES Conference, Proceedings of the Conference, Tehran, Iran, 2004).

Meanwhile, Iran's oil and gas contract framework should consider the need for the rapid infusion of capital, expertise and technology to meet the demands for modernisation. Foreign investment in Iran would clearly increase if the country offered more flexibility in the oil and gas contract frameworks and moved towards contracts that were inherently more flexible than current oil and gas contract in Iran.

6.5.2 Modernising Iran's oil and gas regulation

The failure of the current oil and gas contract to attract sufficient investment, as well as the ever-increasing need for foreign investment and to increase domestic consumption, necessitate the modernisation of the legal system in Iran. Modernising Iran's oil and gas regulations involves a new form of oil and gas contract to attract local and foreign investment. As previously discussed, there is growing recognition that Iran needs to do more to attract IOCs to maintain or even increase current production levels. Some of the changes require legislative reform. Therefore, changes need to be made to the regulatory frameworks to allow for contracts that are more favourable to foreign investors, especially as more and more petroleum reservoirs are being depleted.[151]

Furthermore, highly unfavourable contracts have so far deprived the Iran of much-required FDI in gas and petroleum related projects. This is especially true when non-unitised common oil and gas reservoirs are concerned such as the South Pars which create a competition between the country and its neighbours.[152] However, there appear to be three reasons why Iran will modernise its regulatory framework in the future:

1 Reviewing the history of legislation, particularly *the Petroleum Act 2011* and the *Duty and Authorities of Oil Ministry Act 2012*, towards to foreign investment can attract and utilise new oil and gas contract methods in Iran
2 Consciousness of the governor and nation
3 Iranian authorities tend to introduce more successful contractual mechanism

These reasons show that current regulations and the broader regulatory framework are ready to be modernised. The changes already made, although quite promising in some respects, remain insufficient to significantly alter the pace of foreign investment in the Iranian upstream oil and gas industry. However, some of the changes so far could accelerate the modernisation of Iran's legal frameworks. Perhaps the most often mentioned concern in the barriers section[153] can be resolved by either regulatory reform or the approval a new legislation.

151 Iranpour, above n 145, 161.
152 Common oil and gas reservoir in South Pars is common between Iran, Iraq and Qatar.
153 See Section 6.3.2.

First, the issue surrounding Iran's pessimistic perspective could be resolved by holding international conferences and seminars, as well as the use of mass media, websites and other instruments.[154]

Second, the legal system needs to be reformed. The overall trend in Iran's recent legal developments places emphasis on making Iran more business friendly. Iranian authorities realise the need for intensive (foreign and domestic) private sector activity and appreciate that the required level of such activity can only be achieved with the necessary regulations, and political and economic reforms in place. However, based on the current NCC, some clearer and more transparent legal and regulation frameworks should be enacted.

Third, is the use of concession as mentioned in Article 81 of the Constitution[155] and Article 2(c) of FIPPA.[156] Article 81 prohibits the government from giving foreigners the right to form companies or institutions dealing with mineral extraction.[157] Nevertheless, there was a limit on the number of foreign shares permitted for purchase in Iranian companies according to the company's registration Act. Based on the dominant interpretation of the FIPPA, this restriction has been abolished and this allows foreign companies to have 100 percent foreign investment, a practice currently being implemented. Also, despite the definition of concession in Article 2(c) of FIPPA, this issue has not been resolved.

It should be noted that most countries granted the first oil concessions because of their under-development lacked the required infrastructure to perform the oil operations and to deliver oil to domestic and international markets. Therefore, concession holders, in addition to the oil concession, were permitted by the host state to construct roads, railways, airports, ports and quays.

It is expected that the construction of such installations is welcome in the host country to demonstrate signs of development. However, the mistrust and pessimism surrounding the imperialistic goals of foreign companies and their national governments has seen such clauses regarded as incompatible with the concession system and national sovereignty. The stigma associated with the 'concession' term was such that English companies also avoided using the word when the 1933 concession was in force. In addition, the word 'convention' was used in official correspondence and this became the established term for this contract form in different political, legal and academic settings in the West.[158] With negative impressions of the concession so strong, new titles are applied in contracts

154 Ezzatollah Taher Estakhti, *Concession on Tract and Its Legal Evolution* (Dissertation for LLM of Public Law, Shahid Beheshti Law Faculty, 1999) 74.

155 This article states: The granting of concessions to foreigners for the formation of companies or institutions dealing with commerce, industry, agriculture, services or mineral extraction, is absolutely forbidden.

156 *The FIPP2002*, above n 106, art 2(c).

157 *Iranian Constitution 1979*, above n 90, art 81.

158 William W Jr Bishop, 'The Anglo-Iranian Oil Company Case' (1951) 45(4) *The American Journal of International Law* 749.

currently concluded that have the concession element such as concessionary contracts or licenses.[159]

To modernise Iran's oil and gas legislations, the following steps should be taken:

- Reform the legal obstacles which forbid foreign investment ownership of the well-head or the reservoir
- Revise the regulations which prevent from foreign investment
- Codify an energy strategy by oil and gas authorities
- Clarify a comprehensive plane for national consumption
- Parliament should pass laws and legislation to protect the security of investments and to encourage foreign investment

6.6 Proposing new concession contract (NCC) framework

The main purpose of this section is to propose the NCC framework according to three key considerations: ownership of the oil contract; governmental control and management of oil production and the fiscal regime related to such matters as taxation, royalty and bonus payments.

6.6.1 Ownership of oil and gas in NCC

Ownership of oil in the NCC is divided into two phases: phase one whereby the oil is still in reservoir and in place and phase two when the oil at the well-head. In phase one, the host country maintains ownership of the oil and the concessionaire, despite having exploration and production rights, does not have any right over ownership.[160] In the Oil Acts of some countries, for instance, England's *Petroleum Act 1934* and *Continental Shelf Act 1964*, it states "produced oil in territorial seas and the Continental Shelf belongs to the King".[161] In the second phase, ownership of oil at the well-head is transferred to concessionaire in the NCC.

Therefore, soon after exploitation the oil could be transferred to the concessionaire and IOC after payment of its fiscal commitments to the host country.

159 Taher Estakhti, above n 154, 22.

160 For example: when the NCC was introduced in Brazil (2003) the nation's Constitution (and its *Oil Act*) stated; "the reserves of oil, natural gas and other liquid hydrocarbons existing in the Brazilian national territory, which includes the inland, territorial sea, continental shelf and exclusive economic zone, belong to the federal government" *Brazil's Constitution of 1988 with Amendments through 2014* (Brazil) Articles 20 and 176. (To view the Constitution in English, this is accessible at: <https://www.constituteproject.org/constitution/Brazil_2014.pdf> (accessed 03/05/2017)).

161 *The Petroleum Act 1934* (England), (to view the Petroleum Act 1934, this is accessible at: <http://emrd.portal.gov.bd/sites/default/files/files/emrd.portal.gov.bd/law/c7c4688a_97f6_4442_a417_b4c054cd1a06/petroleumact1934.pdf>).

Whereas, the NCC has the advantage in that the host country could receive oil instead of cash in its fiscal rights from the concessionaire. Moreover, the IOC commits to providing domestic markets as well. This has led to a trend in governments utilising the NCC.[162]

6.6.2 Control and management over oil operations

Controlling and managing oil operations is an important aspect of the host country's sovereignty over its resources. However, developing countries lack the quite fiscal, technological and management knowledge capacity to implement oil operations effectively, and so they vest these affairs to qualified companies who they are satisfied can control the operations.[163]

Some control and management mechanisms are as follows.

6.6.2.1 Control over tender phase

In the CCC, the process for granting concession was simple. The King or governor made the decision to grant a sector of his land to concessionaire and it was done by the signing. However, in the modern NCC, the process for granting the concession is different in that it is implemented via a bidding process. The host country is therefore able to maintain control over the oil operation by way of the pre-defined bidding terms.

The bidding practice to grant a petroleum concession follows from the publication of an international invitation. When foreign oil companies are invited to submit applications they participate in a sealed competitive bidding process.[164] The biddable items include the exploration programme, work expenditure, special advantages, etc. An applicant for a concession must be a company with assets, equipment and expertise, and evidence of its capabilities to produce petroleum.[165]

6.6.2.2 Work programme presentation

One of the phases in which the host country can exercise supervision over its oil operation is when confirming the work programme presented by the concessionaire. According the NCC, the oil operation is divided to the exploration phase and production phases. In turn, the concessionaire should present two individual work programmes for each phase. The work programme must be accompanied

162 F Ameri and M Shirmardi, 'The New Concession Agreements and the Interests of Oil Producer Countries: With Specific Reference to Ownership of the Oil, Host State's Control and Management and the Fiscal Regime of the Agreements' (2016) 4(15) *Journal of Private Law Research* 73.

163 Ibid. 76.

164 In the Thailand NCC case.

165 As in UK and Brazilian NCC cases.

by a proposal for work and expenditures in relation to the area comprised in the block(s) covered.[166]

The concessionaire shall carry out the work programme before the expiry of the initial term of the license. For instance, in the UK, the Ministry of Trade and Industry may at any time serve notice on the concessionaire requiring him to submit an appropriate exploration work programme with respect to a specified period that should fall within the term of the license. If the Minister notifies the concessionaire that he believes the programme submitted by the concessionaire does not satisfy the relevant requirements, the letter must either submit the matter to the arbitration or submit to the Minister an amended programme that satisfies the relevant requirements.

The work programme should specify the following:

- The relevant works the concessionaire proposes to erect or carry out
- The proposed location of the works
- The maximum and minimum quantities of petroleum and gas which in each calendar year or each such period as specified by the Minister and concessionaire[167]

6.6.2.3 Operation progress report and inspection over concessionaire activities

The concessionaire is obliged to submit its petroleum and gas operation progress report to the government. The submission requirement has been expanded to include a detailed report of the petroleum operation results. For instance, in Thailand:

> The petroleum operation progress reports submitted by the concessionaire to the government were treated as confidential for two years from the date of expiry or upon revocation of the contract. Since 1990, the period of confidentiality for the progress reports, production plan and results reports of petroleum operations has been reduced from the original two years from the end of the concession to one year from the date of receipt.[168]

Also, the host country has the right to assign a representative to inspect the concessionaire's oil and gas operational activities. For instance, in Brazil:

> The ANP, directly or through agreements with entities in the states or the federal district, will follow-up and oversee the operation performed in the

166 Ameri and Shirmardi, above n 162, 76.
167 Work programme is already fulfilling in Brazil, Norway and Australia NCC case.
168 Gauult Ian Townsend, 'The Malaysia/Thailand Development Agreement' in Hazal Fox (eds), *Joint Development of Offshore Oil and Gas* (British Institute of International and Comparative Law, 1990) 122.

concession area with the purpose of assuring that the concessionaire is fully and rigorously complying with its obligations under the terms of this agreement and applicable Brazilian legislation.[169]

6.6.2.4 Government participation

The government has the authority to demand as a condition of the grant or license that the state itself or a wholly state-owned enterprise designated for the purpose participates in the venture. This demand for state participation in the license and the venture may be satisfied by the applicant by accepting the state or the designated state enterprise as a co-licensee and by establishing a JV agreement, also known as a state participation agreement. The modes of state participation included in the state participation agreement concern:

i The percentage share from state participation (whether fixed for the duration of the agreement or made dependent on factors such production levels, etc.)
ii The timing of when the state's financial participation becomes effective. A choice must be made between the state participation financial contribution (in accordance with its percentage participation) to start either from the very beginning of authorised operations (i.e. at the start) or not before the first commercial discovery has been made.[170]

The percentage share of state participation may be fixed in law or as a standard condition of the license or state participation agreement. Alternatively, it may be negotiated in the context of a bidding round and so become a condition of the license concerned as is implemented in the UK[171] and Norway.[172]

The government's aims to participate in oil and gas operations are related to political agendas, control over the oil and gas industry, a desire to avoid foreign

169 Federal Republic of Brazil, Ministry of Mines and Energy, *Concession Agreement for the Exploration, Development and Production of Oil and Natural Gas* (2008) clause 14.1 <http://www.eisourcebook.org/cms/Brazil,%20Model%20Concession%20Agreement,%20ANP%2010th%20Rnd,%202008.pdf>.

170 Ameri and Shirmardi, above n 162, 82–85.

171 In the UK, after the *Petroleum and Submarine Pipe-Lines Act 1975* created the British National Oil Corporation (BNOC), the requirements regarding participation by the corporation in the licensee were stipulated as a condition in the *London Gazette*. Under the 5th and 6th round (1976–1979), 51 percent participation by the BNOC was included in the license, if so desired by this corporation, and was made obligatory.

172 The Norwegian government can directly participate in the proceeds arising from the exploration of oil and gas fields under the State Direct Financial Interest (SDFI). This is managed by an entity called Petoro whose participation is decided at the time the licenses are awarded and varies from field to field according to the state's preferences. Once the relevant participation is decided, Petoro behaves like any other licensee; paying its share of costs and participating proportionately in production. This arrangement allows the state to adjust the amount of risk that it wishes to undertake while maintaining a licensing regime.

domination and economic requirements as well as to supply domestic markets, get access to technical skills and knowledge in fulfilling of operations and to access the amount of produced oil.

6.6.3 Financial regime in NCC

In an oil and gas contract, the financial regime plays an important role in determining the mechanism by which profits and losses are shared by the parties.[173] In every oil and gas investment contract, financial clauses dictate revenue distribution and division of risk between the parties and are thus the pillar of each contract. The following sections briefly explain some of the elements of the financial system:

6.6.3.1 Bonus

The bonus is the amount offered by the winning bidder in the proposal for the concession of crude oil and natural gas. The bonus is divided into:

- Signature bonus – the amount offered by the bidder to explore and produce the field, paid when the concession agreement is signed.[174]
- Production bonus – the amount offered in each phase of operations after the exploration phase and commercial fields have achieved a certain production level.

The bonus might be fixed by the agreement or open to negotiation. In addition, the bonus increases the government's bargaining power to take into consideration the importance of oil and gas fields.[175]

6.6.3.2 Royalty

The royalty is a financial compensation to be paid monthly by the concessionaires operating each field. It starts in the month of the respective start-up production date, without the allowance of any deductions. The most common type of payment to the host country made under the concession framework is a royalty, to the extent that the financial framework of the concession contracts supports a royalty. In fact, a royalty was initially the sole payment.

A royalty in the NCC compared to the CCC is basically on the produced production and not profits made by the company. This is unpleasant for the IOC,

173 Le leuch Honore, 'Contractual Flexibility in New Petroleum Contracts' in Nicky Bredjick and Thomas Walde (eds), *Petroleum Investment Policies in Developing Countries* (Graham and Trotman, 1998) 91–93.

174 The signature bonus is the value paid by the company that wins the auction of the determined area of concession.

175 Le leuch, above n 173, 132–136.

especially in areas where production costs are high. Thus, companies tend to pay only part of the host state revenues in the form of royalty so that a royalty will not be the sole source of the host stage income. Therefore, the NCC is the preferred legal regime for Iranian oil and gas fields with no exploration record and high exploration and production costs like in mountain regions.

A royalty constitutes a number between 10 percent and 15 percent of the product. Oil-rich countries, however, design various royalties, paying attention to different strategies for the development of oil fields and the established financial systems in these countries. For example, in Brazil all fields in production currently pay the maximum 10 percent rate; whereas in the US, the oil field owners sometimes submit their fields at auction with a rate of up to 50 percent. In contrast, New Guinea demands a royalty of 1.25 percent and the UK government has abrogated a royalty rate system for new fields since 1982.[176]

In some contracts, a royalty is calculated as a fixed sum for every ton of production; whereas in others, a percentage of the concessionaire's profits is preferred. Indeed, instead of a fixed sum royalty, a sliding scale at specified production levels has been introduced such as the sliding scale in Thailand.[177]

A royalty system has advantages for both parties (especially for some developing countries like Iran) in that relying on the extracted product for the purpose of calculating host state royalty, there is no more need for drawn out accountancy practices to calculate the net income of the company. This has the added advantage for the investing company that host state government bodies have no excuse to supervise the operations of the company and to audit its financial statements to determine the real income of the company.[178]

6.6.3.3 *Taxation*

The rate of taxation for IOCs depends on general income taxation legislation or on specific legislation for petroleum taxation. As in the NCC model in Brazil; "the concessionaire shall be subject to the tax regime at the federal, state and municipal levels, being obligated to comply with their terms, timing and conditions defined by the applicable Brazilian legislation".[179]

According to these legislations, the rate of tax might be different. The concessionaire is subject to payment of petroleum income tax which has remained at a rate of 50 percent of net profit derived from the petroleum business, or 35 percent of profit plus a 23.08 percent remittance tax is the highest among the Asian countries. In the US the rate of income taxation on oil company production is 46 percent, in the UK during the 1960s it decreased from more than 50 percent

176 Keith W. Blinn et al (eds), *International Petroleum Exploration & Exploitation Agreements: Legal, Economic, and Policy Aspects* (Barrows Company Inc, 2nd ed, 2009) 228.

177 As stated in the previous Chapter 4, Table 4.2.

178 Blinn et al, above n 176, 229.

179 Federal Republic of Brazil, above n 465, clause 25.1. <http://www.eisourcebook.org/cms/Brazil,%20Model%20Concession%20Agreement,%20ANP%2010th%20Rnd,%202008.pdf>.

to 30 percent.[180] In Norway, the rate is between 30 percent and 50 percent, and in Pakistan it is around 40 percent.[181] Normally the government decreases the tax rate to leverage incentives. The reason behind this might be the desire of the government to compete for investments and to attract more exploration activities in high cost areas; coupled with the low oil prices at the time.[182]

Taxation as a concessionaire obligation is a substantial part of the NCC. It has two advantages: first, the government takes a substantial rate of profit as taxation; and second, by separating high profit fields from low profit fields, the government can take more tax from the high profit fields.[183]

Other taxation called a *windfall profit tax* is a new supplementary taxation in cases where profits accruing to foreign investors exceed certain limits. The objective of tax diversification is to increase the host country's revenue in relation to the profitability of petroleum operations.

6.6.3.4 Annual benefit

The annual benefit places an obligation on the concessionaire to not claim expenses exceeding a certain amount[184] of the value of petroleum sold or disposed of, excluding royalties and agreed-upon bonuses, during any given year. If expenses are higher than the specified percentage, payment of an amount equivalent to the excess is required as an annual benefit. However, should the deductible costs claimed in each year be less than or exactly equal to certain amounts of the petroleum proceeds, then no annual benefit is payable to the government. This annual benefit is a cost control device as it penalises the concessionaire should it claim expenses higher than the stated percentage of the value of petroleum sold or disposed of in any given year. Such a mechanism is seldom employed in the international petroleum industry.

Thus, produced oil belongs to the IOC after payment of bonus, royalty, taxation, windfall profit tax and annual benefit to host country. The NCC indicates clearly the amount required to be of benefit to the host country. Moreover, the advantages of the NCC can be considered in relation to two more items:

180 Rate of Oil Company's income tax was over 50 percent before 1986 under the Petroleum Revenue Tax (PRT) rate, 30 percent since April 1999 under the Ring-Fence corporation tax rate, and 20 percent since April 2002 under the supplementary charge rate.

181 Global Oil and Gas Tax Guide (2016) 421 and 432 <http://www.ey.com/Publication/vwLUAssets/EY-2016-Global-oil-and-gas-tax-guide/$FILE/EY-2016-Global-oil-and-gas-tax-guide.pdf>.

182 Rami, Abdulkarim, 'The Fiscal Tools in the UK Petroleum Licensing, How Did the UK Attract Investments and What are the Effects of Changing Terms?' (2009) 12(24) *Center of Energy, Petroleum and Mineral Law and Policy* 17.

183 For instance, in Thailand it ranges from 17 percent to 40 percent for small and low profit fields, and from 35 percent to 65 percent for large and more profitable fields.

184 For instance, in Thailand the amount is 19 percent of the value of sold petroleum.

6.6.4 Build-Operate-Transfer (BOT)

One of the most evident types of NCC is BOT. It is very widespread in hydro-electric industry and can also be implemented in the oil industry. This mechanism is a popular tool for financing infrastructure projects. In this type of contract in the oil industry, a consortium can finance the project and perform exploration and exploitation operations within a fixed period. The consortium can pay off its costs and collect the determined profit out of the revenue gained by the project. After termination of the contract, ownership goes back to the host state.

6.6.5 Leasing and license

Other types of NCC more widespread in the oil industry are the leasing agreement and license agreement. In these contracts, ownership of the oil reserves remains with the host state; whereas, the profits from extraction belong to the foreign company. In the leasing agreements, ownership is transferred to the company throughout the duration of the contract; whereas in the license agreements the right to exploit the resources is granted in a limited manner and within the granted license. NCCs are most common in developed countries for political and social reasons.

6.7 Conclusion

The NCC has advantages for the contemporary Iranian upstream oil and gas industry compared to other contractual forms. However, Iran has a unique and distinctive Constitution and legal system. Petroleum and other natural resource laws were developed in an era of strong nationalism as a part of the revolution and response to past abuses by IOCs. Some of the legal barriers to the adoption of the NCC, as a preferred contractual framework, have been considered in this chapter. It has been argued that these barriers can and should be overcome.

The NCC is the preferred arrangement for Iran's oil and gas industry when one consider the issues of ownership, government control and management over oil operations, and the nation's fiscal system. In ownership, the government remains owner of the oil if it is not produced and in government control and management they obtain the right over the exploration and exploitation of their resources. In the fiscal system, involving such matters as taxation, bonuses and royalty, all NCC changes favoured the host country.

Thus, it seems that utilisation of the NCC is permitted in Iran's oil and gas industry implicitly regarding to Constitution, FIPPA, fifth five-ears development plan, and the laws to modify the *Petroleum Act 2011* and the *Duty and Authorities of Oil Ministry Act 2012*. The nature and efficiency of the NCC in Iran's oil and gas industry demonstrates that it is the most appropriate contract form in relation to other issues such as priority of common reservoirs, high cost of investment in oil project, the high-risk factors, limited annual budgets, the geological conditions of the oil fields, and lack of exploration record in many of the regions. Further reforms of Iran's oil and gas contractual frameworks and regulations, and modification of the NCC to meet future needs for the development of Iran's upstream oil and gas industry to comply with Iran's legal framework should be urgent priorities.

7 Conclusion

7.1 Financial issue

A foreign company may not be satisfied with the return of capital in addition to profits from the exploitation of oil and may expect to receive determined revenue independently from the financed project.

State control over all oil production stages, but especially upstream stages, has always been viewed as a target and has some historical credence. However, regard should be given to the high investment costs associated with oil projects as well as the significant risks involved. Governments are generally hesitant to invest public funds in fields where the profitability and return of the capital is doubtful. In addition, oil-rich countries like Iran generally lack the required financial resources for infrastructure investments. In fact, a considerable issue which make conditional the type of involvement and participation states can facilitate in oil and gas contracts is the lack of willingness to make the investment and to assume the risks of the project. The result has been a distortion of negotiations between host country governments and foreign companies, particularly over aspects of financing, infrastructure and the allocation of project risks.

The main result of this position adopted by host countries is the incorporation of a clause into the contracts concluded by states, irrespective of which framework they lie in, which determines that the operating company incurs exploration phase costs up to the time the production becomes commercial. In addition, the state is obligated to pay off the foreign company's investment costs only in cases where the operations achieved the desired result. For this reason, the oil-producing states may be eager to participate in the investment, but will not agree to take investment risks and losses related to the project. Rather, they seek immunity against such matters with the investing company, or the contractor, to bear the investment costs. Therefore, the oil-producing states preferred a contractual form which exempted them from heavy costs of investment while still providing them with a significant share of the profits of the project.

7.2 Geological factors

In this respect, the study of geological conditions of oil fields shows that, in recent decades, only a rather small proportion of resources has been extracted and exploited. As such, large oil fields have remained unexplored, or unused, particularly due to lack of sufficient capital and the preparedness of domestic companies to take investment risks to capitalise on the oil fields. Oil fields form a considerable part of the Iran plateau. In turn, when their lack of exploration record, the impassibility of many of regions, the lack of necessary infrastructure, remoteness from ports and consumption markets and the high-risk factor of the project are taken into consideration, use of the NCC framework appears to most appropriately address the needs and concerns of the Iranian Government.

However, the need for large investment from companies operating in the global oil and gas industry and the need to address the allocation of associated risks demand reforms to Iran's natural resource laws. This can be achieved by amending statutes and removing legal obstacles to FDI and by countering some of the negative historical attitudes regarding concession. This will require the accumulation of evidence and the generation of debate around the advantages of the NCC and its necessity for foreign investment in oil and gas fields.

7.3 Challenging the *Status Quo*

This book argued that no contract should be accepted or not accepted in Iran on the sole basis of its type and the framework it lies in. The contract type is primarily only the framework for profit sharing between parties. Of most importance, and that which represents exactly the structure of financial relations between the host state and foreign company, is the agreed rates and percentages payable to parties. This then points to the need to determine the exact method for keeping payment records and related costs and the determination of the type of exchange which is valid in relation to the parties.[1]

The domestic legal system and enacted laws in the host country play a vital role in promoting the type of contracts and their provisions. These structures can facilitate the conclusion of a contract or present obstacle on the way to its conclusion. Alternatively, the choice of each contractual framework also provides the parties with a wide range of discretions and impediments in regard to their own interests.[2]

Every country with large oil and gas fields gains provisions for more significant recognition of national interests and profits through the NCC. Indeed, in the NCC they seek to attract investors and maximise profit in a win-win

1 Mahmoud Mansouri Naraghi, *Legal Bases and General Terms of Middle East Oil Contracts* (Bita Publication, 1972) Osool –e- Hoghooghi va Sharayete 'omoomi Ghrardadhaye Nafti Dar Khavar-e- Mianeh1350, 147.

2 Faranak Rabiei, *Contracts Law* (translated by author, Behnami, 2002) 71 [trans of: *Hoghoogh-e-Gharardadha* (1381)] 66–68.

negotiation process with the IOC. For instance, Brazil attempted to achieve these outcomes with its own individual bidding round, royalty, local content percentage and level of remuneration for IOC. Thailand used concessionaire the obligations, financial regimes and the SRB and EBG to achieve these outcomes, and Australia utilised the capacity of the MLR to attract capital from IOCs while developing the oil and gas industry at the same time. Furthermore, the UK used government participation and accurate taxation systems, and Norway has applied important taxation regimes which could be practicable in Iran's oil and gas sectors. Particularly, the NCC can be utilised as one of the most appropriate contract forms in common oil and gas reservoirs to maximise production, as demonstrated by the oil contract pattern in the North Sea (under name of license) and in the Thailand/Malaysia Agreement, Australia/Indonesia Agreement, Australia/East Timor Agreement and Iceland/Norway Agreement.

The NCC has been analysed in this book in regard to the extent to which it facilitates the achievement of developed and developing countries' national interests in facing the risks and opportunities of the globalised oil and gas industry. It was argued that the NCC has distinct advantages over the CCC in this regard. The NCC could be utilised to develop some of Iran's oil and gas joint fields such as the joint gas field between Iran and Qatar. This is the largest gas field in the world. Other joint oil and gas fields Iran currently has are with Iraq, Saudi Arabia, Kuwait, Emirate, Oman, Turkmenistan and Azerbaijan.

7.4 Future proposals of NCC

Different projects require different frameworks as using a single type of contractual form in all projects and contracts is not justifiable. Some fields in Iran are in regions with high cost of investment and with no record of exploration or exploitation. The NCC can potentially provide the platform to achieve the national development goals and to address past concerns about the incompatibility of concession system with national interests.

To use an alternative to the NCC, the Iranian government will have to resort to complicated or indirect mechanisms such as buy-back contracts. On many occasions, the rights and duties of parties are subject to misinterpretation because of the complex structure of such mechanisms. In the NCC, because of its long-term functionality, the rights of parties are more transparent. Furthermore, in case of disputes between the parties over the interpretation of contract provisions, a wide range of legal and judicial precedents and customs exist to help them to obtain a resolution.

The biggest advantage of the NCC for a country like Iran is that the state bears no liability for the different risks inherent to every oil project. This avoids costs which may add pressure to the public budget; and important consideration given the problems faced the Iranian government to regulate public finances. In buy-back systems, the government has also tried to discharge its financial obligations by incorporating relevant clauses into the contracts; whereas, discharge of the state's financial liabilities is an essential element in the concession contract.

Therefore, stringent laws and historical grievances should not lead to the rejection of legal frameworks containing interesting financial packages in an absolute way. Indeed, the current circumstances are different to the time the D'Arcy Contract was concluded. This is primarily because of the establishment of a new political and legal system in the country and full independence from foreign relations. In addition to the shrinking geographical scope of the region, the NCC poses little threat to the territorial integrity and political and economic independence of Iran. As such, the NCC can be an effective tool to attract foreign investments, a desirable objective given that Iran is highly dependent on oil resources and remains behind its competitors in the region such as Saudi Arabia. Thus, in the current context, there is a favourable landscape to benefit from the capacities that exist in NCC frameworks, particularly because the competing contractual forms have not been successful in satisfying the expectations of Iranian experts and authorities.

Further reform (modernisation) of Iran's oil and gas contractual frameworks and regulations should be an urgent priority of the Iranian government. Such reforms must include the modification of the NCC to meet the future development needs of Iran's upstream oil and gas industry to comply with Iran's legal framework.

Bibliography

A Articles/Books/Reports

Abdal-Haqq, Irshad, 'Islamic Law: An Overview of Its Origin and Element' in Hisham Ramadan (ed), *Understanding Islamic Law* (Altamira Press, 2006) 1.

Afkhami, Golam-Reza, *Evolution of Iran's Oil Industry: An Industry's View* (translated by author, Iran's Study Institute, 1978) 84 [trans of: *Tahawwole-e- San'te-e Naft: Negahi az Darun* (1357)].

Ahmadov, Ingilab et al, 'How to Scrutinize a Production Sharing Agreement; A guide for the oil and gas sector based on experience from the Caspian Region' (2012) *International Institute for Environment and Development (IIED).*

Al-Attar, Abdulaziz and Osamah Alomair, 'Evaluation of Upstream Petroleum Agreements and Exploration and Production Costs' (2005) 29(4) *OPEC Review: Energy Economics & Related Issues* 254.

Al-Emadi, Talal, 'Joint Venture Contracts (JVCs) among Current Negotiated Petroleum Contracts: A Literature Overview of JVCs Development, Concept and Elements' (8 November 2012) *Georgetown Journal of International Law Online.*

Alramahi, Mohammad, *Oil and Gas Law in the UK* (Bloomsbury, 2013).

Ameri, Faisal and Mohammad Reza Shirmardi, 'The New Concession Agreements and the Interests of Oil Producer Countries: With Specific Reference to Ownership of the Oil, Host State's Control and Management and the Fiscal Regime of the Agreements' (2015) [Gharardadhaye emtiazi jaded va manafe' Keshvarhay–e Tolid konande Naft (1393) 4(15) *Journal of Private Law Research*] 89.

Amin, Sayed Hassan, *Commercial, Arbitration in Islamic and Iranian Law* (Vahid Publication, 3rd ed, 1988).

Anglo-Persian Oil Company, *Agreement of 28th May, 1901 (the D'Arcy Concession) between, the Governments of His Imperial Majesty the Shah of Persia ad William Knox D'Arcy* (Publisher Is the Company, Digitized 2009).

Ashong, Marcia, 'Cost Recovery in Production Sharing Contract: Opportunity for Striking It Rich or Just Another Risk Not Worth Bearing?' (2011) *Centre of Energy Petroleum and Mineral Law Policy* 2.

Atai, Ardeshir, 'A New Paradigm for Attracting Foreign Investment: Restructuring Investor-State Arbitration for Resolution of Petroleum Dispute: Dynamics of the New Iranian Investment Contract' (2015) 12(2) *Transnational Dispute Management.*

Atighetchi, Dariusch, *Islamic Bioethics: Problems and Perspectives* (Springer, 2007).

Azadi, Kamran and Mohammad H. Yarmohammadi, 'Analysis of Iran's Crude Oil Export Future Capacity' (2011) 39(6) *Energy Policy Journal* 33.

Baderin, Mashood, *International Human Rights and Islamic Law* (Oxford University Press, 2003).

Bamberg, John, *The History of the British Petroleum Company* (Cambridge University Press, 1994).

Barrows Company, *World Petroleum Arrangements* (Barrows Company Inc, 1989).

Batista, Ana et al, 'Cross Border Unitisation and Joint Development Agreement: An International Perspective' (2007) 29 *Houston Journal of International Law* 411.

Bindemann, Kristen, *Production-Sharing Agreements an Economic Analysis* (Oxford Institute for Energy Studies, 1999).

Birnie, Patricia and Alan Boyle, *International Law and the Environment* (Oxford University Press, 3rd ed, 2009).

Blinn, Keith W et al (eds), *International Petroleum Exploration & Exploitation Agreements: Legal, Economic, and Policy Aspects* (Barrows Company Inc, 2nd ed, 2009).

Bowett, Derek William, 'State Contracts with Aliens: Contemporary Developments on Compensation for Termination or Breach' (1988) 59 *British Year Book of International Law* 49.

Bradbrook, Adrian, 'The Relevance of the Cuius est Solum Doctrine to the Surface Landowner's Claims to Natural Resources Located Above and Beneath His Lands' (1988) 11 *Adelaide Law Review* 462.

Brexendorf, Alexander et al, 'The Iranian Buy-Back Approach' (2009) 7(1) *Oil, Gas & Energy Intelligence* 22.

Bunter, Michael, *The Promotion and Licensing of Petroleum Prospective Acreage* (Kluwer Law International, 2002).

Bunter, Mike, 'Sovereignty over Minerals and Petroleum in the Islamic Law and the Question of Ownership' (2006) 4(1) *Oil, Gas &Energy Law Intelligence.*

Bunter, Michael A G, 'The Iranian Buy Back Agreement' (2009) 3(1) *Oil, Gas & Energy Law Intelligence.*

Burmester, Henry, 'The Zone of Co-Operation between Australia and Indonesia: A Preliminary Outline with Particular Reference to Applicable Law' in Hazal Fox (ed), *Joint Development of Offshore oil and Gas* (British Institute of International and Comparative Law, 1990) 128.

Burns, Robert E, *Introduction to Research Methods* (Longman, Cheshire, 4th ed, 2000).

Cameron, Peter, 'North Sea Oil Licensing: Comparisons and Contrasts' (1985) 4 *Oil & Gas and Law Taxation Review.*

Campbell, Henry, *Black's Law Dictionary* (MINN West, 4th ed, 1951).

Carlston, Kenneth S, 'International Role of Concession Agreements' (1958) 52 *Northwestern University Law Review* 618.

Chandler, Albert T, 'Current Development in the Thai Petroleum Concession' (1988) *Oil and Gas Law and Taxation Review* 7.

Chandler, Albert T, 'Evolution of the Thai Petroleum Concession' (1987/88) 10 *Oil & Gas Law & Taxation Review* 10.

Chandler, Albert T, 'The Thai Petroleum Concession' (1984) 2 *Journal of Energy and Natural Resources.*

Chandler, Albert T, 'Thailand: Oil and Gas Concessions Special Conditions', (1985) 3 *Journal of Energy and Natural Resources.*

Chapman, Simon, 'Oil in Middle East and North Africa' in Lucy Dean (ed), *The Middle East and North Africa 2004* (Europa Publication, 50th ed, 2004) 321.

Corley, Thomas Anthony Buchanan, *A History of the Burmah Oil Company* (London, Heinemann, 1983).

Coulson, Noel J, *History of Islamic Law* (Edinburgh University Press, First Transaction Paperback Printing, 2011).

Crommelin, Michael, 'The Legal Character of Resource Titles' (1998) 17 *Australian Mining and Petroleum Law Journal* 57.

Daintith, Terence, *Finders Keepers? How the Law of Capture Shaped the World Oil Industry* (RFF Press, 2010).

Daintith, Terence et al (eds), *United Kingdom Oil & Gas Law* (Sweet & Maxwell, 2nd ed, 1984).

Daintith, Terence, Geoffrey Willoughby, and Adrian Hill, *United Kingdom Oil and Gas Law* (Sweet & Maxwell, 3rd ed, 2009).

Dam, Kenneth W, 'The Evolution of North Sea Licensing Policy in Britain and Norway', (1974) 17(2) *Journal of Law and Economics* 213.

Davis, Jerome, *Does One Size Fit All? Reflecting on Governance and North Sea Licensing Systems*, 2004, Background Paper: BC Offshore: Potential and Problems a MASC Workshop for Lawyers, Dunsmuir lodge, Sidney BC, 18–21 March 2004.

Deuteronomy [Correspondence] (1931) 47 *Law Quarterly Review*.

Dien, Mawil, *Islamic Law: From Historical Foundations to Contemporary Practice* (Edinburgh University Press, 2004).

Duval, Claude et al, *International Petroleum Exploration and Exploitation Agreement* (Barrows Company Inc, 2nd ed, 2009).

Ebrahimi, Seyed Nasrollah and Abdolhossein Shiroui, 'The Contractual Form of Iran's Buy-Back Contracts in Comparison with Production Sharing and Service Contract' (2003) 2 *SPE International Society of Petroleum Engineers*.

El Chiati, Ahmed Zaki, *Protection of Investment in the Context of Petroleum Agreement* (1987) Brillonline Revise Works 204 Hague Recueil Des Cours <http://referenceworks.brillonline.com/entries/the-hague-academy-collected-courses/protection-of-investment-in-the-context-of-petroleum-agreements-volume-204-ej.9789024737420.009_170>.

Elm, Mostafa, *Oil, Power, and Principle: Iran's Oil Nationalization and Its Aftermath* (Syracuse University Press, 1992).

Entessar, Nader, 'Criminal Law and the Legal System in Revolutionary Iran' (1988) 8(1) *Third World Law Journal*.

Esmaeili, Hossein, 'Boundaries of Land, Fixtures and Ownership of Minerals and Resources' in Hossein Esmaeili and Brendan Grigg (eds), *The Boundaries of Australian Property Law* (Cambridge University Press, 2016) 95.

Farnejad, Hooman, 'How Competitive Is the Iranian Buy-Back Contracts in Comparison to Contractual Production Sharing Fiscal Systems?' (2009) 7(1) *Oil, Gas and law Intelligence*.

Farrokhrouz, Mehran, 'Foreign Investment Contracts in Oil and Gas Sector' (2015) 8(5) *Humanities and Social Sciences*.

Fatouros, Arghyrios A, 'Government Guarantees to Foreign Investors' (1962) 63(3) *Colombia Law Review*.

Ferrier, Ronald W, *The History of the British Petroleum Company* (Cambridge University Press, 1982).

Fischer, Peter and Thomas Waelde, *A Collection of International Concessions and Related Instruments* (London Oceana, 3rd ed, 1982).

Gary, James H et al, *Petroleum Refining Technology and Economics* (Taylor & Francis, 2007).

Gasiorowski, Mark, *Mohammad Mosaddeq and the 1953 Coup in Iran* (Taylor & Francis, 4th ed, 2009).

Geiger, Rainer, 'The Unilateral Change of Economic Development Agreements' (1974) 23(1) *The International and Comparative Law Quarterly* 73.

Geiger, Rainer and Aril Seren, *Basic Elements of a Law on Concession Agreements* (Organization for Economic Co-Operation and Development (OECD), Multilateral Centre for Private Sector Development Istanbul, 2001).

Glenn, Patrick, *Legal Traditions of the World* (Oxford University Press, 5th ed, 2014).

Gordon, Greg, ' Petroleum Licensing' in Greg Gordon, John Paterson and Emek Usenmez (eds), *Oil and Gas Law Current Practice and emerging Trends* (Dundee University Press, 2001) 65.

Goudarzi, Z, 'The Effects of New Legislations on Iranian Buybacks' (2014) 11(5) *Oil, Gas & Energy Law Intelligence.*

Gray, Kevin, 'Property in Thin Air' (1991) 50(2) *Cambridge Law Journal.*

Greig, Donald W, *International Law* (Butterworths, 2nd ed, 1976).

van Groenendaal, Willem J H and Mohammad Mazraati, 'A Critical Review of Iran's Buyback Contracts' (2006) 34(1) *Energy Policy Journal.*

Guasch, J Luis et al, 'Renegotiation of Concession Contracts in Latin America' (2008) *International Journal of Industrial Organization.*

Haddadi, Mahdi, 'The Nature of Iranian Petroleum Contracts in Upstream Section' (2015) 44 *International Letters of Social and Humanistic Sciences* 45.

Hallaq, Wael B, *An Introduction to Islamic Law* (Cambridge University Press, 2009).

Hanssensvei, Olav, 'General Information on the Norwegian Regulatory Regime Pertaining to Fiscal Measurement of Oil and Gas from the Norwegian Continental Shelf' (2014) *The Norwegian Petroleum Directorate* <http://www.npd.no/global/engelsk/5-rules-and-regulations/fiscal-measurement/fiskal-measurement.pdf>.

Heiss, Mary Ann, *Empire and Nationhood: The United States, Great Britain, and Iranian Oil* (Columbia University Press, 1997).

Henniker, Edward, 'Nationalisation: The Anglo-Iranian Oil Company, 1951 Britain vs. Iran' (2013) 2(2) *Moral Cents: The Journal of Ethics in Finance* 16.

Hossain, Kamal, *Law and Policy in Petroleum Development. Changing Relations between Transnationals and Governments* (Nichols Publishing Company, 1979).

Hunt, Michael, *Minerals and Petroleum Law* (Butterworths, 1996).

Hunter, Tina and John Chandler, *Petroleum Law in Australia* (Lexis Nexis, 2013).

Hussain, Jamila, *Islam, Its Law and Society* (Federation Press, 2011).

Hutchinson, Terry, *Researching and Writhing in Law* (Thomson Reuters, 3rd ed, 2010).

Johnston, Daniel, *International Petroleum Fiscal Systems and Production Sharing Contracts* (Pennwell, 2nd ed, 1994).

Jennings, Anthony, *Oil and Gas Exploration Contracts* (Sweet & Maxwell Publish, 2002).

Kamali, Mohammad, *Shari'ah Law: An Introduction* (Oneworld, 2008).

Karine, Mette, 'Norway; Petroleum Regime' (2015) *Ministry of Petroleum and Energy* 8–11. <http://www.congreso.es/docu/docum/ddocum/dosieres/sleg/legislatura_10/spl_76/pdfs/19.pdf>.

Kemp, Alexander G, 'An Assessment of UK North Sea Oil and Gas Policies' (1990) 18(7) *Energy Policy Journal* 599.

'Key World Energy Statistics' (2012) *International Energy Agency* <http://alofatuvalu.tv/FR/12_liens/12_articles_rapports/IEA_rpt_2012_us.pdf>.

Khadduri, Majid, *The Islamic Conceptions of Justice* (Johns Hopkins, 1984).

Khan, Arif, *Concept of Islamic Law* (Pentagon Press, 2007).

Khatinoglu, Dalga, 'Legal Aspects of Iran's New Oil Contracts' (18 July 2016) *Natural Gas Europe* <http://www.naturalgasworld.com/legal-aspects-of-irans-new-oil-contracts-30651>.

Kinzer, Stephen, *All the Shah's Men: An American Coup and the Roots of Middle East Terror* (John Wiley & Sons, 2008).

Kuehne, Gunther, 'Oil and Gas Licensing: Some Comparative United Kingdom German Aspects' (1986) 4(3) *Journal of Energy and Natural Resources Law* 29 and it is published online on (8 June 2015) <https://www.tandfonline.com/doi/abs/10.1080/02646811.1986.11433555>.

Kuhn, Maximilian and Mohammadjavad Jannatifar, 'Foreign Direct Investment Mechanisms and Review of Iran's Buy-Back Contracts: How Far Has Iran Gone and How Far May It Go? (2012) 5(3) *Journal of World Energy Law & Business.*

Le leuch, Honore, 'Contractual Flexibility in New Petroleum Contracts' in Nicky Bredjick and Thomas Walde (eds), *Petroleum Investment Policies in Developing Countries* (Graham and Trotman, 1998) 81.

Le leuch, Honore, 'Recent Trends in Upstream Petroleum Agreements: Policy, Contractual, Fiscal, and Legal Issues' in Andreas Goldthau (ed), *The Handbook of Global Energy Policy* (John Wiley & Sons Ltd, 2013) 127–145.

Lenczowski, George, 'Oil and State in Middle East' (1963) 14(3) *Middle East Journal* 87.

Likosky, Michael B, *Law, Infrastructure, and Human Rights* (Cambridge University Press, 2006).

Lyster, Rosemary and Adrian Bradbrook, *Energy Law and the Environmental* (Cambridge University Press, 2006).

Macini, Paolo and Ezio Mesini, *The Petroleum Upstream Industry: Hydrocarbons Exploration and Production* (Encyclopedia of Life Support Systems (EOLSS), 2008).

Mafi, Homayoun, 'Iran's Concession Agreements and the Role of the National Iranian Oil Company: Economic Development and Sovereign Immunity' (2008) 48 *Natural Resources Journal.*

Mann, Frederick Alexander, *Further Studies in International Law* (Oxford University Press, 1990).

Manning, William, 'Assignment Clauses in Mining and Petroleum Joint Venture' (1986) *AMPLA Yearbook* 119.

Mansouri Nraghi, Mahmoud, *Legal Bases and General Terms of Middle East Oil Contracts*, (Bita Publication, 1972) Osool –e- Hoghooghi va Sharayete 'omoomi Gharardadhaye Nafti Dar Khavar-e- Mianeh1350.

Me, M. 'The Iranian Buyback Model and Its Efficiency in the International Petroleum Market - A Legal View' (2009) 7(1) *Oil, Gas and Law Intelligence.*

Merralls, James, QC, 'Mining and Petroleum Joint Venture in Australia: Some Basic Legal Concepts' (1988) 62 *ALJ.*

Meurs, Pedro Van, 'Financial and Fiscal Arrangements for Petroleum Development on Economic Analysis' in Nicky Beredjick and Thomas Walde (eds) *Petroleum Investment Policies in Developing Countries* (Graham & Trotman, 1988) 47.

Milenkovic, Tamara, 'Drafting an International Buy-Back Agreement' (2004) 2(2) *FACTA Universitatis Series Economic and Organisation.*

Miyoshi, Masahiro, 'The Basic Concept of Joint Development of Hydrocarbon Resources on the Continental Shelfs' (1988) 3(1) *International Journal of Estuarine and Coastal Law.*

Moinifar, Hashmat S. and Amir Ashraf Vaghefi, 'Gamete Donation and the Role of Religious Leaders in Iran' (2010) 8(3) *Journal of Women of the Middle East and the Islamic World* 247.

Mommer, Bernard, Fiscal Regimes and Oil Revenues in the UK, Alaska and Venezuela (Oxford Institute for Energy Studies, 2001).

Nasr, Hossein, *Expectation of the Millennium: Shi'ism in History* (State University of New York Press, 1989).

Nasrollahi Shahri, Nima, 'The Petroleum Legal Framework of Iran: History, Trends and the Way Forward' (2010) 8 *China and Eurasia Forum Quarterly* 111.

Nazhad, Arash. 'The Link between Islamic Law and Hydrocarbon Agreements' (2008) 10(2) *Journal of Islamic Law and Culture*.

O'Connell, Daniel Patrick, 'A Critique of the Iranian Oil Litigation' (1957) 60(4) *The International and Comparative Law Quarterly* 267.

O'Connor, Harvey, How the International Oil Cartel Carved Up the Oil Resources of Iran after the Overthrow of Mossadegh: A Full Account of a Little-Known Story by an Expert in the Oil-Industry Field: The Iranian Oil Grab (American Socialist, 1995).

Omorogbe, Yinka, 'The Legal Framework for the Production for the Petroleum in Nigeria' (1987) 5(4) *Journal for Energy & Natural Resource Law*.

Otman, Waniss A, 'The Iranian Petroleum Contract: Past, Present and Future Perspectives' (2007) 44(5) *Oil, Gas & Energy Law Intelligence*.

Production Sharing Contracts and Concession in the Brazilian Subsalt Region (University of Oslo, 2010).

Pearce, David W (ed), *The MIT Dictionary of Modern Economics* (MIT Press, 1986).

Rabiei, Faranak, *Contracts Law* (Behnami, 2002) 71 [trans of: *Hoghoogh-e- Ghharardadha* (1381)].

Ramazani, Rouhollah K, 'Choice-of-Law Problems and International Oil Contracts: A Case Study' (1962) 11(2) *The International and Comparative Law Quarterly*.

Rami, Abdulkarim, 'The Fiscal Tools in the UK Petroleum Licensing, How Did the UK Attract Investments and What Are the Effects of Changing Terms?' (2009) 12(24) *Center of Energy, Petroleum and Mineral Law and Policy* 12.

Rich, Loretta D, 'American Oil Interests in China' (1983) 119(6) *Loyola of Los Angeles International and Comparative Law Review* <http://digitalcommons.lmu.edu/cgi/viewcontent.cgi?article=1058&context=ilr>.

Roggenkamp, Mike, 'Energy Law in the Netherlands' in Mike Roggenkamp et al (eds), *Energy Law in Europe* (Oxford University Press, 2001) 304.

Rouhani, Foad, *The History of OPEC* (Moanouchehr Roohani trans, 1975) [trans of: Tarikhcheh E OPEC (1353)].

Russell, Brian and others (eds), *An Introduction to Business Law in the Middle East* (Drake, 1976).

Sa Reberio, Marilda Rosaldo, 'The New Oil and Gas Industry in Brazil: An Overview of the Main Legal Aspects' (2001) 36(14) *Texas International Law Journal* 141.

Sanjabi, Karim, *Political Diary* (Zohreh Publication, 1963) [trans of: Khaterat Siasi (1342)].

Sereni, Angelo Piero, *International Economic Institutions and the Municipal Law of States* (Leyden Sijthoff, 1959).

Shafiei Khah, Maryam and Ali Amini, 'Petroleum Contracts in Iran' (2014) 3(3) *European Online Journal of Natural and Social Sciences*.

Shiravi, Abdolhossein and Seyed Nasrollah Ebrahimi, 'Exploration and Development of Iran's Oilfields through Buyback' (2006) 30(3) *Natural Sources Forum*.

Smith, David N. and Louis T. Wells, 'Mineral Agreement in Developing Countries, Structures and Substance' (1975) 69(3) *The American Journal of International Law* 560.

Smith, Ernest E. and John S Dzienkowski, 'A Fifty-Year Prospective on World Petroleum Arrangements (2005) 3(1) *Oil, Gas & Energy Law Intelligence OGEL.*

Sornarajah, Muthucumaraswamy, *The Pursuit of Nationalized Property 79* (Ian Brownlie, 3rd ed, 1986).

Tabataba'i, Hossein, *An Introduction to Shi'i Law* (Ithaca Press, 1984).

Taverne, Bernard, *Petroleum, Industry and Government: A Study of the Involvement of Industry and Governments in Exploring for and Producing Petroleum* (Kluwer Law International, 3rd ed, 2013).

Terki, Nour E, Comment, 'The Algerian Act of 1986 and the Encouragement of Foreign Investment in the Area of Hydrocarbons' (1988) 3(80) *Oil & Gas Law Tax.*

'Thailand Oil Prospects Brighten' (1992) *Oil& Gas Journal* 33 <http://www.ogj.com/articles/print/volume-90/issue-38/in-this-issue/drilling/thailand39s-oil-prospects-brighten.html>.

Toloui, Mahmoud, *Power Game, Oil War in the Middle East* (Elm Publication, 1993).

Townsend, Gauult Ian, 'The Malaysia/Thailand Development Agreement' in Hazal Fox (ed), *Joint Development of Offshore oil and Gas* (British Institute of International and Comparative Law, 1990) 102.

United Nations, Centre on Transnational Corporations, *Alternative Arrangements for Petroleum Development. A Guide for Government Policy-Makers and Negotiators* (UN Publications, 1982).

Vagts, Detlev F, *Transnational Business Problem* (Foundation Press, 1986).

Vassiliou, Marius S, *The A to Z of the Petroleum Industry* (Scarecrow Press, 2009).

Walden, Jerrold L, 'The International Cartel in Iran: Private Power and the Public Interest' (1962) 11 *Journal of Public Law.*

Wall, E H, 'The Iranian-Italian Oil Agreement of 1957' (1958) 7(4) *The International and Comparative Law Quarterly* 736.

World Petroleum Arrangements (The Barrow Company Inc., 1985).

Zabbah, Leila, 'Investment Challenges in Iranian Oil & Gas Sectors – A Legal Approach' (2011) 10 *Institute for International Energy Studies (IIES).*

Zhiguo, Gao, *International Petroleum Contracts* (Graham and Tortman Ltd, 1994).

B Cases

Anglo-Iranian Oil Co. Case (U.K. v. Iran) (Judgment) [1952] ICJ Rep. 501, 521.

Barnard v Monongahela Natural Gas Co (1907) 216 Pa 65 A 810.

Batten Pooll v Kennedy [1907] 1 Ch 256 and *Eardley v Granville* (1876) 3 Ch d 826, 834.

Bocardo SA v Star Energy UK Onshore Ltd [2009] 3 WLR 1010 [59] and [69].

Brown v Humble Oil Co (1935) 126 Tex 296 at 305.

Bury v Pope (1586) Cr Eliz 118; 78 ER 375.

Bush and Bush v Taylor (1981) Warden's Court Report 1.

Case Concerning the Payment in Gold of the Brazilian Federal Loans Issued in France (France v Brazil) (Judgment) [1929] P.C.I.J (Ser. A) Nos. 20/21.

Cross v Mason and CRA Exploration Pty Ltd (1978) Warden's Court Report 22.

Elliff v Texon Drilling (1948) 146 Tex 575.

Lord Provost and Magistrates of Glasgow v Farie (1888) 13 App Cas 657, 689.

Ohio Oil Co v Indiana (1990) US 190.

South Australia Land Commission v Burton and Taylor (1980) Warden's Court Reports 41.

United Dominions Corporation Ltd v Brian Pty Ltd (1985) 157 CLR 1 at 14.

Westen Australia v Ward (2002) 213 CLR 1, 185 [382].

C Legislation

1 Australia

Atomic Energy Act 1953 (Cth).
Crown Lands Act 1989 (NSW).
Crown Lands Alienation Act 1861 (NSW).
Commonwealth Native Title Act 1993.
Constitution Act 1902 (NSW).
Local Government Act 1993 (NSW).
Mine Resources (Sustainable Development) Act 1990.
Mineral Resources Act 1989 (Qld).
Mineral Resources Development Act 1995 (Tas).
Minerals Acquisition Act 1981 (NT).
Mining Act 1971 (SA).
Mining Act 1978 (WA) ss 9(1).
Offshore Petroleum and Greenhouse Gases Storage Act 2006.
Petroleum (Onshore) Act 1991 (NSW).
Petroleum and Geothermal Energy Resources Act 1967 (WA).

2 Brazil

Brazil's Constitution of 1988 with Amendments through 2014.
Federal Republic of Brazil, Ministry of Mines and Energy, *Concession Agreement for the Exploration, Development and Production of Oil and Natural Gas* (2008).
Oil Act 1997.
Oil and Gas Law 2010.

3 Iran

Budget Act of 1994.
Commercial Law 1932.
Direct Taxation Act 1995.
Iranian Constitution 1979.
Law of the Fifth Five-Year Economic, Social and Cultural Development Plan 2010–2015.
Law of the Fifth Five-Year Economic, Social and Cultural Development Plan 2005–2010.
Law Regarding Exploration, Discovery and Extraction of Oil in All Regions of the Country and Continental Shelf 1957.
Mining Law 1998.
Petroleum Act 1957.
Petroleum Law 1974.
Petroleum Law 1987.
The Act to Modify Petroleum Act (1987) 2011.
The Act of Duty and Authorities of Oil Ministry 2012.
The Foreign Investment Promotion and Protection Act 2002.

4 Norway

Petroleum Act 1985.
Petroleum Act 1996.
Petroleum Act 2007.
Petroleum Act 2012.

5 *Thailand*

Ministerial Regulation 1971.
Ministerial Regulation 1989.
Petroleum Act 1971.
Petroleum Act 1988.
Petroleum Income Tax Act 1971.
Triton and Gopher concessions 1987.

6 *United Kingdom*

Budget Act 2011.
Corporation Tax Act 2010.
Finance Act 1993.
Finance Act 1999.
Finance Act 2004.
Finance Act 2007.
Finance Act 2009.
Finance Bill 2011.
Finance Act 2014.
Oil Taxation Act 1975.
Petroleum Act 1934.
Petroleum Regulation 1988.
Taxation Act 1983.

D Thesis

Ansari, Abbas, *The Nature and Efficiency of Buy-back Contracts* (Dissertation for LLM of International Trade Law, Shahid Beheshti University, Persian Abstract, 1387).

Fayadh, Khaled Hamad, *The Legal Regulation of Assisted Reproductive Technology in Iraq-Lessons From the Australian Approach* (PhD Thesis, Western Sydney University, 2015).

Ghosh, Sunil Kanti, *The Anglo-Iranian Oil Dispute: A Study of Problems of Nationalization of Foreign Investment and their Impact on International Law* (Master Thesis/ Dissertation, Calcutta K. L. Mukhopadhyay, 1960).

Hassanzadeh, Elham, *Export of Iranian Natural Gas to Regional and International Markets a Study of Political, Legal and Economic Barriers* (PhD Thesis, The University of Dundee, 2013).

Hedayati Kakhki, Mohammed Mehdi, *A Critical Analysis of Iranian Buy-Back Transactions in the Context of International Petroleum Contractual Systems* (PhD Thesis, The University of Durham, 2008).

Karim, Muhammad S, *Oil, Islamic and International Petroleum Industry Legal, Economic, Political and Cultural Issues* (LLM Dissertation, The University of Dundee, 2001).

Sakhaei, Ehsan, *Oil Contracts of Production Sharing and their Applicability in the Oil Industry of Iran* (Dissertation for LLM of International Trade Law, Shahid Beheshti University, 2009).

Savana, Sinturug, *World Petroleum Arrangement and the Role of the State* (Dissertation submitted to the CEPMLP, University of Dundee, 1986).

Taher Estakhti, Ezzatollah, *Concession on Tract and Its Legal Evolution* (Dissertation for LLM of Public Law, Shahid Beheshti Law Faculty, 1999).

E Internet Material

ABC News, 'Mining Act Review: What Does It Mean for Grain Farmers across South Australia?', *ABC Rural* (6 February 2017) Courtney Fowler <https://www.abc.net.au/news/rural/2017-02-03/sach-mining-act-review/8239998>.

Addison, Joanna, 'The New Iranian Petroleum Contract (IPC)' (January 2017) DOC Player <http://docplayer.net/29992304-The-new-iranian-petroleum-contract-ipc.html>.

Alfred, Randy, 'May 26, 1908: Mideast Oil Discovered – There Will Be Blood' (21 March 2012) <http://www.wired.com/2008/05/dayintech-0526/>.

Alveberg, J Lars, 'Norwegian Petroleum History' (2013) FACTS, 10 <http://www.npd.no/Global/Engelsk/3-Publications/Facts/Facts2013/FACTS_2013.pdf>.

Bain & Company, 'Studies of Regulatory, Corporate and Financial Alternatives for the Exploration and Production of Oil and Gas and the Industrial Development of the Oil and Gas Production Chain in Brazil' (2009) DOC Player <http://docplayer.net/8345768-Studies-of-regulatory-corporate-and-financial-alternatives-for-the-exploration-and-production-of-oil-and-gas-and-the-industrial-developmentof-the.html#show_full_text>.

Berittan Bevan, 'The New Concession Contracts Regulations and Utilities Contracts Regulations Come into Force Today' (2016) <http://www.legislation.gov.uk/uksi/2016/273/contents/made>.

British Petroleum (BP), 'Statistical Review of World Energy' (June 2015) bp <http://www.bp.com>.

British Petroleum (BP), 'Statistical Review of World Energy' (June 2016) bp <http://www.bp.com>.

CCOP EPF, 'Thailand Exploration/Development History' (2002) <http://www.ccop.or.th/epf/thailand/thailand_explor.html>.

Corbett, Michael, 'Oil Shock of 1973–74' (22 November 2013) Federal Reserve History <http://www.federalreservehistory.org/Events/DetailView/36>.

Department of Resources, Energy and Tourism, 'Offshore Petroleum Acreage Release' (07 August 2012) Ningaloo Atlas <http://ningaloo-atlas.org.au/content/offshore-petroleum-exploration-acreage-releases>.

Exigency Council, 'General Policies of Article 44 of the Constitution of the Islamic Republic of Iran' (1 July 2006) Iran Data Portal <http://irandataportal.syr.edu/the-general-policies-pertaining-to-principle-44-of-the-constitution-of-the-islamic-republic-of-iran>.

Federal Republic of Brazil, Ministry of Mines and Energy, 'Concession Agreement for the Exploration, Development and Production of Oil and Natural Gas' (2008) clause 14.1 <http://www.eisourcebook.org/cms/Brazil,%20Model%20Concession%20Agreement,%20ANP%2010th%20Rnd,%202008.pdf>.

Ghush, Palash, 'Iran: The Long Lasting Legacy of the 1953 U.S./CIA Coup' (20 March 2012) International Business Times <http://www.ibtimes.com/iran-long-lasting-legacy-1953-uscia-coup-214329>.

Global Oil and Gas Tax Guide (2015) 421 and 432 <http://www.ey.com/Publication/vwLUAssets/EY-2015-Global-oil-and-gas-tax-guide/$FILE/EY-2015-Global-oil-and-gas-tax-guide.pdf>.

Global Oil and Gas Tax Guide (2016) 421 and 432 <http://www.ey.com/Publication/vwLUAssets/EY-2016-Global-oil-and-gas-tax-guide/$FILE/EY-2016-Global-oil-and-gas-tax-guide.pdf>.

Key Terms, 'The New Iranian Petroleum Contract (IPC)' (February 2016) Herbert Smith Freehills <file://ad.uws.edu.au/dfshare/HomesPTA$/90923458/Downloads/%C3%9D%C3%A4%C3%A4%C3%A8%C3%B1%C3%AE%C3%AD_%C3%A0%C3%AD%C3%A3%C3%AB.pdf>.

'Key World Energy Statistics' (2012) International Energy Agency <http://alofatuvalu.tv/FR/12_liens/12_articles_rapports/IEA_rpt_2012_us.pdf>.

Malek, Mohammad, 'Oil in Iran between the Two World Wars' (9 March 2016) Iran Chamber Society <http://www.iranchamber.com/history/articles/oil_iran_between_world_wars.php>.

Ministry of Finance, Statistic Norway, *The Petroleum Tax System* (Updated 22 February 2017) <http://www.norskpetroleum.no/en/economy/petroleum-tax/>.

'Oil Agreements in Iran' (20 July 2004) Encyclopaedia Iranica <http://www.iranicaonline.org/articles/oil-agreements-in-iran>.

Oil and Gas Authority, *Taxation of Exploration For, and Production of, Oil and Gas in the UK and on the UK Continental Shelf* (9 October 2015) GOV.UK <https://www.gov.uk/guidance/oil-and-gas-taxation>.

'Oil and Gas Taxation in Norway' (2014) Deloitte <https://www2.deloitte.com/content/dam/Deloitte/global/Documents/Energy-and-Resources/gx-er-oil-and-gas-taxguide-norway.pdf>.

OPEC, 'Annual Statistical Bulletin' (2012) <http://www.opec.org/opec_web/static_files_project/media/downloads/publications/ASB2012.pdf>.

OPEC, 'Annual Statistical Bulletin' (2016) <https://www.opec.org/opec_web/static_files_project/media/downloads/publications/ASB2016.pdf>.

OPEC, 'Annual Statistical Bulletin' (2017) <http://www.opec.org/opec_web/static_files_project/media/downloads/publications/ASB2017_13062017.pdf>.

Sharafodin, Bozorgmehr, 'Iran's Supreme Leader Says Reform in New Oil Contracts Are Necessary' (3 July 2016) Reuters <http://www.reuters.com/article/us-iran-oil-contract-idUSKCN0ZJ067>.

'Sultanate of Muscat and Oman' (Oil Concession Agreement 1937) Qatar National Library <https://www.qdl.qa/en/archive/81055/vdc_100000000833.0x00001b>.

Tavana Energy, 'Iran Petroleum Contract' (21 July 2016) Tehran University <http://tavana energy.com/iran petroleum-contract/>.

The Petroleum Act 1934 (England), to view the Petroleum Act 1934, this is accessible at: <http://emrd.portal.gov.bd/sites/default/files/files/emrd.portal.gov.bd/law/c7c4688a_97f6_4442_a417_b4c054cd1a06/petroleumact1934.pdf>.

Tumnde, Taylor, *Petroleum License in United Kingdom* (30 July 2014) linked in <https://www.linkedin.com/pulse/20140630151031-137158292-petroleum-licensing-in-the-united-kingdom>.

Unravelling the Carbon Web, *About Production Sharing Agreement* <http://www.carbonweb.org/showitem.asp?article=58&parent=4&link=Y&gp=3>.

World Petroleum Arrangements (1985) The Barrow Company, INC, New York 574 <http://www.barrowscompany.com/>.

F Other

Abu Dhabi Concession Contract 1980 (The United Arab Emirates UAE) article 9.

Akhlaghi, Behrooz, 'Iran Petroleum Contract (IPC)' (Bi-Weekly News & Analysis of the International Law Office No. 1, Behrooz Akhlaghi & Associate, 2015).

Brumberg, Daniel, 'The National Iranian Oil Company in Iranian Politics' (Prepared in Conjunction with an Energy Study Sponsored by Japan Petroleum Centre and the James A. Baker III Institute for Public Policy Rice University, 2007).

DIARIO OFICIAL DA UNIAO (Brazil) [Lei No. 9,478, art 44, 111, de 6 de Agosto de 1997, de 7.8.1997 Brazil] <http://www.planalto.gov.br/ccivil_03/leis/19478.htm>.

Directive 94/22/EC of 30 May 1994 of the European Parliament and of the Council on the Conditions for Granting and Using Authorisations for the Prospection, Exploration and Production of Hydrocarbons article 3.

Gopher Oil Ltd. Petroleum Concession (Thailand) [No. 4/2528/29 dated November 21, 1985]).

Mirmoezi, 'Role of Middle Eastern NOCs in World Oil Industry and Necessity of Structural Reforms and Productivity' (Paper presented at the Ninth international IIES Conference, Proceedings of the Conference, Tehran, Iran, 2004).

Paliashvili, Irina, 'The concept of Production Sharing' (Paper presented at the Seminar on the Legislation on Production Sharing Agreements, the Russian-Ukrainian Legal Group, 14 September 1998).

República de Angola, 'Lei das Actividades Petrolíferas' [No. 10/2004, de 12 de novembro de 2004].

Smock, David, 'Applying Islamic Principles in the 21st Century' (Special Report No. 150, United States Institute of Peace, September 2005).

'The Price of Oil-In Context' (Media Released, 18 April 2006) 1 <https://web.archive.org/web/20070609145246/http://www.cbc.ca/news/background/oil/>.

Triton Oil and Gas Corp Concession 1973 (Thailand) [No. 8/2512/12].

UNCITRAL, *Legislative Guide on Privately Financed Infrastructure Projects* (2001).

UNCTAD, *Public Monopolies, Concessions, and Competition Law and Policies* (2009).

Yeganeh, Mohammad, Farokh Najmabadi, and Parviz Mina, 'The Development of The Iranian Oil Industry' (Proceedings of the Conference held at the School of Oriental Studies London in March 1990, Published by Society for Contemporary Iranian Studies, Middle East Center, University of London, 1991).

Index

Note: **Bold** page numbers refer to tables and *italic* page numbers refer to figures.

For Product Safety Concerns and Information please contact our EU
representative GPSR@taylorandfrancis.com
Taylor & Francis Verlag GmbH, Kaufingerstraße 24, 80331 München, Germany

www.ingramcontent.com/pod-product-compliance
Ingram Content Group UK Ltd.
Pitfield, Milton Keynes, MK11 3LW, UK
UKHW011012180926
475701UK00004B/693

9781032240398